D0174610

Understanding
the Enneagram

Understanding the Enneagram

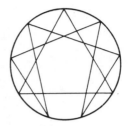

The Practical Guide to Personality Types

DON RICHARD RISO

Houghton Mifflin Company
Boston

Library of Congress Cataloging-in-Publication Data

Riso, Don Richard.
Understanding the enneagram : the practical guide to
personality types / Don Richard Riso.
p.   cm.
Includes bibliographical references.
ISBN 0-395-52026-6.—ISBN 0-395-52148-3 (pbk.)
1. Enneagram.   2. Self-evaluation.   I. Title.
BF698.3.R57   1990   89-38806
155.2'6—dc20   CIP

Printed in the United States of America

VB 11 10 9 8 7 6 5 4

The author is grateful for permission to reprint material
from the following sources: *Essence: The Diamond Approach
to Inner Realization* by A. H. Almaas. Copyright © 1986 by
A-Hameed Ali (York Beach, Me.: Samuel Weiser, 1986).
Used by permission. *Diagnostic and Statistical Manual of
Mental Disorders,* Third Edition, Revised. Copyright ©
1987 by American Psychiatric Association. Reprinted with
permission. *Personality Types: Using the Enneagram for Self-
Discovery* by Don Richard Riso. Copyright © 1987 by
Don Richard Riso. Reprinted by permission of
Houghton Mifflin Company.

For
C.S.A., R.St.G., G.E.,
B.L.T., M.M., B.P.M., and
A.M.D.G.

This thing we tell of can
never be found by seeking,
yet only seekers find it.

Sufi saying

ACKNOWLEDGMENTS

In *Personality Types*, I acknowledged my indebtedness to many people. Since I had so many to thank for what they had given me up to that notable point in my life, it was a pleasure to remember them all. They are remembered here again because they have continued to play an important role in my life and work.

In a sense, however, I have both more and fewer people to acknowledge here. Those who have written to me about *Personality Types* and who have attended my workshops and seminars have played a more important role in the formation of this book than they realize since it has been written in large part in response to them. The Enneagram has brought me into contact with many wonderful people; it has been a privilege to become part of their lives and gratifying to have my work touch them so deeply.

I continue to be indebted to Houghton Mifflin for its support of my work, and I am grateful in particular for the wise counsel and support of my editor, Ruth Hapgood. Her talented assistant, Tara Hartnett, is also always a pleasure to work with. Becky Saikia-Wilson, Gretchen Hachmeister, Lynn Krise, and Mab Gray have been helpful in many ways that have gone beyond professionalism to include kindness and personal interest. Thanks also go to Barbara Flanagan, my manuscript editor, for her unflagging work to make mine seem effortless.

I want to take this opportunity to thank Helena Bentz who, among a handful of others at Houghton Mifflin, perceived the potential of *Personality Types* when it was a manuscript and gave it special attention. And I will always remain indebted to Austin Olney, the former editor in chief, for discovering that book and allowing it a chance to be.

Once again, I would like to thank Mark Desveaux, who executed the line drawings and the new set of caricatures of the personality types, Gene Bagnato for my photograph, Brian Taylor for his help and advice at every turn, and Maux and Buster for all that they are.

Above all, I have been supported in the work of understanding human nature by the first Author by whose Word all has been created and sustained. Without realizing it, every writer imitates this most original of authors by seeming to bring something out of nothing. To move from the first inspiration for a book to the moment when it comes into existence has much in common with the mysteriousness of the original act of creation itself. May this book add both to human understanding and to the glory of that Author's Word.

CONTENTS

New Developments

ONE

The Practical Guide to Personality Types

WE ARE LIKE prisoners in an unguarded cell. No one confines us against our will, and we have heard that the key that would release us is also locked inside with us. If we could find the key, we could open the door and be free. Yet we do not know where it has been hidden, and even if we knew, part of us is afraid to break out of our prison. Once out, where would we go, and what would we do with our new-found freedom?

This is not a meaningless metaphor: we are truly prisoners of our ego, enchained by our fears, restricted in our freedom, suffering from our condition. No one prevents us from searching for the key that would free us. We must, however, know where to look for it and be willing to use it once we have discovered where it is.

With the Enneagram, we have found a master key, one that will unlock many doors. It will give us access to the wisdom we need to escape from our self-imposed prison so that we can embrace a fuller life.

This book will take us further with the Enneagram than we have ever gone before. It will help us use this ancient system of human understanding to unlock hidden parts of ourselves so that we can become freer, more fully functioning persons. But how we use the Enneagram in our lives—indeed, whether or not we use it at all—depends entirely on us. If we want to use it, we must be willing to explore what the Enneagram unlocks in us. And as the process of liberation continues, we will be increasingly freed from our fears and conflicts, from our wayward passions and compulsions, from our disordered desires and inner confusions.

No part of this process is automatic, however. Even after we have identified our personality type, it still may not be clear how to use the insights we have been given. People often ask, "Now that I know my type, what do I *do* with it? Where do I go with it now?" Or, as someone in an Enneagram workshop once asked, "Why are we here?"

The answer to that unsettling question is "Because we are not all there." Some part of us knows that we are "not all there"—we are not complete, not fully in command of ourselves, not "perfect" persons. We are sometimes afraid and uncertain about which direction to move in life. We are sometimes inexplicably unhappy, or even if we are relatively happy much of the time, we find it difficult to maintain our happiness all the time. Sometimes we feel alienated and acutely sense our deep aloneness in life, despite being surrounded by family and friends. Sometimes we get into conflicts with others and are stymied in our attempts to reach out to them to heal our relationships. In short, we turn to the Enneagram, as we do to other forms of psychology, *because we are not all there*. As a mandala of the self, the Enneagram can serve as a guide to our personal development. It holds out to us an image of the wholeness to which we unconsciously aspire.

Understanding the Enneagram can yield profound insights into human nature. Nevertheless, despite its remarkable richness, we do not turn to the Enneagram simply because it is an interesting psychological system but because by having insight into ourselves and others we hope to live happier, more productive lives. My intention in this book is not only to reveal more about the Enneagram but to indicate how our lives can be enriched with the help of this remarkable tool.

To orient ourselves properly to the Enneagram, we should remember several important things. We must have patience since we are trying to explain the virtually inexplicable— human nature and the great number of different forms in which human nature expresses itself. At best, we can come only to partial, incomplete understandings of ourselves and others—not total comprehension or final illumination. There is, and will always be, an element of mystery about human nature, so we will never be totally satisfied with the answers we arrive at.

Acquiring self-knowledge is an inherently difficult, subtle matter. As we know from *Personality Types*, to the degree that we open ourselves up to the process of self-discovery, we will be surprised, rewarded, enriched—and possibly disturbed —by what the Enneagram stirs up within us. Understanding ourselves more objectively is exhilarating *and* frightening, so we must be aware of the seriousness of the process we are undertaking. (Actually, the more emotionally moved we are by the Enneagram, the more valuable our experience will be.) If we allow ourselves to be affected, the Enneagram can become a catalyst for personal growth and liberation. However, before we are able to use the Enneagram, we must understand it in depth and with insight so that we will not be misled or do more harm than good. Like any tool, the Enneagram can be misused. Like any key, it can unlock a door we later realize we should never have opened.

The two principal areas in which to use the Enneagram are first, *for self-understanding* (to know what to change in ourselves), and second, *for understanding others* (so that we will be able to deal with them more effectively).

By far, the most legitimate use of the Enneagram is in our

own lives. The ancient Sufi masters who discovered the personality types supposedly taught them to their disciples to help them understand themselves so that they could make progress toward psychological and spiritual liberation. This is fundamentally the same use we make of the Enneagram today since human nature (and the need to resolve our typical problems) has not changed. The Enneagram can help us understand our fears and desires, strengths and weaknesses, defenses and anxieties, how we react to frustration and disappointment—and, more positively, what our truest capacities and greatest strengths are so that we can build on those rather than on misjudgments and illusions.

There are three stages of our work. First, we need to learn *self-observation* so that we can have more distance from ourselves and see our behavior as objectively as possible. Second, we need to increase our *self-understanding* so that we can know the true motives for our behavior. And third, we need to be motivated to start our *self-transformation* so that we can actually change what needs to be changed. Self-observation and self-understanding merely provide us with insight to get us to the threshold of changing ourselves. Ultimately, our motive for making the effort to change is not only so that we will be happier but also so that we will be able to make a contribution to others and to the world, furthering and enriching the human enterprise.

Although self-understanding is the most proper use of the Enneagram, naturally we will also want to use it to understand others. The Enneagram is so interesting and so powerful that it is too much of a temptation *not* to apply it to others (although when we do so, the complexities multiply and we are on less sure ground).

Indeed, we want to use the Enneagram in our dealings with others precisely because it affords so much insight into them. Understanding others more profoundly allows us to appreciate the good we find in them as well as to become more objective about the things we do not like about them. Since we all tend to think that other people are basically like ourselves, it is helpful to realize that different types think and feel and react quite differently. As a result of understanding personality types, we can see people more objectively, connecting deeply with them while remaining in our own center, true to ourselves. By understanding the Enneagram, we paradoxically become both more self-possessed and more capable of reaching out to others.

Using the Enneagram in all our relationships is endlessly fascinating and complex because there are so many people in the world and so many different circumstances in which we deal with them. In fact, it is for the best that we use the Enneagram in our relationships since it is as important to understand others as it is to understand ourselves. We simply cannot (and do not) go through life without a clue about "what makes others tick"—about how they are likely to react in various circumstances, about their motivations, about how genuine or truthful or good they are. Whether or not we are conscious of it, everyone uses some kind of "personality theory" all the time. It is therefore extremely helpful to recognize what our implicit theory is and to make sure that it is as accurate and comprehensive as possible.

Another reason to understand the Enneagram is that it is to our advantage to recognize our negative tendencies before they become self-defeating habits *so that we can avoid the tragic consequences of those habits*. The Enneagram can become an "early warning system" of potentially harmful behavior, allowing us to do something about it before we become unhealthy. If our attitudes and behavior did not have potentially tragic consequences, we could think, "Well, why should I care about self-knowledge? What difference does it make to know more about myself or my personality type?"

The answer is that our attitudes and our actions *always have consequences*, some of which can affect the whole of our lives. This makes acquiring self-knowledge and insight into others an extraordinarily practical thing to do. Without self-knowledge, we can make choices that may turn out disastrously. If we do not know our own motives and do not have control over our behavior, we can do harmful things to ourselves, our spouses, our children, our friends and acquaintances—even to people we may never meet.

Furthermore, if we are not good judges of the characters of others, we can also be terribly hurt and abused. So many marriages end in bitterness and divorce because people do not know either themselves or each other. How often have we heard something like "If I had only known what my husband was really like before I married him, I would never have married him." Or "If I had only known the Enneagram twenty years ago, my life would have been so different. . . ." We can console ourselves with the thought that at least we know the Enneagram now—and with its help, we will be much more likely to avoid the suffering caused by our lack of self-knowledge and the unwise actions that may result. With insight, we have a much better chance to avoid tragedy and become happier.

Each of the great spiritual traditions uses different metaphors to express many of the same discoveries about human nature as well as to express its insight into the way out of our predicaments. At its deepest, the Enneagram is not only profound psychology but a path toward the spiritual since self-transcendence is the first step toward spirituality. Despite the Enneagram's apparent origin in the Sufi tradition of Islam, it is not overtly religious. It can be adapted to many different religions and religious expressions because the most important thing it does is reflect the patterns found in human nature. By helping us more clearly understand the human side of the relationship between God and human nature, the Enneagram can become an integral part of any spirituality.

While it can say very little about the revealed truths of religion, the Enneagram can say a very great deal about the forms that the human ego takes—one of the primary obstacles between human beings and the Divine. It demonstrates both the need for transcending ourselves and the direction we must take if we are to do so. The Enneagram is a tool that, when used properly, can guide us toward self-transcendence with more assurance. That is all it is. But considering the sublimity of this work, the Enneagram is a treasure—more valuable than anything we could have hoped to discover.

Even in a purely psychological, nontheological frame of reference, we want to understand the Enneagram so that we can become *more free*—more liberated—from whatever is blocked, negative, and destructive—from whatever is unfree, conflicted, fearful, and wounded—in ourselves. The Enneagram can aid our healing so that we can use our growing freedom in ennobling and constructive ways.

Once we begin to be liberated from our ego states and conflicts—from the darkness and fear inside—with each step we take toward the light we will gain that much more freedom and create new capacities in ourselves. Strength will build upon strength, grace upon grace, virtue upon virtue, and each new capacity will summon forth yet another as we become the persons that we are meant to be.

In the end, however, the Enneagram will be as useful and rewarding as *we* make it. The Enneagram will enrich us to the degree that we understand it correctly and use it properly in our lives. We can be confident that we will find endless insights and great riches here.

It was not possible to include in *Personality Types* all the new material that I have developed over the years. Nor would it necessarily have been a good idea to reveal all my discoveries, even if I had been able to. That book would have been double its size—and probably only half as intelligible.

Understanding the Enneagram is a practical guide to that first book, taking the information contained there as its starting point. We are not concerned here with the basic structure and theory of the Enneagram or with comprehensive descriptions of the nine personality types since they have already been provided. While it is not strictly necessary to have read *Personality Types*, the present book will mean more to you if you are familiar with the first.

Indeed, very little material is repeated from *Personality Types*, and what little was necessary to repeat is completely revised and expanded. For example, the Profiles at the beginning of each description in *Personality Types* have been more than doubled in length to become the Expanded Profiles found here. This book is also cross-referenced to *Personality Types* so that you can return to that longer resource if you want to find out more about something. Furthermore, much of the new material is completely independent of the earlier book (the Expanded Profiles, the Questionnaire, and the Recommendations for Personal Growth, for example) and can be used without reference to it.

Above all, the emphasis here is twofold: *Understanding the Enneagram* is meant to be both a *practical guide to* and an *expansion of Personality Types*. It is still not possible, for instance, to explore all the abstract theoretical aspects of the Enneagram (that will have to wait for a full-length book on theory), nor can this book make every possible application of the Enneagram for every reader—a book devoted entirely to relationships is also in the future. Instead, this book is concerned with uses that most people will be likely to find helpful in their daily lives. More applications can be expected as the Enneagram continues to be developed by psychologists, by those in the business world, and by teachers and writers.

This book is also intended as an expansion of *Personality Types*. To appreciate the clarifications introduced here, this book should be used in conjunction with that more detailed book. In *Personality Types*, I took the traditional teachings as my starting point, clarified them, and demonstrated how the Enneagram corresponds with the findings of contemporary psychology. I felt that what was most important was to present accurate descriptions of the nine basic personality types so that future work on this typology could be done with more assurance. In this second book, I want to give readers a clearer understanding of many aspects of the Enneagram that I could only briefly touch on before. A great deal of information was presented "between the lines" in *Personality Types* or was simply stated without being explicitly pointed out. It has come time to be more explicit about the types, about their inner structure and dynamics, and about the Enneagram as a whole.

In deciding what to include in this book, I have listened to suggestions from readers. Some requested more information about how to type themselves and others and how they can be certain about the diagnoses they have made. Some asked for guidance in applying the insights they have gained to their psychological and spiritual development; others, for guidelines about how they can become more healthy. Still others wanted information about how to distinguish more clearly between different personality types; individuals of one type sometimes resemble those of another (at least superficially), and beginners often have difficulty telling various subtypes apart.

I have answered these requests by including a Questionnaire (Chapter 4) to serve as a check on your self-diagnosis, a chapter with recommendations for each personality type to aid personal growth (Chapter 8), and a chapter that includes workbook space for assessing your personality type or that of someone else (Chapter 6). The request for information about distinguishing between similar types is covered in Chapter 5, which compares and contrasts easily misidentified types. In short, many of the requests readers have made for more information about the Enneagram are fulfilled in this book.

Aside from the new material presented here, I thought that

readers would find it useful to have a place to record their observations about themselves, the types, and the Enneagram in general. Some workbook space has therefore been included so that you may jot down your own observations. The more you make this information your own, the more the Enneagram will become a living, useful part of your life.

As well received as *Personality Types* has been, it is still worth mentioning that it will always be impossible to produce adequate descriptions that account for every characteristic of human nature. This is why it will always be necessary to reflect on the personality types to discover more about them in your life. If a book were able to describe everything about a person, the description would have to be as long as the individual's life — and take as long to read as the person has time to live. There would be as many books as there are people in the world. Complete specificity is impossible; generalization and, therefore, incompleteness are inevitable.

Although I have attempted to honor most readers' requests, it has, of course, been impossible to fulfill all of them. For instance, it is not feasible to give a set of ironclad rules for diagnosing people or to provide foolproof advice to each type that will infallibly "enlighten" them. While it is natural for us to want simple answers, if there is one thing in the world which is not — and cannot be — simple, it is human nature.

Even with the clarity the Enneagram provides, there are no easy answers to many of the most important problems we face. Not only is it impossible, but it would be dishonest, to offer oversimplifications or empty promises. Unfortunately, many self-help books (including some based on the Enneagram) offer facile solutions that seem to help but later fail us when the complexities of reality reassert themselves.

It is necessary to avoid promising more than the Enneagram can deliver by not raising false hopes about attaining "enlightenment" or final personal integration, since there can be no fulfillment or happiness for anyone, following any system, without wisdom, courage, fortitude, self-discipline, and patience—qualities that are not now (and have never been) in vogue. The simple fact is that it takes time and effort to undo whatever problems were created in our past as we learn to live more authentically in the present.

In the end, no matter what truths we attain with it or what practical purposes we put it to, we will find that the Enneagram is deeply valuable. Nevertheless, possessing complete self-understanding is, by definition, beyond human capacity since to understand ourselves completely we would have to stand outside ourselves to comprehend ourselves as a whole. This is impossible because the person observing is the same one being observed. We cannot see ourselves as a whole because our life does not exist as a whole at any point in time. We see fragments of ourselves, catch glimpses of ourselves, only hints of who we are.

Perhaps the most we can hope for is to be liberated from whatever holds us back from being more whole, more open, more free—and, ultimately, more capable of moving beyond ourselves to embrace all that lies beyond.

The Traditions of the Enneagram

Despite the publication of several books, much still remains secret and much is in dispute about the Enneagram. Several teaching "traditions" have sprung up, all varying in form and emphasis—from the tradition begun by Gurdjieff in the 1920s to the tradition begun by Oscar Ichazo (and supplemented by the psychiatrist Claudio Naranjo) at the Arica Institute beginning in the 1970s, to the religious tradition presented by various Jesuit priests throughout North America, to a recent emphasis on pious spiritual direction (which, in the view of many, has gotten away from the rigorous psychological and spiritual roots of the Enneagram), to my own interpretation of the Enneagram (a clarification and extension of the psychological and implicitly spiritual Enneagram of Ichazo and Naranjo, as later elaborated on by the Jesuits).

The continued publication of books about this system has sparked a debate about which book better presents the original authentic oral tradition, about which author studied with which Enneagram master, about which changes have been made in the presentation of the Enneagram from the early Arica tradition (which has implicitly been taken as "basic"), even about whether the Enneagram is primarily a psychological system or a spiritual one, since different books emphasize one aspect over another. Readers of different interests approaching the Enneagram from their different points of view are rightly confused by the welter of claims and counterclaims being made about "the traditional teaching." There is no need, however, to erect a barrier between its psychological aspects and its spiritual ones since both are already implied by the Enneagram, just as both are implied in human nature itself — the very thing the Enneagram so elegantly and accurately reflects.

Indeed, the debate about psychology versus spirituality is misdirected since the best evidence indicates that the Enneagram came from the mystical Sufi tradition of Islam, after being discovered and developed by untold generations of spiritual seekers in secret brotherhoods that used it to aid their search for union with God. Knowing ourselves so that we can transcend ourselves and attain balance and integration is what psychology is about — while transcending ourselves to make room for the Divine is what spirituality is about. Both go together and are not at odds with each other.

Even so, the psychological aspects of the Enneagram should be approached first since our psychology colors and shapes our spirituality. Seen from this point of view, the Enneagram is simply a system of personality types, an ancient psychological typology, a way of understanding human personality. However, we must be clear that psychology is not spirituality, or vice versa. They are related disciplines but certainly not the same thing. Psychology is an important prelude and adjunct to spirituality, and it is from that point of view that *Personality Types* was written—to lay the groundwork for a more mature spirituality by providing a more accurate understanding of each personality type. The descriptions were a guided tour of the states of ego that inexorably lead to a descent into the hell of neurosis. Each description was an unvarnished account of the entire range of personality from the self-transcending states of integration to ordinary healthy states of ego, to average states in which ego inflation and various kinds of conflicts occur, to unhealthy states in which people suffer and make others suffer. The descriptions were not intended to include everything but to lay out the foundations of each type clearly so that we would have something solid on which to build.

Just as the debate about psychology versus spirituality has been misguided, so is the issue of which tradition of the Enneagram is truest. Even among the several competing traditions now in existence, it is difficult to say which is the most authentic. For instance, it is impossible to say whether the Arica presentation of the Enneagram accurately reflects the ancient Sufi understanding of it. To know that, we would have to discover the ancient Sufi sources—or their allegedly more ancient sources—to discover the very earliest teachings. But would a teaching traced to Babylon nearly five thousand years ago necessarily be the ultimate truth, the immutable teaching that everyone must accept? Since it is probably impossible to find the original source of the Enneagram, we are free to approach each modern interpretation as a separate point of view on this remarkably rich symbol. All may not be equally valid (indeed, all cannot be), but all have a right to be heard.

While we should be aware of historical traditions, it is much more important to be concerned with the essential truths conveyed by the Enneagram in whichever tradition we find them. We must remember that the most significant thing about the Enneagram is that it reflects human nature—the objective, natural laws of the psyche. Its amazing ability to illuminate and deepen insights discovered independently in modern psychology is another of its most valuable and exciting properties. Indeed, its correspondence with contemporary psychological categories goes far to prove its objective validity. There is no need to adhere dogmatically to a tradition that itself may be incomplete, in error, or the result of teachings that have intentionally been only partially revealed by its founder(s).

Furthermore, *Personality Types* never claimed to be presenting the "traditional" interpretation since none of the then available traditions provided an adequate description of each personality type, much less a satisfactory explanation of the theory of the Enneagram as a whole. Over the years I have become convinced that a full and accurate description of each personality type is the *sine qua non* for the future of this system. Accurate descriptions are essential since they constitute the core of the teaching about the Enneagram—and any teaching that describes the nine types wrongly is, to that degree, not a true source of knowledge about the Enneagram. The personality descriptions are what draw most people to the Enneagram in the first place, and if the descriptions are wrong or incomplete, the claims made for the Enneagram are ultimately empty.

During the years in which I developed my interpretation of the Enneagram, I took nothing for granted, accepted nothing on faith, questioned every "traditional" teaching, and critiqued every claim. In a sense, I rediscovered the Enneagram for myself and expressed my insights in ordinary language and, where necessary, in the language of modern psychology.

I translated the essence of the various traditions that have sprung up into something that people can understand and use.

Because it is not always clear where the older traditions leave off and where my contributions begin, and rather than go into detail about my contributions, the following rule of thumb can be used. The way to distinguish between the "traditional" teaching and my work is simple: everything in *Personality Types* and this book that has not been explicitly attributed to someone else or to a specific traditional source is the result of my original work. For instance, the nine Levels of Development within each type and their names; the method of describing the personality types along the Continuum of traits in their healthy, average, and unhealthy states; the Childhood Origins of each type; the overall type names assigned to each, and so forth are original with me. This rapidly growing field is in need of a history of the Enneagram that will examine the many contributors to it. Until such a history appears, a great deal of misinformation will unfortunately continue to be passed around.

Even so, despite the errors and mistakes of all sorts that are being made, the essential truth of the Enneagram speaks for itself because it touches the human heart. As individuals continue to respond to the Enneagram, there will inevitably be more discoveries, more elaborations—and more distortions and mistakes.

This cannot be avoided and is, in fact, an important part of the process of disseminating and refining knowledge. We should not attempt to preserve the Enneagram in some doctrinally pure state even if we could know what that state is (since doing so would limit us to the insights of the ancients who supposedly first formulated it). On the contrary, we must have confidence that as the Enneagram becomes more developed and refined over time, its essential truths will continue to be communicated. Distortions will, in time, die away.

Changes and New Terminology

In the interest of accuracy, I would like to make some corrections to *Personality Types* in this book. My interpretation of the Enneagram is a "work in progress," with each successive book modifying and complementing those preceding it. Happily, very little of what has already appeared needs to be revised, much less retracted. However, I would like to introduce some changes.

It became clear that it would be helpful to give each type an overall label so that each could be introduced quickly to readers. More distinctions and subtleties could be made later in the descriptions themselves. So I attempted to find *le mot juste* for each of the types, a single noun that would reveal something of its essence. Ideally, I felt that each of the type names should reflect a healthy trait. Thus, the Eight became "The Leader"; the Nine, "The Peacemaker"; the Two, "The Helper"; the Five, "The Thinker"; the Six, "The Loyalist"; and the Seven, "The Generalist."

But I was also forced to use a more "average" term when a healthier, more positive word simply eluded me or did not seem appropriate. Thus, for the One I chose "The Reformer"; for the Three, "The Status Seeker"; and for the Four, "The Artist." Not only did these words seem to give an accurate flavor of those types, but they also were better than anything else that had occurred to me at that time.

With the exception of the Three's label, I am going to retain the former type names while pointing out that other labels could just as well have been used. For example, I labeled the Four "The Artist," and while accurate enough, this label has confused people of other types who are also artistic (see Chapter 5 for more about misidentifications). Perhaps a better label for the Four would have been "The Aesthete" or "The Individualist." But the former seemed too negative, although accurate, while the latter seemed accurate, but potentially misleading. Better would have been "The Aesthetic Individualist" since this precisely gives the flavor of the Four. But this grammatical form would not have been consistent with the other names, so for the sake of consistency among the types I adopted "The Artist" for the Four. There is no need to change it if you keep in mind that this one-word label is simply a starting place for understanding this type.

Similarly, I chose "The Reformer" for the One. Another equally accurate term could have been "The Teacher," but that word seemed to raise problems analogous to those raised by "The Artist"—that it described people of more than one type. I might have named the healthy One "The Principled Teacher," although this would have caused the same stylistic problem as "The Aesthetic Individualist," so I discarded it. Only "The Reformer" seemed to be adequate, and so I retained it.

In the case of the Three, however, shortly after the completed manuscript for *Personality Types* had gone into production, a better, less negative phrase than "The Status Seeker" occurred to me. While "Status Seeker" is the correct designation for average Threes (at Level 4), the term has a pejorative connotation and some people were rightly put off by it. A more positive label for the Three as a whole is "The Motivator," and I am introducing it in this book as the overall type label for the Three. If a second edition of *Personality Types* is in its future, I will revise my description to incorporate this change of terminology.

It might also be helpful to introduce new terminology relating to the Enneagram. For example, it would be good to have a more economical way of referring to the type with its wing. Instead of writing "Four with a Three-wing," we can use the abbreviation "4w3," although we would read this shorthand notation the same way. For example, "5w6" would be read "Five with a Six-wing," and so forth for all eighteen subtypes. Whenever it is necessary to refer to a type with its wing in this book, and in the future, this designation will be used.

More important, in *Personality Types* I recast the terminology associated with the Jesuit tradition. Among the things I changed, for example, were the terms for the "head, heart, and gut centers" to the "Feeling, Doing, and Relating Triads." Not only is this terminology more elegant, it is—and this is the important point—more precise and accurate as a description of what the three types in each group have in common. (Furthermore, the terminology introduced by the Jesuit interpretation was itself a change from the earlier Arica interpretation, which calls them the "Living, Doing, and Being Groups," so the language used in the religious tradition does not seem to have any claim to historical authenticity of its own.)

In any event, Eights, Nines, and Ones do not have in common the fact that they operate from their "gut" or instinctual center (whatever that might actually be) but that they all tend to relate to the world, the self, and other people in an imbalanced way. It is the quality of their "relating" (especially their thinking and judging) that is characteristic of these types, not their common "gut center."

Furthermore, the term "center" seems to denote an almost physical place or connection. A more abstract word such as "Triad" does not become confused with a quasiphysical area of the body. Using "Triad" also makes it clear that the three personality types making up each subgroup of the Enneagram do so because they are related to the others in a special way, like three notes in a chord. The Triads are as they are because they are *interrelational*—the types are in a dialectic relationship with each other. They are not things or "centers." (There will be a brief review of the Triads in the next section of this chapter.)

Both the Arica and the Jesuit traditions present the descriptions in a rather negative light. The negative side of the personality types is emphasized because it is our ego inflation that causes problems in our lives. Once our egos are inflated, they need to be defended, and we begin to get into conflicts with other people, with reality, and with ourselves as this process continues and worsens. In short, the negative aspects of the types are essential to present since in many ways we are our own worst enemies, and our ego and its illusions must be stripped away if any psychological or spiritual progress is to be made.

As true as this is, each type also has a positive side, as demonstrated in *Personality Types*. We are not disembodied spirits; we live in the real world with other people with whom we need to communicate. Our healthy ego states (found in the first three Levels of Development) are a reflection of the human need to have an individual identity as well as the need to relate to others. The Arica presentation of the Enneagram sees all ego states as negative and is therefore unrealistic about the possibility of maintaining a healthy, balanced ego. The Jesuit tradition tends to misinterpret ego states by calling average states healthy ones and by misattributing traits from one Level to another. Both interpretations need to reassess these and other aspects of the personality types more carefully.

To understand personality types is to understand general patterns. This understanding is enormously useful, but we must keep in mind that the types are generalizations and that no person is precisely like the description of his or her type. General descriptions must walk a fine line between being specific enough to convey precise information about each type and being general enough so that all the individuals who belong to each type can find themselves in it. The rule, then, is this: the types are general patterns; individuals are unique variations on those patterns.

An analogy might help. Just as we all know what we mean when we say that something is the color "red," once we have understood the personality types, we are given similarly specific information when we say that someone is a "Five." In both cases, the words "red" and "Five" give us only a general idea of the particular class under consideration; in both cases, there are hundreds of possible individual variations. For example, crimson, brick, scarlet, maroon, pink—and many more hues—are variations on red, and yet we know very clearly what someone means when he or she says that something is "red." Even if we cannot be certain of the precise shade of red the person is referring to, we still know enough to distinguish a red object from a black one or a yellow one. Red is clearly not black, and yellow is certainly not red—just as a Five is not an Eight or an Eight a One. Categories such as these are different and distinct. To further the analogy, just as we can distinguish between types, we can distinguish between individuals within a type. I might be a cobalt blue while someone else is an aquamarine blue: we are both still in the "blue family" and therefore have a number of traits in common. And yet we are still different, still ourselves, and still unique. Once we know the Enneagram, we know that we are talking about general patterns when we refer to different types.

Seen from this point of view, the personality types of the Enneagram are as diverse and distinct as the colors of the rainbow, only much more complicated. Each one of us is an individual, unique person, and yet a moment's reflection will reveal some of the many ways in which we are alike. In fact, we should expect to find that human beings are alike in many ways. After all, we share the same biological basis for our common human nature. We all have blood and bones, the same basic male or female anatomy, we all use language and are able to deal with abstract ideas, we have all had parents, and we have all had to learn to relate to ourselves, the world, and other people. Even though cultural differences influence us a great deal, certain underlying qualities are common to all human beings.

Nor is uniqueness denied by the Enneagram. Uniqueness is to be found in the different facts of our lives: no two individuals in the history of the human race have been born at the same instant, to the same parents, into the same family and culture, with the same genetic endowments, educated in the same way, and the subject of precisely the same influences. What makes us unique is our unique history. But what makes us part of a personality type is the fact that we also share certain traits with other human beings. Although we are unique, we are not totally different. It would be an impossible world if everyone were literally *completely unique*, that is, if everyone were a totally dissimilar entity unto himself or herself. Language, literature, the arts, commerce, communication—all of society—would be impossible if people did not have a great many qualities in common.

From the point of view of psychology, if people were totally unique, they would have totally different neuroses, and no general theories or techniques could be devised to help them. The fact that we are like each other (and are especially similar to those of our personality type) is shown most clearly by how much alike neurotics are. Depressives are like other depressives—thinking and saying things very similar to other depressives. Hysterics resemble other hysterics; those who dissociate from reality are like others who do the same, even in their appearance and their responses to the world around them.

Freedom is one of the keynotes of healthy functioning and, with freedom, individuality. People who are healthy are truly most themselves, and they are never more themselves than when they are transcending themselves. Thus, we discover a paradox: in self-transcendence we find our deepest freedom and our deepest self. And the reverse is equally true: as we deteriorate down the Levels of Development into neurosis,

we gradually lose our freedom and become increasingly unfree and "compulsive." Neurotics act under constraint and
cannot find who they are. Healthy human beings are free to
enjoy the quest.

Reviewing the Enneagram

This section is included so that readers can review the basics
and refresh their memories about the Enneagram—and also
so that I can make some additional comments about the theory. (For more details, consult *PT*, 23–46.)*

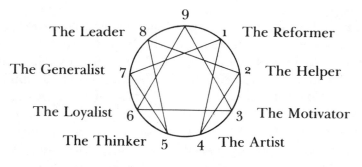

THE ENNEAGRAM

As already mentioned, I have given the personality types
these names, just as other authors have given the types different names. The names I have chosen reflect traits of each

*Parenthetical references to *Personality Types* are abbreviated *PT* and include
page numbers from that book.

type that are relatively *healthy*. In the Arica presentation, by contrast, the types are given names based on their "ego-fixations"; for example, the One is given the name "Ego-Resentment." (See Lilly and Hart or Wagner for the other correlations;* due to copyright restrictions, it is impossible to quote Arica material or to present a scholarly examination of the Arica interpretation.)

The names that I have assigned to each type were also chosen to help focus on the type's most prominent role. In the Gurdjieff tradition, the name of each type is that type's "chief feature," that central flaw that is its most important weakness—and is related to (but not the same as) its most important strength.

You may find a little of yourself in each type, although *one* type should stand out as most typical of yourself. That is your *basic personality type*.

Three common problems are seen time and again. First, people tend to pick the personality type they would like to be rather than the one they actually are. You can avoid this by being objective about yourself, although this is, of course, very difficult—nevertheless, objectivity is one of the very things we are ultimately trying to achieve with the Enneagram. (More guidelines for identifying your type are given in Chapter 4.)

Second, people tend to make an identification based on a single trait. For example, someone might say, "Twos are kind, and I'm kind, so therefore I must be a Two." While it is true that Twos are kind, so are Nines—and Fours and sometimes Ones, Threes, Fives, and all of the types. It is not sufficient to make a diagnosis based on one trait: it is important to see the larger pattern of traits as well as the motivations behind them. Once you have discovered your personality type, you will find that it really does describe you better than any of

---

*Works contained in the Bibliography are referenced in the text by their authors' last names, and page numbers are given where appropriate.

the others. Of course, it will also contain traits that you may not have recognized in yourself before as well as traits that are as familiar as old clothes. (For more guidelines about distinguishing between similar types, see Chapter 5.)

A third common problem is that people are tempted to pick and choose among the traits as if the descriptions were a smorgasbord. This approach does not work because the personality types are not arbitrary. The traits that constitute each of the types have not been haphazardly thrown together by human nature. On the contrary, they grow out of each other, proceeding from each other like the colors of the rainbow. They are expressions of our basic fears and desires, our fundamental needs and values and reactions to ourselves and the world around us. While there may well be strange and contradictory traits found among the types, they are all of a piece.

Nor are the nine types of the Enneagram arbitrary; they fall into three groups of three, each group being one of the Triads of the Enneagram. (The Jesuit teaching refers to each group as a "center"—the head, heart, and gut centers, as I have already noted.) Each Triad indicates some of the most important traits common to the three types making up that Triad. For example, types Two, Three, and Four are found in the Feeling Triad—and their common assets and liabilities involve expressing (or not) their genuine emotions. Types Five, Six, and Seven constitute the Doing Triad—and their strengths and weaknesses involve their ability (or inability) to do and make decisions on their own. Finally, types Eight, Nine, and One are the types of the Relating Triad—and their assets and liabilities involve their ability to relate in a more or less balanced manner with the environment, especially with other people. The Triads can be understood more clearly on the Enneagram itself.

Each Triad has an inner structure based on a dialectical relationship among the three types in it (*PT*, 25). In each Triad, one type overexpresses the characteristic faculty of the

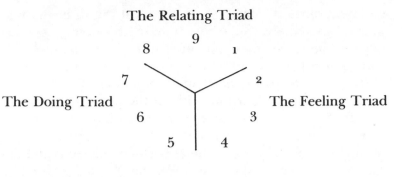

THE TRIADS OF THE ENNEAGRAM

Triad, another type underexpresses the faculty, and the third type is most out of touch with the faculty (this is the "primary type" of each Triad and is the type on the equilateral triangle).

If we move around the Enneagram Triad by Triad (beginning by my convention with personality type Two in the Feeling Triad), you will see these dialectical relationships more clearly. The Two is the type that tends to overexpress its feelings. Twos become effusive and overly friendly, expressing only their positive feelings for others while repressing any awareness of their own needs or ulterior motives. The Three is the primary type of the Feeling Triad (*PT*, 26). Because Threes are most out of touch with their feelings, they project an impression of feelings and attitudes to others instead. The Four is the dialectical opposite of the Two; Fours are painfully self-conscious and underexpress their feelings, revealing themselves instead through various forms of art or creativity. All three types have common problems with their identities and with hostility, both of which are expressed differently and have different causes (*PT*, 30–31).

In the Doing Triad, the Five is the type that, in a sense,

underexpresses its ability to do practical things in the real world. Instead, Fives substitute thinking for doing, generating ever more complex, yet often unrealistic, theories that may have little to do with reality. The Six is the primary type of this Triad. Sixes are most out of touch with their ability to make decisions on their own without the permission and approval of an authority figure of some kind. (Once Sixes get that "permission," however, they have no problem with "doing"—in fact, they sometimes become rebellious and deviate from the rules they have been taught to follow.) The Seven is the type that overexpresses its ability to do. Sevens do things to a fault, often too many things at once, until they become hyperactive and manic, addicted to staying in motion until they are out of control. These three types have common problems with insecurity and anxiety which are expressed differently and have different causes (*PT*, 31–32).

And, finally, in the Relating Triad, the Eight is the type that overexpresses its ability to relate to the environment by completely dominating everything and everyone around it. Eights relate to the world by seeing themselves as stronger and more powerful than everyone else. The Nine is the primary type of the Relating Triad. Nines are most out of touch with their ability to relate to the world without identifying with another, living through someone else rather than becoming independent and autonomous. The One is the type that underexpresses its ability to relate to the environment in the sense that it needs to feel justified by being right before it acts. Ones constantly measure themselves against ideals of various sorts that they strive to attain. All three types have in common aggression and repression, which are expressed differently and have different causes. (More about the Triads can be found in *PT*, 24–27, 30–34, 321–22, and 339–41, and in the Overview of the description of each type.)

In the Enneagram, as in life, there are no pure types. Everyone is a unique mixture of his or her basic type and one of the two types adjacent to it, called a "wing." Second in importance to the basic type, the auxiliary type, or wing, provides the basic type with other psychological functions, sometimes complementing the basic type, sometimes working in opposition to it. Of all the theoretical aspects of the Enneagram, the so-called "wing theory" is the most controversial since some writers feel that there is no wing, some (such as myself) feel that there is only one wing, and others feel that there are two wings, one on each side of the basic type.

The truth of this dispute (as with others regarding the theory of the Enneagram) can be discovered only by looking to human nature: what are human beings really like? If someone is correctly identified as a One with a Two-wing, for example, does the person also clearly possess the traits of a Nine and therefore also have a Nine-wing? If we cannot discern a second wing in real people, then either it does not exist or its influence is so minimal as to be negligible. (It is theoretically possible that each of us has two wings; if so, one wing has developed to a greater degree than the other. The potential "second wing" therefore need not be given much attention as we use the Enneagram in our daily lives.)

Furthermore, from a theoretical point of view, the wing develops as the result of the relationship with a second parent or parent figure. This explanation of why we have only one wing is an elaboration of my theory of the Childhood Origins of each type. For example, Ones are negatively oriented to their fathers (or father figures); I believe that Ones with a Nine-wing are negatively oriented to their fathers while also having a positive orientation to their mothers; Ones with a Two-wing have a negative orientation to their fathers and an ambivalent orientation to their mothers. If a One had a negative orientation to both the father and the mother, he or she would no longer be a One but a Four (since this type is negatively oriented to both parents). To give another example, Sixes have a positive orientation to their fathers; Sixes with a Seven-wing also have a secondary negative orientation to their mothers, while Sixes with a Five-wing have an ambivalent orientation. If either wing provided the Six with a positive relationship to his or her mother, the Six would no longer be a Six but a Nine—the type that has a positive orientation to both parents. A full explanation of the eighteen subtypes, including these primary and secondary parental orientations, will have to wait for a book on theory. In the meantime, this brief explanation of the wings and why it seems that each of us has only one wing will have to suffice.

Also remember that on one level of analysis we possess the entire Enneagram in our psyches. Seen from this point of view, it would be true to say that we have "two wings" since (to return to our example) a One with a Two-wing would also automatically have something of the Nine by virtue of possessing all of the human potentials symbolized by the Enneagram. More than this is meant, however, by those who believe that each type has two wings, and it remains for them to make convincing arguments and to present descriptions to support their theoretical position.

There has also been some question about whether it is possible to change your basic personality type, especially as you become older. Some people feel that they were one type when they were children but became another type as adults owing to various factors in their lives.

I remain convinced that people do not change from one basic personality type to another. We develop from childhood as an example of a certain personality type—as a unique individual within a larger group—and we essentially remain that type for the rest of our lives. We grow or deteriorate from that beginning point, our basic type, which reflects who we have become as the result of genetics and our childhood experiences, especially the relationships we have had with our parents. Which type we have become is profoundly who we are, and this does not change to a radically different type.

But of course, in reality, people do change, and the Enneagram accounts for psychological change of various sorts. We evolve and mature, becoming who we can be or failing that essential task. When we do evolve or deteriorate, the direction in which we change is predicted by the lines on the Enneagram. Everyone "moves" in specific Directions of Integration and Disintegration as indicated by the lines of the Enneagram from the basic type.

The Direction of Disintegration (which signals the further deterioration or breakdown of your basic personality type) is indicated on the Enneagram by the sequence of numbers 1-4-2-8-5-7-1 and 9-6-3-9. The Direction of Integration (which marks the further integration and personal growth of your basic type) is indicated by the reverse of these two sequences: 1-7-5-8-2-4-1 and 9-3-6-9. For example, a One who disintegrates will move to Four, the type in its Direction of Disintegration, while a One who integrates will move to Seven, the type in its Direction of Integration; a Nine will go to Three if it integrates and to Six if it disintegrates.

While it is helpful to have separate Enneagrams for each of these sequences, it is really not necessary once you know what the two lines from each basic personality type mean — one indicates that type's Direction of Integration, while the other indicates its Direction of Disintegration (*PT*, 36–39) — and the arrows can be eliminated.

Thus, *four* of the personality types are pertinent for a full analysis of any individual — the basic type, the wing, the type in the Direction of Integration, and the type in the Direction of Disintegration. We must attempt to see how these four types (at their various Levels), along with other important personality factors (such as intelligence, which the Enneagram does not categorize), combine in ourselves to help make us the unique persons we are. The Enneagram is subtle and open-ended — although it is also highly specific and detailed. We must take more than the basic personality type into account, although for most purposes this alone is enough to

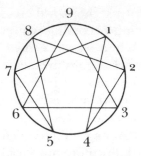

The Direction of Integration   The Direction of Disintegration
1-7-5-8-2-4-1   1-4-2-8-5-7-1
9-3-6-9   9-6-3-9

**THE DIRECTIONS OF INTEGRATION
AND DISINTEGRATION**

handle. As we continue our quest for self-understanding, the wing and the types in our Directions of Integration and Disintegration must also be taken into consideration.

It is also important to have a sense of the movement within our own personality. The many hundreds of traits that make up our type are part of a larger pattern — our type as a whole. The traits found in each type are not arbitrary: they are interrelated in extremely complex and subtle ways. Moreover, people fluctuate among the traits that constitute their type along a Continuum from health to unhealth.

Because people are constantly changing and are in different places along the Continuum, not everything in the descriptions will apply to them equally. When you are healthy, the unhealthy traits will not apply to you as you are right now. Nevertheless, you should be able to recognize all of the traits of your basic type as genuine *tendencies* inherent in yourself. Our unhealthy traits should strike us as accurate reflections of what would happen to us—of how we would become—if we were to become unhealthy or neurotic. Likewise, the traits of the types in the Directions of Integration and Disintegration should also strike us as accurate predictions of our potentially more integrated or disintegrated states, if we should either grow or deteriorate psychologically. The Continuum (with the nine Levels of Development that make it up) can be pictured as follows:

To the Direction of Integration

HEALTHY
Level 1:
Level 2:
Level 3:

AVERAGE
Level 4:
Level 5:
Level 6:

UNHEALTHY
Level 7:
Level 8:
Level 9:

To the Direction of Disintegration

THE CONTINUUM

As you get to know the personality types—and yourself—in more depth, you will find that on a very profound level, the Enneagram lays out the full range of psychological possibilities, revealing the many different potential parts of yourself *in all of the types*. While it remains true that everyone emerges from childhood as a unique member of only one basic personality type, it is equally true that as we develop over our lifetimes, it is possible to integrate the healthy psychological aspects of the other types as we activate new capacities. We can move beyond the type in our Direction of Integration to the next type and then to the next, around the Enneagram in an endless upward spiral of integration (*PT*, 40 and 309).

The Enneagram is not imposing a narrow theory on human beings. Rather, it is a framework within which we can understand the subtle dynamics that make each of us who we are. Everyone constantly changes, and the very structure of the Enneagram reflects the fact that human nature is in process, always coming into being.

TWO

The Nine
Personality Types

THE NINE personality types are reviewed in this chapter—although with a difference from *Personality Types*. The descriptions given here are condensed and are presented with several new features that approach the types thematically rather than analytically. Those familiar with the full descriptions in *Personality Types* can use this chapter to augment the essentials, since much new material is presented here for the first time. For those not familiar with the types, this chapter can be used as a brief introduction.

The most important new feature is the Expanded Profiles. Instead of merely duplicating the Profiles as they appeared in *Personality Types*, I have expanded them substantially so that readers will be given more of the essential traits. These Expanded Profiles are, in effect, the "core traits"—the complex cluster of related traits that is the essence of each type—in the healthy, average, and unhealthy Levels of Development. The development of the Enneagram as a typology depends a great deal on arriving at some agreement about which traits constitute the essential core of each personality type. One of the fundamental problems with the traditional descriptions has been that traits have often been misattributed from type to type; there has been little understanding of which trait goes with which type and why. While the Expanded Profiles presented here are not encyclopedic, they present a core of the essential traits of each type. This chapter and the following one on the Levels of Development should help finally establish some sort of agreement about what traits constitute each type.

However, even though the Expanded Profiles have been substantially enlarged, they may not necessarily contain *all* of the "core" traits of each type. More can always be said, and different practical or analytic approaches might well emphasize different traits, although finding an objective "core" of each type remains an ultimate goal. Since the Expanded Profiles cannot satisfy everyone's needs, you can note other traits you have observed. (If more space is needed, you may want to use the space provided in Chapter 6, "Assessment Guides.")

Another new feature in this book is the inclusion of female caricatures. Male caricatures were used in *Personality Types*; however, since all of the types apply equally to both males and females, it is appropriate to present female figures too, thereby avoiding a sexist bias. The female caricatures also embody entirely different traits for each type, giving a more rounded impression of the types.

Following the Expanded Profile of each type are very brief sketches of that type's Direction of Disintegration and Direction of Integration. The longer explanations in *Personality Types* are much more complete, but for readers who want to understand the essence of the movements toward further integration or disintegration, these short entries should be helpful. Of course, you can add your own insights to them as well.

Childhood Origins have already been given in the Overview to each type in *Personality Types*. This section has nevertheless been included as a very brief restatement of the fundamental relationship that each child has had with his or her parents. (For a longer discussion of the Childhood Origins of each type, refer to the cross-referenced pages in *Personality Types*.)

A word of explanation about how the Childhood Origins came about is also probably in order. During the years that I was researching the Enneagram, I was always on the lookout for "three times three" patterns that could be applied to the nine personality types. Two of the most basic categories of parent-child relationships in early formation are child-to-mother and child-to-father relationships. Yet, to my knowledge, no one had perceived that children could be related to mother and father taken together. Thus, children could be related primarily to their mothers or primarily to their fathers or to their mothers and fathers equally. That third category was a major breakthrough, as obvious is it now seems.

Then I realized that in addition to the positive and negative orientations that can exist between parents and children, there can also be an "ambivalent" one, even at an early age—and this yielded another group of three. The result was two groups of three whose permutations yielded nine theoretical combinations for the Childhood Origins of the nine Enneagram types (*PT*, 336–38).

The next step was to discover if these nine new theoretical categories actually occur in real life: do the theoretical origins match the childhood development of real people? While not proving anything scientifically, the anecdotal evidence presented by people in workshops and in counseling and my ongoing observations have borne out my theory—that, for example, Sixes have had a positive orientation to their fathers, Threes a positive orientation to their mothers, and so forth, as they have been given in *Personality Types* and as recapitulated briefly in this chapter. Formal research has yet to be done on these theoretical categories but, at least informally, they are being confirmed and will give researchers a fertile, clear set of hypotheses to work with. Importantly, my explanation of the Childhood Origins of each type correlates with the findings of other psychological systems; while this in itself does not prove anything, it is an encouraging indication that theories are converging on objective facts about the development of the personality types.

Several more clarifications must be made about the Childhood Origins. First, the genetic basis for personality may be very strong, and to the degree that it is, it offsets the purely psychological influence of our parents. Research on individual twins reared apart, for example, indicates that they seem to have the same personality type. If further research bears this out, the biology of personality may prove to be the most important single factor in our Childhood Origins. Second, there may be exceptions to the general patterns given in *Personality Types*, although evaluating someone as an exception to the general childhood pattern must be done only after assessing whether the person's Enneagram type has been correctly diagnosed and whether the person is influenced by an undue amount of resistance or denial. Many people do not know what their true relationship with their parents was, or their memories have been distorted for one reason or another. (For example, my hypothesis is that Sevens have developed as they have, at least in part, because of a negative relationship with their mother or a mother figure. The denial typically present in average to unhealthy Sevens makes facing this fact of their lives difficult, and their every tendency is to glibly dismiss that they ever had negative feelings toward their mother. Often it is only after years of therapy that the true picture emerges, and so it is not surprising that a person for whom denial is a defense mechanism simply would not be able to admit the truth about himself or herself.) Because of resistance, our initial reaction to the theory of Childhood Origins may not reflect the reality of our past.

Third, no one should make a diagnosis based on the theory of Childhood Origins alone. It is but one factor among many and should not be given undue weight. But neither should it be ignored, especially since it has important implications about the origins of other characteristics in the personality types.

Last, remember that the theory is about our parents *or parent figures*, not always literally about one or both of our actual parents. For instance, Threes may have been positively oriented not to their biological mother but to a grandmother who was, in effect, a mother figure in their life. Likewise, a One may have been negatively related not to his or her father but rather to a father figure such as a minister, a stern and forbidding image of God the Father, or a particularly severe teacher or early disciplinarian who played the role of the father in the child's life. While we should not disregard the possibility that the childhood orientations are accurate as they have been given, we must also admit the possibility that, in some cases at least, they are symbolic and that some kind of parent figure must be taken into account.

One of the many implications of the Childhood Origins is that they give rise to our fundamental motivations, to our sense of self, and, in a way, to the entire orientation of our lives (or "life script"). Without getting involved with theory, it is worth understanding that our ordinary conscious motivations have their roots in an unconscious Basic Fear and Basic Desire that have arisen from childhood experiences, particularly in our responses to our parents. The inspiration for this insight came from Karen Horney's work on the concept of "basic anxiety"; I took it a step further by discovering that an underlying Basic Fear and Basic Desire are unique to each personality type and that this twin source of negative and positive motivation is responsible for the subsequent secondary (derivative) motivations and behaviors (traits) that constitute each type at each Level of Development. In *Personality Types* I only alluded to the Basic Fear and Basic Desire in the descriptions; I have made them explicit here for the first time.

As just mentioned, the Basic Fear and Basic Desire produce the secondary, or derivative, fears and desires that appear at each Level in each type. An expanded list of Secondary Motivations has therefore been provided. These motivations are especially noteworthy since traits alone do not help us to understand each type: we must comprehend the range of related motivations that underlie the traits we observe. Failure to understand the different motivations for similar behavior in different types has been a persistent source of confusion for readers as well as for those who have written about personality types, whether from the viewpoint of the Enneagram or of other systems. Without understanding each type's underlying motivations, it is difficult to discriminate between types: their behavior may seem arbitrary or unmotivated or otherwise difficult to account for.

Another new feature of this chapter is how each personality type sees itself—that is, its Healthy Sense of Self. Each type has a different sense of self, and maintaining a stable sense of self is an underlying, unconscious goal for everyone; it constitutes one of the most important areas for understanding ourselves and others. The Healthy Sense of Self (given here) arises from our Basic Fear and Basic Desire as well as from our cognitive functions and defense mechanisms. (The sense of self is discussed further in Chapter 3.)

Although only the Healthy Sense of Self of each type is given here, our sense of self shifts as we move up or down the Levels of Development. Many of our intrapsychic conflicts result from a disparity between the sense of self that we consciously maintain and the sense of self that our actual behavior and attitudes warrant—just as many of our interpersonal conflicts result from the discrepancy between the sense of self that we have and the perception of us that others have. Sometimes our sense of self is inflated, while at other times it is too negative; in either case, it must become more realistic if we are to be healthy. When it is not realistic, anxiety results, triggering defense mechanisms and the complex interplay of more secondary fears and desires. In short, our sense of self and how we defend it (and many other related issues) are important factors not only for understanding but for changing ourselves.

Besides the characteristic Healthy Sense of Self that has been listed for each type, there is a related typical Hidden Complaint that points to a frustrated or unfulfilled claim made about the self, particularly as the person begins to deteriorate down the Levels of Development toward neurosis. The Hidden Complaint is an unstated source of many of the underlying attitudes a person holds toward others; as a result, the Hidden Complaint is the unacknowledged source of many interpersonal conflicts. It is useful to be aware of the Hidden Complaint (and other "hidden complaints" you may become aware of) as another key both to self-understanding and to change.

The traditional teaching of the Enneagram lists one defense mechanism for each type, attributed to Claudio Naranjo. My own investigations indicate that there are at least three key defense mechanisms for each type—and there are probably more. In addition, even though all nine types employ many of the same defense mechanisms, precisely which of the dozen or so basic defenses they employ produce a different pattern for each type. Two similar types have one or two defense mechanisms in common, providing yet another explanation for their similarities and differences.

The Defense Mechanisms give us insight into the motivation and behavior of each type, into how the sense of self is characteristically defended, into interpersonal relations, and into other important matters. Furthermore, the Defense Mechanisms help explain why each type is what it is: the traits are not arbitrary because the underlying structures of the personality are not arbitrary. Traits grow out of the unique pattern of motivations and defenses.

The type names used in the traditional Arica presentation of "Ego-Fixations" were renamed in *Personality Types* and given a more positive general descriptive title, as we saw in Chapter

1. Other features of the traditional teaching have also been reformulated so that they will be clearer and more accurate. For example, the traditional idea of a type's "trap" has been reconceptualized as the Characteristic Temptation. What traditionally has been called the "idealized self-image" (probably following Karen Horney) has been reformulated as the Sense of Self (which, as already noted, besides being idealized, also manifests itself at different Levels of Development in other than idealized states).

Unfortunately, because of copyright restrictions on Enneagram material, I am unable to compare and contrast my new features with the corresponding features in the traditional Arica presentation. (Those interested in learning more about this approach should consult the doctoral dissertations and the Lilly and Hart article listed in the Bibliography for more information.)

The following sections have been included in this chapter to round out the picture of each type and to further indicate how my interpretation of the personality types corresponds to the "traditional" approach, where applicable: Characteristic Temptation, Characteristic Vice, Characteristic Virtue, Saving Grace, Structural Patterns, and Inevitable Consequences.

A Characteristic Temptation arises at the beginning of the average Levels of each type, at Level 4. The Characteristic Temptation is a way of thinking or behaving (or both) that initiates the type's downward spiral into progressively unhealthy states. If a type succumbs to its Characteristic Temptation, it gradually becomes entrapped in attitudes and behaviors that will, like getting caught in quicksand, eventually spell disaster. The Characteristic Temptation can therefore function as an early warning signal of potentially destructive behavior—while there is still time and psychological strength left to avoid it.

The Characteristic Vices are roughly equivalent to the capital sins in traditional theology. Each personality type can be characterized by one capital sin that is the linchpin of its psychology—much as Gurdjieff adapted the concept of capital sins to become each type's "chief feature."

The Characteristic Virtue of each type often acts as an antidote to its Vice and as a focal point for its positive traits. While the discussion of the Characteristic Temptations, Vices, and Virtues may seem to have more to do with traditional (or even medieval) theology, it is nevertheless helpful to include them and to use them in psychological settings, since these aspects of the personality are a reflection of significant themes found in the type as a whole. Furthermore, the practice of virtue and the avoidance of vice are central to any spiritual use of the Enneagram.

The last three features are not part of the traditional presentation of the Enneagram since these kinds of insights are possible only by understanding the Levels of Development, which are not an element of the traditional interpretation.

Each type's Saving Grace is the kernel of strength that remains in the person after he or she has deteriorated fairly far (to Level 6) and is in danger of deteriorating into the unhealthy Levels of Development. The Saving Grace is the positive quality that still remains and can be drawn on to help the person out of his or her predicament. The neurotic condition itself does not have the potential to save a person from being neurotic (an absurdity that some Enneagram teachers propound); rather, a remaining source of strength that is active despite deterioration becomes the anchor that not only prevents a person from deteriorating further but can help restore the person to healthier functioning. By being aware of the Saving Grace and acting on it, the deteriorating person can begin to reverse the downward movement toward neurosis.

The type's Structural Patterns make explicit its psychological patterns of intrapsychic and interpersonal conflicts. As has been mentioned, it is essential to understand larger patterns if we are to understand each type as a whole. Understanding each type's internal and external conflicts more explicitly is therefore very helpful.

Last, Inevitable Consequences describe the inexorable results of the type's deterioration into the unhealthy Levels of Development. This section makes explicit the "self-fulfilling prophecy" that is each type's tragic element — how the person loses the very thing he or she most desires (Basic Desire) while bringing on himself or herself the thing most feared (Basic Fear). This process began when the person succumbed to his or her Characteristic Temptation and continued to gather momentum if the person did not act on the Saving Grace (among other, more complicated reasons).

I will begin the Expanded Profiles and other new features of each type with personality type Two, the first type in the Feeling Triad (*PT*, 24–26 and 30ff.). By my own convention, I always start with the Two since doing so allows us to see the types within their Triads and thus to understand larger patterns both within the Enneagram and within each type.

Personality Type Two:
The Helper
The Concerned-Helpful-Possessive-Manipulative Person

EXPANDED PROFILE

Healthy: Healthy Twos are empathetic, compassionate, full of feeling with and for others. Put themselves in others' place, are caring and concerned about others' needs. Sincere, warm-hearted, appreciative, and encouraging: play a parenting role, seeing the good in others where they may not see it in themselves. Service is important; they are extremely generous, giving, and helpful. Loving and thoughtful, they give people what they really need, even if it means going out of their way to do so. *At their best:* Become profoundly disinterested, unselfish, and altruistic: giving unconditional love with no expectation of reward. Feel it is a privilege to be in other people's lives. "Saintly," deeply charitable, and humble, "Good Samaritans."

Average: Average Twos begin to do more talking about their feelings than helping: "love" is their supreme value, and they talk about it constantly, becoming emotionally demonstrative (histrionic), gushy, too friendly, full of "good intentions" about everything. Give attention, approval, flattery. Begin to get overly intimate, too solicitous, and intrusive: they need to be needed, hovering, meddling, and interfering with others under the guise of being a "caring friend." Become the self-sacrificial mothering person who cannot do enough for others, creating needs to fulfill and wearing themselves out for everyone yet possessive and jealous of those they have "invested" in. Want people to depend on them, to keep them informed about everything, to come for permission and advice. Increasingly self-important and self-satisfied, they begin to feel indispensable (while overrating what they do for everyone) and to feel that others owe them for what they have been given. Patronizing, overbearing, imperious, high-handed. Begin to expect to be constantly thanked and honored for their goodness. May become hypochondriacs or play the role of martyrs who have suffered because of their good works on behalf of everyone else.

Unhealthy: Feeling unappreciated, unhealthy Twos become resentful and complain bitterly. Begin to be extremely self-deceptive about their motives and how aggressive and egocentric they can be, becoming manipulative and self-serving, undermining people and playing on their guilt and weaknesses. Begin to make belittling, disparaging remarks; gradually become coercive and domineering, feeling entitled to get anything they want: old favors must be repaid, money given as tokens of thanks, special favors granted. Able to rationalize and excuse whatever they do since they feel victimized and abused by the ingratitude of others. Repressed anger becomes evident in psychosomatic problems ("conversion reactions").

Direction of Disintegration: Unhealthy Twos are resentful and enraged at the ungrateful treatment they feel they have received from others. When they move to Eight, they strike out at those who have not responded to them as they wanted. Deteriorated Twos can become physically violent, even murderous, usually to those closest to them, the very people for whom they think they have had nothing but the kindest, most tender feelings.

Direction of Integration: When healthy Twos go to Four, they get in touch with their genuine feelings and become aware of themselves as they really are. They become emotionally honest, acknowledging their aggressions and mixed motives as fully as they have accepted their positive view of themselves. By unconditionally loving themselves for their real value, they realize that they do not have to be all good to be loved. They can be themselves and reveal themselves more fully; thus, their relationships become more honest, human, reciprocal, and satisfying.

Childhood Origins: Ambivalently identified with the father or a father figure (*PT*, 54). The key element is that as children, Twos learned to fit into the family by serving others, thus winning their love and praise, beginning with the father. They may have learned to play the role of "little mommy" or "little daddy" to other siblings, thus also winning the praise of an absent, or otherwise distant, father.

Basic Fear: Of being unloved and unwanted for themselves alone (*PT*, 53).

Basic Desire: To be loved (*PT*, 53).

Secondary Motivations: Twos want to express their feelings for others, to help people, to be appreciated for what they have done, to be an important influence on others, to be intimate with others, to be necessary to others, to control people, and to justify the demands they make on others.

Healthy Sense of Self: "I am a caring, loving person."

Hidden Complaint: "I am always loving, although people don't love me as much as I love them."

Key Defense Mechanisms: Identification, reaction formation, denial.

Characteristic Temptation: To think that they are always well intentioned. Average Twos begin to think of themselves as entirely well meaning and always completely loving toward others, totally without any ulterior motives or emotional needs of their own. They do not acknowledge their own needs or that they tend to use others to fulfill them.

Characteristic Vice: Vainglory. The form of pride in which Twos take special satisfaction in their virtues and virtuous activities. This is goodness that calls attention to itself so that they will be admired for being virtuous, praised for being humble, rewarded for being self-sacrificial, repaid for being generous, and so forth.

Characteristic Virtue: Disinterested charity. Very healthy Twos love others disinterestedly, without any thought of self, of being thanked or repaid, or of even having the good regard and appreciation of the people they do things for. They strive to do good unselfishly, helping others for others' sake, without ego or the thought of reward getting in the way.

Saving Grace: Despite growing pride and self-importance, average Twos may still have enough genuine empathy for others to prevent them from deteriorating any further into outright manipulation or coercive behavior. Their healthy capacity to identify with others can act as a catalyst to help them return to healthier attitudes and behavior.

Suggestions for Personal Growth: See Chapter 8.

Structural Patterns: The keynote here is *indirection*. Personal needs and desires are expressed indirectly, through service to others. Average to unhealthy Twos communicate what they want from others without saying so openly. Unacknowledged needs, covert claims, and ulterior motives cause tensions and conflicts between their loving, empathetic, positive feelings and their unconscious resentments and aggressions—often toward the same people. These internal conflicts may become expressed in aggressive acts against others (expressed as overbearing, coercive behavior) as well as in aggressions turned against the self (in self-sacrifice and moral masochism). Although their inner conflicts are consciously repressed, their aggressive impulses take their toll at an unconscious level and in their relationships. Therefore, the pattern is interpersonal and intrapsychic tension, often producing conscious suffering and physical ailments.

Inevitable Consequences: As with everyone who deteriorates down the Continuum, unhealthy Twos inevitably lose their Basic Desire (to be loved) while bringing on themselves their Basic Fear (that they are unloved and unwanted for themselves alone). The more manipulative and coercive they become, and the more domineering and inflated with self-importance they are, the less others can stand being around them. (Ironically, the reactions of others indicate how loving or how ego-inflated Twos actually are, rather than their self-deceptive claims about themselves. If they are consistently having interpersonal conflicts, the source of their problems is most likely in themselves, not in others.)

The single most important thing for Twos to remember is that if they claim to be loving and want only to serve others, they have committed themselves to the very highest ideal and will be judged by that standard. If they want to be loving, they must freely give to others. To do so, they must constantly transcend their ego. The instant they begin to call attention to themselves or expect praise for whatever they give to others, they are going in the wrong direction and will only be frustrated and suffer as a result.

Personality Type Three:
The Motivator
The Self-Assured-Ambitious-Narcissistic-Psychopathic Person

EXPANDED PROFILE

Healthy: Healthy Threes are self-assured, feel desirable, and enjoy high self-esteem, believing in themselves and their own value. Adaptable, energetic, often attractive, charming, and popular. Ambitious to improve themselves, to be the best they can be: often become outstanding in some way, truly admirable, a human ideal, embodying widely admired qualities. Others want to be like them, to imitate their achievements. Good communicators, motivators, and promoters, know how to present something in an acceptable and compelling way. *At their best:* Self-accepting, inner-directed, genuine, and authentic: everything they seem to be. Accept their limitations and live within them, within their own "center."

Average: Average Threes begin to become competitively concerned with rising above others: compare themselves with others in search for success, status, and prestige. Social climbers for whom exclusivity, career, and being a "winner" is important. Pragmatic, goal-oriented, and efficient, but also calculating and affectless beneath the cool, polished facade.

Become image-conscious, highly concerned with how they are perceived by others; concerned with credibility, with projecting the right image, saying the right thing, packaging themselves according to expectations that will be rewarded. Become chameleons, depending on jargon and projecting style over substance. Problems with commitment and intimacy, dishonesty and phoniness, emerge. They want to impress others with their complete superiority and so constantly promote themselves and make themselves appear better than they actually are. Narcissistic and pretentious, feel "special," full of inflated self-regard, with grandiose expectations about themselves and their potential. Arrogant and exhibitionistic, as if saying "Look at me!" as hostility and contempt for others surface.

Unhealthy: Fearing failure and humiliation, unhealthy Threes can be exploitative and opportunistic, out for themselves, using others to stay on top. Sleazy, immoral, pathological liars, taking advantage of others however they can. Completely untrustworthy, maliciously sabotaging and betraying people, stabbing friends and colleagues in the back, ruining reputations and relationships for the feeling of triumph it gives them. Unconsciously they become delusionally jealous of others. Devious and duplicitous to protect their image and to be sure their deceptions will not be exposed. Finally, become vindictive and diabolically sadistic, attempting to ruin others. Violent, psychopathic tendencies: torture, mutilation, murder ultimate possibilities.

Direction of Disintegration: Unhealthy Threes become so malicious, so intent on the destruction of others, and so consumed by their hostility that they may well strike out at others. They suddenly realize that they have gone too far, and, rather than feel anxiety or guilt, any feelings they have suddenly "turn off" completely. When they go to Nine, disintegrating Threes dissociate from their hostile feelings, with the result that they feel nothing. Rather than feel guilt or anxiety about whatever they may have done, they "blank out" and become depersonalized and catatonic, revealing their inner emptiness.

Direction of Integration: When healthy Threes go to Six, they become committed to others and in doing so find more of value to affirm in themselves. Their love for another, paradoxically, creates more value within themselves. Integrating Threes begin to become real—more genuine and more developed as persons—by sustaining a mutual relationship. They no longer are competitive but cooperative; no longer falsely superior but equal; no longer tending to exploit people but committed to others and their welfare.

Childhood Origins: Positively identified with the mother or with a mother figure (*PT*, 81–82). The essential element is that as children Threes were taught to have high self-esteem and to expect attention and praise from others because of the attention and praise lavished on them by their mothers, at least during their early formation.

Basic Fear: Of being rejected (*PT*, 104).

Basic Desire: To be accepted (affirmed) (*PT*, 84).

Secondary Motivations: Threes want to improve themselves, to rise above others and distinguish themselves, to get attention, to be admired, to impress others, to use or do whatever they need to stay on top, to ruin others if they themselves cannot be superior.

Healthy Sense of Self: "I am a desirable, admirable person."

Hidden Complaint: "I am a superior person, and other people are jealous of me."

Key Defense Mechanisms: Repression, projection, displacement.

Characteristic Temptation: To compete with others. Average Threes want to distinguish themselves in some way to maintain their high self-esteem and feelings of superiority. They begin to compare themselves with others, looking down on them and attempting to beat them in overt and covert competitions that will prove their total superiority.

Characteristic Vice: Sloth in self-development. Average

Threes develop their image and the perfection of their "package" rather than their real self. Beneath the seeming perfection, however, they are less perfect than they seem because they have developed not their genuine self and talents but only what will "go over" and get them what they want. (Other writers list "deceit" as the vice of Threes; this is correct, although sloth in genuine self-development underlies the Three's deceitfulness. It is therefore given here as the fundamental vice.)

Characteristic Virtue: Proper love of self. If healthy Threes love themselves properly, they invest time and energy to make the most of themselves without competing with anyone else and without overshooting their own limitations. Their proper love of self is based on humility and a truthful assessment of their capacities, not on a narcissistic, inflated notion of themselves. Proper love of self also leads Threes to love others genuinely and hence to move in their Direction of Integration.

Saving Grace: Despite increasing narcissism and arrogance, the desire of average Threes to be accepted by others may prevent them from deteriorating any further into exploiting people or acting with hostility toward them. Their healthy desire to be accepted by others may guide them back to balanced, healthier behavior.

Suggestions for Personal Growth: See Chapter 8.

Structural Patterns: The keynote is *changeability*. Threes form their identities and interact with others by adapting to people, by responding to others' expectations, and by adjusting to the "feedback" they are given. Beneath what appears to be a highly functional, independent facade, average to unhealthy Threes are covertly dependent on the acceptance of others and change like chameleons to assure themselves of receiving as much attention and affirmation as possible. The inner pattern for average Threes, therefore, is of emotional deficits concealed by a superb capacity for social interaction and adaptability. Outwardly, their interpersonal image changes constantly depending on whom they interact with and what social expectations are placed on them.

Inevitable Consequences: The inevitable result of ego inflation is that Threes will lose their Basic Desire (to be accepted) while invariably bringing on themselves their Basic Fear (of being rejected) (*PT*, 104). Their search for acceptance will end not in a demonstration of their superiority but in rejection because they are not who they seem to be. If they play others falsely, they will be seen not as the paragons they wish to be but for what they truly are: fraudulent and empty persons.

It is important for Threes to remember that if they wish to enjoy the admiration of others they must accomplish something genuinely worthy of being admired. They must work at a worthwhile goal and become everything they seem to be. Anything less is false, and if Threes go too far in making false claims about themselves, they will likely be exposed and bring about their own downfall. Only to the degree that they embody genuine values will Threes be genuinely admirable. Anything less invites humiliation and rejection.

Personality Type Four: The Artist
The Creative-Individualistic- Introverted-Depressive Person

EXPANDED PROFILE

Healthy: Healthy Fours are introspective, self-aware, in a "search for self," in touch with feelings and inner impulses. Sensitive and intuitive both to self and others: compassionate, tactful, discrete, and respectful of others. Self-expressive, highly personal, individualistic. Enjoy being alone, taking time for their unconscious impulses to surface into consciousness. Self-revealing, emotionally honest, authentic, and true to self. Have an ironic view of life and self: can be serious and funny, easily touched, and yet emotionally strong. *At their best:* Profoundly creative, expressing the personal and the universal, possibly in an inspired work of art. On the personal level, they become regenerative and self-renewing—possessing a self-creating, redemptive quality, able to transform all their experiences into something valuable.

Average: Rather than risk expressing themselves, average Fours begin to take an artistic, aesthetic, and romantic orientation to life, revealing personal feelings indirectly through something beautiful. Intensify reality through fantasy, imagination, and by heightening passionate feelings. May begin to be emotionally overwhelmed: to deal with their feelings, they withdraw, becoming self-absorbed, self-conscious, and shy. Begin to question self constantly (self-doubt) and take everything personally, getting hypersensitive, feeling they are "different," "outsiders." Moody, easily hurt, and emotionally vulnerable. Yearn to break free of self-consciousness and the melancholy suffering it brings. Feel increasingly different from others and therefore exempt from living as others do. Self-pity leads to different kinds of self-indulgence—to becoming decadent and sensual, to wallowing in a world of dreams, illusions, and unrealistic expectations. Yet they are perversely willful, disdainful, effete, impractical, and unproductive.

Unhealthy: If their dreams (fantasies and expectations) fail, unhealthy Fours become angry at themselves and severely depressed, ashamed of themselves, and alienated from others because of self-inhibitions and emotional paralysis. Profoundly fatigued, mentally confused, emotionally "blocked," and unable to work or function, they develop a deep sense of futility and meaninglessness. Racked with delusional self-contempt, self-hatred, self-reproaches, morbid thoughts, and tormented by their failures: everything becomes a source of withering self-accusations. Feeling worthless and hopeless, they despair and become self-destructive, possibly abusing alcohol or drugs to escape their crushingly negative self-hatred. In the extreme, emotional breakdown or suicide is likely.

Direction of Disintegration: Unhealthy Fours despair of ever actualizing themselves; when they move to Two, it may well be as the result of an emotional breakdown. Since they can no longer function, in effect they coerce someone else to take care of them. Severe problems result, however, because deteriorated Fours hate themselves and may ruin even the relationships on which they have become dependent. They may live with their parents or with a friend or become institutionalized, either until they get the professional help they need or they finally go mad or commit suicide.

Direction of Integration: When healthy Fours go to One by transcending their self-consciousness and their introversion, they are no longer controlled by their ever-changing feelings. They act on objective principles rather than subjective moods; rather than becoming self-indulgent, they are self-disciplined. They no longer see themselves as different and no longer feel exempt from the need to work; thus they make a place for themselves in the real world. By learning self-discipline, they are able to bring their emotional riches to others more often, with a creativity they themselves can depend on.

Childhood Origins: Negatively identified with both parents, feeling abandoned or misunderstood by them in some way (*PT*, 110). The key element in their early formation is that, because of their lack of role models, Fours were forced to create their own identities by looking inward to their feelings and imagination.

Basic Fear: Of being defective or inadequate in some way (*PT*, 110).

Basic Desire: To understand (and "actualize") themselves (*PT*, 114).

Secondary Motivations: Fours want to express themselves, to create something beautiful that will communicate themselves to others, to withdraw from people so that they can sort out and protect their feelings, to cope with their emotions before dealing with anything else, to indulge themselves to make up for what they are missing in the real world.

Healthy Sense of Self: "I am an intuitive, sensitive person."

Hidden Complaint: "I am different from others, and I feel I don't really fit in."

Key Defense Mechanisms: Introjection, displacement, turning against the self.

Characteristic Temptation: To overuse their imaginations in the search for self. Average to unhealthy Fours think that they will find themselves and the meaning of their feelings by retreating into fantasies. But they only lose themselves in their imaginations rather than find themselves by engaging in the real world. By becoming engrossed in fantasies, rather than deal with reality they retreat into an imaginary world where they give themselves permission to feel and be anything, thus wasting their time and energies on illusions.

Characteristic Vice: Envy. Average to unhealthy Fours envy others because they seem so normal and easygoing; others seem to fit in and are not socially awkward or self-conscious, as Fours feel they are. Fours tend to feel like outsiders who never belong anywhere, and they envy those who do.

Characteristic Virtue: Emotional balance. Healthy Fours realize that they are able to cope with life, that they do not have to be so vulnerable and "storm-tossed" by every feeling. Even negative experiences can be made into something positive, and they find peace in knowing that they are able to transform everything into something worthwhile and valuable.

Saving Grace: Despite their growing self-indulgence, their withdrawal from people, and the many bad habits they have gotten into, average Fours may still have enough self-awareness to know what they are doing to themselves. Their honesty with themselves may prevent them from deteriorating further.

Suggestions for Personal Growth: See Chapter 8.

Structural Patterns: The keynote is *subjectivity*, and the overall pattern is of conflicts between subjective feelings and impulses—and between the need to express them and to hold them back. The self-inhibitions of Fours are due to the aggressions they direct toward themselves for the guilt they feel for not being worthy of the love of their parents. As they deteriorate, the pattern is of spiraling inward down the Levels of Development into an increasingly self-enclosed negative state until they become completely alienated from others and, ironically, from themselves. In the end, if they cannot break the pattern of introversion and self-absorption, they will be worn down by a negative self-evaluation that does not allow anything positive to offset it.

Inevitable Consequences: The inevitable consequence of their ego inflation (in fantasies and subjective withdrawal) is that Fours lose their Basic Desire (to actualize themselves) while bringing on themselves their Basic Fear, that they are fundamentally defective in some irredeemable way (*PT*, 133). The more solipsistic Fours become in their endless "search for self," the more they unwittingly perpetuate habits that become increasingly difficult to change. Once they withdraw into fantasies and avoid engaging themselves in realistic ways, they should realize that they are going in the wrong direction.

Fours will find themselves only by transcending their feelings. They must get beyond self-consciousness by taking the "leap of faith" that they will actualize themselves if they involve themselves with the real world. Rather than indulge in useless dreams, they must start taking an active, realistic interest in their own lives—as paradoxical and strange as that may seem. However, Fours know what it means: they must stop imagining life and start living it.

Personality Type Five:
The Thinker
The Perceptive-Analytic-
Eccentric-Paranoid Person

EXPANDED PROFILE

Healthy: Healthy Fives are able to observe everything with extraordinary perceptiveness and insight. Mentally alert, curious, with an acutely searching intelligence — asking the right questions while using extraordinarily fine perceptions. Able to concentrate, to become engrossed in what has caught their attention, and to foresee and predict how some chain of events will likely turn out. Love learning, excited by possessing knowledge, and often become experts in some field. Independent thinkers, innovative, inventive, producing extremely valuable, original ideas. *At their best:* Become discoverers, broadly comprehending the world while penetrating it profoundly. Visionaries, open-minded, taking in things whole, in their true context, making the right connections, seeing things as they actually are. May make pioneering discoveries of something entirely new: often brilliant, possibly geniuses of historical magnitude.

Average: Average Fives become specialized, analytic, constantly dissecting things intellectually, "making a science" of things: involved in research, scholarship, the scientific method, gathering empirical data, building theories. As they speculate about highly complicated, abstract ideas, become more detached, preoccupied with interpretations and possibilities rather than with actual data or facts. Immerse themselves in details, esoteric, abstruse subjects, and elaborate theories, beginning to "lose the forest for the trees," not seeing the true, broader context. Become "disembodied minds," although very high-strung and sharply aggressive as a defense against being emotionally involved or overwhelmed. Want to have certitude about their ideas so they can have something secure to hold on to: jump to conclusions, interpreting facts according to their theories, becoming reductionistic, imposing ideas on the facts. If others disagree, they become highly contentious, abrasive, and cynical: others are too stupid to understand. Litigious to protect their "discoveries." Their provocative, extreme, iconoclastic interpretations may contain valuable insights, but also far-fetched half-truths.

Unhealthy: Rejecting and repulsing all social attachments, unhealthy Fives become reclusive and isolated from people and reality: increasingly secretive, strange, eccentric, and mentally unstable. Highly antagonistic and vituperative, yet fearful of aggressions from others, they become increasingly suspicious and mentally overwrought. Get obsessed with yet frightened by (their own) projected ideas that seem to threaten them, becoming paranoid and prey to gross distortions, phobias, and hallucinations. Finally, lose touch with reality: insanity with schizophrenic tendencies is possible.

Direction of Disintegration: Unhealthy Fives have become extremely isolated and incapable of acting effectively in their environment; when they go to Seven, they become impulsive, acting erratically and hysterically. Thinking too much has gotten them into many problems, so they no longer think but act mindlessly. Deteriorated Fives become unstable and reckless, lunging out at an apparent solution to their problems, although often doing only more harm to themselves than good.

Direction of Integration: When healthy Fives go to Eight, they act from a realization of their own mastery; they feel that they have learned enough to act and to lead others with confidence. (They also realize that while they do not know everything, they still probably know more than anyone else.) They no longer identify with their theories but with objects in the real world; as a result, they feel more secure than they did from theorizing about the world or detaching themselves from it.

Childhood Origins: Fives are ambivalently identified with both parents or parent figures (*PT*, 138). The key element is that Fives feel uncertain of people (beginning with their ambivalence toward their parents) and have learned to defend themselves and their security by being aware of potential threats from others. (As with the other types, there is probably also a genetic foundation for the Five's personality formation, although in this type it seems that an overactive brain chemistry plays a particularly important role.)

Basic Fear: Of being threatened or overwhelmed by another (*PT*, 136).

Basic Desire: To understand the world around them (*PT*, 134 and 141).

Secondary Motivations: Fives want to understand everything, to observe everything, to have intellectual certitude, to interpret everything according to a unifying idea, to reject that which does not agree with their ideas, to isolate themselves from whatever seems to threaten them.

Healthy Sense of Self: "I am an intelligent, perceptive person."

Hidden Complaint: "I am so smart that no one else can understand the things I understand or appreciate the things I know."

Key Defense Mechanisms: Displacement, projection, isolation.

Characteristic Temptation: To analyze everything. Average to unhealthy Fives literally "think too much," in inappropriate categories and circumstances. They are persuaded that by analyzing everything they will attain insight and thus be able to control their environment by predicting what will happen next—and therefore will be able to defend themselves against it, if necessary. However, as they abstract from reality, average to unhealthy Fives become increasingly fixated on more minute details until they lose all perspective. Excessive analysis is therefore the potential prelude to distortion and paranoia.

Characteristic Vice: Avarice. Fives are avaricious for knowledge (retentive: to hold on to what they have) and want to possess all knowledge. They would like to be omniscient, to have everything in the environment figured out, to have The Answer so that they can be completely defended. They think that nothing would be able to surprise, threaten, or overwhelm them if they were able to foresee it and defend themselves against it.

Characteristic Virtue: Understanding. This virtue is related to wisdom, although it is not the same. Understanding allows healthy Fives to comprehend many points of view at the same time, to understand both the whole and its component parts. (Wisdom is the virtue of knowing which choice will be most conducive toward one's end, the virtue of the One.) The understanding of healthy Fives also allows them to be compassionate and tolerant (*"Tout comprendre c'est tout pardonner"*— "to understand all is to forgive all") instead of being cynical and detached from others.

Saving Grace: Despite their overelaborate explanations and detached preoccupations, average Fives may realize that they have begun to introduce distortions into their thinking rather than coming closer to correct conclusions. The understanding of their own thought processes may prevent them from deteriorating further and getting out of touch with reality. Their healthy capacity for observation may help them reassess their ideas; their perceptiveness may help them return to a more balanced, healthier state.

Suggestions for Personal Growth: See Chapter 8.

Structural Patterns: The keynote is *involvement.* The outside world is the focus of their attention; however, the world of thought is the arena Fives inhabit. Therefore, the inner pattern is of thinking oriented to the outer world but impelled by subjective impulses (including aggressions). (Conflicts arise if and when their subjective impulses overpower and distort their perceptions.) Their minds are highly active, intensely driven, and yet defensive—and as their minds become increasingly overheated, Fives unconsciously project subjective ideas into their perceptions. Outwardly, the pattern is of increasing distance from reality as Fives reject attachments with the world, particularly with other people. Thus, the overall pattern is of paradoxical curiosity and withdrawal, involvement and detachment, immersion and defense, aggression and fear of aggression, attraction and repulsion, and so forth.

Inevitable Consequences: If Fives cease observing reality and do not check their ideas against objective facts, they are in danger of becoming completely immersed in their own ideas and consequently of getting out of touch with reality. As with every personality type, Fives may end by losing their Basic Desire (to understand the world around them), while unwittingly bringing on themselves their Basic Fear (of being overwhelmed by the outside world) (*PT,* 161). As they get out of touch with reality, their mental distortions make it inevitable that they will feel threatened either by someone else or by reality. Rather than be more safely defended by their analysis and foresight, they are literally driven mad by it.

Personality Type Six:
The Loyalist
The Likable-Loyal-Dependent-Masochistic Person

EXPANDED PROFILE

Healthy: Healthy Sixes are able to elicit strong emotional responses from others: they are engaging, appealing, endearing, lovable, friendly, playful, and ingratiating. Trust is important, as is bonding with others and forming permanent relationships. Others feel warm toward them and want to help and protect them. Become committed and loyal to those with whom they have identified: family and friends important, as is the feeling that they "belong" somewhere. Respond to others by being cooperative, reliable, responsible, trustworthy, hardworking, and dependable. *At their best:* Become self-affirming, trusting of self, independent yet symbiotically interdependent as an equal. Faith in self leads to having a positive attitude as well as manifesting courage, leadership, richness in creativity, and self-expression.

Average: Average Sixes begin to fear making decisions, taking responsibility for themselves: identify with an authority figure (or a group), becoming obedient to it. Become traditionalists, "team players," and members of organizations, dutifully doing what they are told. Begin to be ambivalent and to react against the authority, through indirect passive-aggressive behavior, giving contradictory, mixed signals. Ambivalence makes Sixes vacillate and react unpredictably: they procrastinate, become indecisive, cautious, and evasive about everything. As tensions increase, they get grumpy, negativistic, and obstructionistic. To overcome doubts and tensions, they become counterphobic and reactionary, taking a tough, rebellious stance to overcompensate for growing insecurities. Become belligerent, aggressively reacting to apparent threats to their security. Can be highly partisan, defending in-groups (with a "them against us" siege mentality, while attacking out-groups); get mean-spirited and bigoted, scapegoating others and lashing out at anyone who seems to threaten them, as a way to silence their fears and insecurities.

Unhealthy: Fearing condemnation and rejection by the authority figure if they have gone too far or if their counterphobic defenses have failed, unhealthy Sixes feel highly insecure and become clingingly dependent and self-disparaging, with acute inferiority feelings. Have a low self-image and become depressed, feeling cowardly, worthless, incompetent, plagued by fears. Overreact to everything, exaggerating problems: their irrational actions may actually bring about the very thing they fear. Extremely anxious, feel persecuted and attacked by others, imagining that people are "out to get them." To be rescued from anxiety, abandonment, and the consequences of their actions, they become self-defeating and may abase and humiliate themselves to the authority figure to be rescued. Self-punishing, masochistic behavior as pathology.

Direction of Disintegration: Unhealthy Sixes feel extremely anxious and become masochistic, filled with feelings of inferiority and worthlessness. When they go to Three, they strike out violently at others both to overcome their inferiority feelings and to hurt anyone who has hurt them. Their aggressions (formerly seen as authoritarian bigotry and mean-spiritedness) now come out in a much more dangerous form as psychopathic and sadistic violence.

Direction of Integration: When healthy Sixes go to Nine, both their ambivalence toward others and their tendency to overreact to anxiety have been overcome. They are much more emotionally stable as well as receptive and trusting of others. They become supportive and reassuring, beacons of stability and maturity. Their problems with anxiety have largely been resolved, and as a result they are more peaceful, secure, generous, and relaxed than ever.

Childhood Origins: Sixes have positively identified with the father or a father figure (*PT*, 167–68). The key element in their development is that Sixes look to an authority figure for security, approval, and rewards for obedience. However, their self-esteem requires that they also learn to act independently, to resist being completely obedient to or dependent on an external authority, creating the ambivalence seen in average Sixes.

Basic Fear: Of being abandoned and alone (*PT*, 170 and 188).

Basic Desire: To have security (*PT*, 167 and 188).

Secondary Motivations: Sixes want to be liked, to have approval, to test the attitudes of others toward themselves, to assert themselves to overcome their fears, to gain reassurance if they are afraid, to have the authority figure come to their aid.

Healthy Sense of Self: "I am a likable, dependable person."

Hidden Complaint: "I am dependable and I follow orders, although other people don't."

Key Defense Mechanisms: Identification, displacement, projection.

Characteristic Temptation: To be dependent on others. Despite occasional overcompensations, average to unhealthy Sixes are basically dependent on others for emotional security. But looking to someone else to take responsibility, although reassuring in the short run, undermines their self-confidence in the long run. Once Sixes become dependent on someone else and cannot act without "permission," they have succumbed to this temptation.

Characteristic Vice: Sloth in self-reliance. Sixes do not put their energy and attention into building proper self-esteem, into having faith in themselves. It is easier to look to an authority and protector who will take care of them; hence their vice is a form of sloth. (Other writers list "fear" as the vice of the Six, and while true, this does not go deep enough. The reason Sixes are afraid is that they have not developed self-reliance.)

Characteristic Virtue: Courage. The courage of healthy Sixes is extremely hard-won, achieved by resisting their constant tendency to become anxious and afraid. When Sixes are courageous they become "fighters" who, although they may be knocked down, always get back up and try again. Self-affirmation is the basis for their courage—the ability to believe not merely in others but in themselves and their own genuine capacities.

Saving Grace: Despite increasing tensions and overcompensations, average Sixes may still want to build genuinely secure and cooperative relationships with others. Their healthy capacity for maintaining committed relationships may prevent them from deteriorating further or from doing something that would bring about rejection and potential abandonment.

Suggestions for Personal Growth: See Chapter 8.

Structural Patterns: The keynote is *reactivity*. The Six has the most complex and ever-changing psychological pattern because of constant emotional and interpersonal shifts from Level to Level. Outwardly, Sixes oscillate from one state to another as they interact with people and react to their own feelings and anxieties. To find security, Sixes feel they must engage others emotionally. But to maintain their self-esteem, Sixes also become defensive and resist the influence of others, tending to overcompensate in the opposite direction by acting forcefully to prove that they are not dependent on anyone. They can be tough and belligerent to prove that they are their own masters, while still wanting to feel that they are approved and that others care for them. Internally, they experience constant reactions between their aggressive and compliant feelings, between their fears and their aggressions, between their desire to be close to people and their desire to be on their own, and so forth. The overall pattern is one of ever-changing double circles—an external circle of interpersonal interactions and an internal circle of emotional reactions, both of which constantly react with each other as well as with the external world, particularly other people.

Inevitable Consequences: By giving in to their fears, Sixes unwittingly bring about their Basic Fear—that they will be abandoned—while they lose their Basic Desire—emotional security (*PT*, 188). Fear and anxiety are the twin monsters that threaten Sixes, and unless Sixes defeat them, they will be eaten alive. They must remember that anxiety is inescapable: either they must cope with it and resolve its causes, or, if they attempt to flee from it in some way, they will likely bring more of it on themselves. However, rather than fear anxiety so much, they should try to see it as an invigorating force. Anxiety consciously used and worked with can become the "shock" they need to help boost them to a higher level of accomplishment and independence.

Personality Type Seven: The Generalist
The Accomplished-Extroverted-Excessive-Manic Person

EXPANDED PROFILE

Healthy: Highly responsive, excitable, and enthusiastic about their experiences, healthy Sevens are classic extroverts, oriented to the real world of things and sensations. They are spontaneous and exhilarated by every experience. Every stimulus brings an immediate response, and they find everything exciting and invigorating. Happy, vivacious, stimulating people: resilient and lively. Become accomplished achievers and generalists who do many different things well: multitalented, Renaissance people, gifted with virtuosic talents and prodigious skills. Practical, productive, prolific, versatile, cross-fertilizing their many areas of interest. *At their best:* They assimilate experiences in depth, becoming appreciative and grateful, enthralled (awed) by the wonders of life. Life-affirming, joyful, and ecstatic. Begin to have intimations of a life beyond the physical, a spiritual reality, and a deep sense of the goodness of life.

Average: As their appetites increase, average Sevens want to amuse themselves with things and a wider variety of experiences, becoming avid consumers, acquisitive materialists, playboys and socialites, worldly-wise sophisticates, connoisseurs, "trendsetters," and sensation seekers. Having money to afford new amusements is important. Become unable to say no to themselves, to deny themselves anything: begin to be hyperactive, throwing themselves into constant activity, doing and saying whatever comes to mind. Fear being bored and try to heighten their stimulation and excitement by staying in perpetual motion, distracting themselves with something fun and new, although they do too many things, becoming superficial, glib dilettantes merely dabbling around. Uninhibited, "flighty," flamboyant, outrageous, outspoken, loud, and brash — constantly talking, wisecracking, joking, and "performing" to stay in high spirits. Begin to feel that they never have enough, so they become excessive and extravagant, engaging in conspicuous consumption, yet are greedy for more. Self-centered, selfish, demanding, and impatient. Jaded and hardened by their lavishness and excesses, yet unsatisfied. Insensitive to others: can be rude, ill-mannered. Addictive tendencies, especially to alcohol and drugs.

Unhealthy: Unhealthy Sevens are very easily and quickly frustrated, getting offensive and abusive as they demand whatever they want to keep themselves busy and distracted. Become infantile escapists, impulsive and insulting, flying into rages and tantrums: have serious problems controlling themselves. Addictions to alcohol, drugs, and other excesses take their toll as they become dissipated, dissolute, debauched, and depraved. They act out impulses rather than dealing with anxiety, going out of control, prey to wildly erratic, volatile mood swings and compulsive (manic) actions (the "manic-depressive" defense). They engage in wild sprees of various sorts, grandiose and delusionally unrealistic, as if there could be no limits on them. They are in flight from the self and subject to sudden panic attacks if defenses fail.

Direction of Disintegration: Unhealthy Sevens are out of control of themselves (manic) and of their actions. When they go to One, they try to impose an arbitrary order, becoming obsessive, punitive, and vindictive toward others. They also become obsessively fixated with someone or something that seems to them to be the solution to their unhappiness.

Direction of Integration: When healthy Sevens go to Five, they become involved with their experiences in depth, contributing to the environment rather than merely consuming it. Integrating Sevens no longer fear that they will be deprived of happiness unless they are constantly grabbing after things for themselves. They delve into their experiences more profoundly, getting to the heart of things, comprehending more, and therefore enjoying reality on a deeper level than ever before.

Childhood Origins: Sevens have negatively identified with their mothers or with a mother figure (*PT*, 194–95). The key element in their early development revolves around their fear of being deprived (for some reason) by their mothers. The deprivation may have been material or emotional, and it could have been caused in any number of ways. It also may have been more feared than actual, and yet the determination never to feel insecure or in need becomes a major force in their development.

Basic Fear: Of being deprived (*PT*, 194 and 216).

Basic Desire: To be happy (satisfied) (*PT*, 198 and 216).

Secondary Motivations: Sevens want to enjoy themselves, to be amused and to have fun, to put no limits on themselves, to get whatever they want, to repress anxiety by staying in motion regardless of the consequences, to give in to impulses, to flee from anxiety.

Healthy Sense of Self: "I am a happy, enthusiastic person."

Hidden Complaint: "I am happy, although I would be a lot happier if I got everything I wanted."

Key Defense Mechanisms: Repression, externalization, acting out.

Characteristic Temptation: To be acquisitive (greedy). Sevens are tempted to think that they will be happier if they have more of everything that has pleased them (whether it is a thing or an experience). However, as they attempt to acquire more, they only increase the strength of their appetites without really satisfying them.

Characteristic Vice: Gluttony. Stuffing themselves with an excess of food is both literally and metaphorically their capital sin, the one that inevitably leads to self-defeating behavior. The tragedy is that the more they attempt to fill themselves with things and experiences (some sort of external sustenance for the self), the more Sevens become grotesquely depraved and incapable of finding the happiness they seek.

Characteristic Virtue: Gratitude. Very healthy Sevens are grateful for everything they have. Life is a gift, full of wonders, and they realize that they have more than their share of blessings and are grateful for them. Anything and everything *if used rightly* can fill them with joy.

Saving Grace: Despite their increasing excesses, average Sevens may still have enough genuine enthusiasm for things that their very love of the material world will prevent them from deteriorating further into mere escapism or manic hyperactivity. Their healthy capacity to enjoy the world may act as a brake on their desire for mere stimulation, helping them to return to healthier levels of functioning.

Suggestions for Personal Growth: See Chapter 8.

Structural Patterns: The keynote is *responsiveness*. The Seven's psyche is extraordinarily externalized since most of its energies are invested in the external world. Sevens move outward toward ever-new, different, and more exciting experiences. They are not empty; rather, they are completely extroverted, turning all of their energy and attention outward to the real world of material objects. As they deteriorate, they get caught in a flight from self, anxiety, unconscious impulses, aloneness, and insecurities while demanding that the material world (including other people) fulfill their every need. The overall pattern, therefore, is of a buzzing, humming vibrancy, full of energy and vitality, but tending to be shallow and impulsive. Thus, average to unhealthy Sevens consume their experiences with little or no personal internalization of them—and are in constant danger of being frustrated and lashing out at the very "hand that feeds them."

Inevitable Consequences: If Sevens deteriorate into unhealth, they bring about their Basic Fear (of being deprived), while losing their Basic Desire (happiness and satisfaction) (*PT*, 216). Yet who will have denied them happiness? The truth is that average to unhealthy Sevens bring much of their unhappiness on themselves by allowing their appetites to run away with them. Once they become unwilling to control themselves—to say no to themselves—to put limits on what they should or should not do, they cross a boundary that can have the direst consequences. The only way to become healthier is to control themselves and their desires. If they still refuse, at some point reality itself will certainly say no to them.

Personality Type Eight:
The Leader
The Powerful-Expansive-
Dictatorial-Destructive Person

EXPANDED PROFILE

Healthy: Self-assertive, self-confident, and strong, healthy Eights have learned to stand up for themselves for what they need and want. Action-oriented, with a "can-do" attitude and inner drive. They love a challenge and are resourceful self-starters, taking the initiative and making things happen. They are natural leaders that others respect and turn to for decisions and direction: decisive, authoritative, and commanding. Earn respect by being honorable, by using power constructively, by championing and protecting people, by acting as providers, sponsors, and promoters of worthwhile causes and valuable enterprises. *At their best:* Become self-restrained and magnanimous, merciful and forbearing, mastering themselves, carrying others and fulfilling others' needs with their strength. Courageous, they put themselves in jeopardy to achieve vision: possibly heroic and historically great.

Average: Average Eights want to be self-sufficient, to use their power and strength only for self-interest. Financial self-sufficiency is very important: become "rugged individualists," enterprising wheeler-dealers, and entrepreneurs. Audacious, they love adventure and risk-taking to test and prove themselves. Begin to want to dominate the environment completely (including others) by becoming forceful, aggressive, and more expansive: the empire builder and power broker whose word is law. Proud, egocentric, imposing their will and vision on everything, arrogantly ordering others around as if chattel, not seeing people as equals or respecting their needs, creating master-slave relationships (and tending to mix sex and aggression in crude vulgarity, machismo, and bravado). Feel they must get their way, becoming confrontational, belligerent, bullying, and defiant, creating and relishing adversarial relationships. They make everything into a test of will and do not back down. Use threats and fear of reprisals to extort compliance from others, to keep them off balance and feeling powerless. Others feel insecure and oppressed: unjust treatment makes people resent and hate bullying Eights and possibly to band together against them.

Unhealthy: Unhealthy Eights want to hold on to their power and prevail no matter what the cost: become completely ruthless, violent, immoral, and hardhearted, defying guilt, fear, and any other human feelings. Dictatorial, tyrannical, espousing the totalitarian "might makes right," "law of the jungle" philosophy. Begin to develop delusional ideas about themselves (megalomania), feeling omnipotent, invincible, and invulnerable; become increasingly reckless, overextending themselves and their resources. Finally, if in danger, they may vengefully and brutally destroy everything that has not conformed to their will. Sociopathic, barbaric, murderous.

Direction of Disintegration: Unhealthy Eights have dominated their environment so completely that they have made enemies of everyone around them. When they go to Five, they become paranoid about their continued survival since their many enemies may well have joined together against them. They finally realize how insecure and threatened they really are. From being fearless, they begin to fear everyone.

Direction of Integration: When healthy Eights go to Two, they use their power and strength for others rather than against them. They become caring, generous, and personally concerned for the welfare of others instead of being motivated only by self-interest. They understand the power of love rather than succumbing to the love of power, becoming the servants of others (in some sense) rather than their masters.

Childhood Origins: Ambivalently oriented to the mother or to a mother figure (*PT*, 223–24). The most important element in their development is their successful testing of wills against their mothers. As they exercise their wills like muscles, Eights grow up with enormous willpower and strong egos, with an unquestioned belief in themselves and confidence in their ability to get their way.

Basic Fear: Of submitting to others (*PT*, 244).

Basic Desire: To be self-reliant (*PT*, 226).

Secondary Motivations: Eights want to assert themselves, to prove themselves and their abilities, to be respected, to dominate the environment, to get their way, to be feared by others, to fight for their survival, to have absolute power, to be invulnerable.

Healthy Sense of Self: "I am a strong, assertive person."

Hidden Complaint: "I am fighting for my own survival, and others would take advantage of me if I let them."

Key Defense Mechanisms: Repression, displacement, denial.

Characteristic Temptation: To think that they are completely self-sufficient. Average to unhealthy Eights increasingly act solely on self-interest, attempting to be in no one else's power or control. They want to be utterly self-sufficient and independent of others so that they will need no one, although, ironically, they want to become so powerful that everyone else will be dependent on them.

Characteristic Vice: Lust. Although the lust for power is typical of Eights, sexual lust is a significant part of the picture since sex and aggression are mixed in their attitudes and behavior. In its broadest sense, lust is the desire to utterly possess and control another, to be God-like in total power over others.

Characteristic Virtue: Magnanimity. Healthy Eights have a largeness of heart that allows them to transcend their self-interest, to take the needs and rights of others into equal consideration. Their magnanimity is seen in their self-restraint, forbearance, mercy, benevolence, and protection of others.

Saving Grace: Despite increasing confrontations and their ability to intimidate everyone, average Eights may realize that their own survival is increasingly threatened because of the very confrontations they are creating. Their desire to be self-reliant may act as a catalyst for returning to a healthier state by asserting themselves in a more balanced way, and only in really necessary matters. Furthermore, their desire for self-reliance may cause them to be concerned that others become similarly self-reliant and may lead them to help others achieve that end constructively.

Suggestions for Personal Growth: See Chapter 8.

Structural Patterns: The keynote is *expansiveness*. The psyche of Eights is "volcanic," as if a massive force were constantly moving outward to dominate the environment. The primary force is aggression (mixed with sexual elements) that is directed toward the external world by the Eight's formidably strong ego. Eights generally experience little internal conflict since the structure of their psyches allows them to discharge their aggressions outwardly rather than to repress them or turn them against themselves. However, while conflicts seldom exist in Eights, interpersonal conflicts frequently arise when Eights pit themselves against others in confrontations and displays of will, ego, or sexual dominance. (Such a conflict may produce momentary feelings of anxiety and fear, although Eights will deny and defy them.) Thus, the overall pattern is of relentless expansion into the environment (including other people) to dominate it completely.

Inevitable Consequences: Although Eights fear submitting to someone else (their Basic Fear), they bring this about by their ruthless and oppressive behavior since they will inevitably be stopped, either by society and its justice or by death. Moreover, unhealthy Eights also lose their Basic Desire—to rely solely on themselves—so that they can assert themselves as they see fit (*PT*, 244). But by acting unjustly, they inevitably curtail their freedom and ability to act. Ironically, as they deteriorate, they are not self-sufficient or self-reliant but become ever more dependent on others to do their bidding. Far from being the masters of their worlds, they live like prisoners, in constant fear of retaliation and retribution.

What Eights must remember is that others are fundamentally like themselves and that others have the same rights, needs, and desires as they. Once Eights begin to violate others, only escalating inhumanity and barbarism will be the result and, ultimately, they will surely topple.

Personality Type Nine: The Peacemaker
The Peaceful-Reassuring-Passive-Repressed Person

EXPANDED PROFILE

Healthy: Healthy Nines are deeply receptive, open, unselfconscious, emotionally stable, and serene. Accepting, trusting of self and others, easygoing, at ease with self and life. Patient, gentle, unpretentious, they have an innocence and simplicity about them and are genuinely nice people. Optimistic, reassuring, kind, supportive, they make people feel comfortable and have a calming, healing influence, harmonizing groups and bringing people together. Good mediators, comforters, and sustainers. Have enormous dignity, deep serenity, and real peace that come from acceptance of their human condition. *At their best:* Become self-possessed and have great equanimity and genuine contentment. Feel autonomous and fulfilled, paradoxically at one with themselves yet able to form more profound relationships because of their union with themselves. Become more alive, awake, alert to self and others.

Average: Average Nines become self-effacing, accommodating themselves and going along with others too much. Submissive, too agreeable and conciliatory, accepting conventional roles and expectations naively and unquestioningly— subordinating themselves to the other, idealizing the other, and living through the other. Conservative and fear change, upset, or pressure of any kind. Become passive, phlegmatic, unresponsive, and complacent, walking away from conflicts and sweeping problems under the rug. Slothful, emotionally indolent, unwilling to exert the self (and stay focused), they exhibit indifference and lazy procrastination, stalling until problems go away on their own. Begin to "tune out" reality, becoming oblivious to what they do not want to see. Disengaged, inattentive, and unreflective: thinking becomes hazy, unfocused, and ruminative, mostly about idealized notions of how harmonious and "pleasant" everything should be. If problems don't go away, Nines begin to minimize the seriousness of the problems to calm and appease others, to "get problems behind them," and to have "peace at any price." Become stoic, fatalistic, and resigned, as if nothing can be done to change anything. Have poor judgment, responsible for sins of omission and wishful thinking, looking for a magical solution that will solve problems without their effort or response.

Unhealthy: Unhealthy Nines become too repressed, and inadequate personal development results: become helpless and ineffectual, and others must step in to save them from themselves. Become obstinate, stubbornly denying that problems and conflicts exist or that anything is wrong. Seriously neglectful and irresponsible, dangerous to anyone who needs them. If problems persist, they dissociate from anything threatening so that they eventually cannot function, becoming severely disoriented, depersonalized, catatonic, and immobilized. Emotional breakdown, personality fragmentation, with multiple personalities possible.

Direction of Disintegration: Unhealthy Nines have become so dissociated from reality that they can no longer function. When they go to Six, they become overwhelmed by anxiety that erupts into consciousness. They overreact and become irrational and masochistic, lashing out at others while also becoming more dependent than ever on others to take care of them and solve their problems. Deteriorated Nines may become masochistic so that others will save them from themselves and once again establish some sort of relationship with them.

Direction of Integration: When healthy Nines go to Three, they become interested in developing themselves and their potential. They take control of their lives instead of being complacent. As their sense of self develops, Nines become more self-assured, self-assertive, and independent; their self-esteem also increases. They are more conscious and live in the real world rather than in their idealizations. Moreover, they find that they can be themselves and cease living through someone else.

Childhood Origins: Positively identified with both parents or with other parent figures (*PT*, 249–50). The key element in their development is that, because Nines have had close, supportive relationships with their parents (at least in early childhood), they have learned to identify with other people. Nines establish their identities by identifying with someone else and by living through that other person. Their profound receptivity gives Nines deep emotional stability and peace-fulness but is also the reason they wish to ignore anything that threatens their peace.

Basic Fear: Of separation from the other (*PT*, 250 and 272).

Basic Desire: To find union with the other (*PT*, 250).

Secondary Motivations: Nines want to have harmony and peace, to mediate conflicts and bring people together, to pre-serve things as they are, to allow nothing upsetting to get to them, to minimize problems and conflicts, to deny the exis-tence of anything that would be difficult to accept or deal with realistically.

Healthy Sense of Self: "I am a peaceful, easygoing person."

Hidden Complaint: "I am content with the way things are, although everyone else is always pressuring me to change."

Key Defense Mechanisms: Repression, dissociation, denial.

Characteristic Temptation: To be too accommodating. Av-erage Nines begin to think that by being conciliatory and subordinating themselves to others, they can maintain their relationships and their own emotional peace. But by accom-modating themselves too much, they put themselves in dan-ger of becoming passive and neglectful when problems and conflicts arise.

Characteristic Vice: Sloth of self-remembering. Nines are the most literally slothful of the types—indolent and phleg-matic, slow to respond adequately to the world around them. On a deeper level, slothfulness refers to a lack of energy put into self-awareness or self-remembering. They do not put energy into making contact either with themselves or with others as they really are; as a result, they gradually live in a world of false hopes and comfortable illusions.

Characteristic Virtue: Patience. A hopeful, eager watch-fulness rather than any form of passivity or disengagement. Profound patience is a deep "letting be" of the other so that the other can develop in his or her own way. It is full of hope and expectancy, of the kind shown by a good parent who patiently teaches its young new skills while watching over it at a respectful but watchful distance.

Saving Grace: Despite their growing unresponsiveness and fatalism, average Nines may still want to retain relationships with others so much that they learn to exert themselves and respond to people as they really are rather than deteriorate into serious negligence. Their healthy capacity to be receptive to people may allow them to truly put the needs of others first, even at the expense of sacrificing their own peace of mind in the short run.

Suggestions for Personal Growth: See Chapter 8.

Structural Patterns: The keynote is *self-effacement.* There are two aspects to the psyche of Nines: first, the inner life of subjective feelings and fantasies, and second, the interpersonal relationships that give rise to their subjective states. Of these, the dominant aspect is their inner world: only the very healthiest Nines are able to keep their attention on reality rather than on their idealizations of it. As they deteriorate, their attention becomes focused not on identifications with people but on their idealizations of them. For average to unhealthy Nines, the outward pattern becomes one of accommodation and self-effacement to others, but only to maintain their peace and ignore the outside world. Their inner life is dominated by fantasy, while they remain completely defended against reality, impregnable and immovable.

Inevitable Consequences: It is one of the oddities about Nines that their actions and omissions do not seem to have negative consequences for them. Indeed, Nines seem to have uncanny good fortune, always seem to land on their feet and be untouched by disasters: reality seems not to affect them. However, despite appearances, Nines are not exempt from the long-range effects of their actions, even if they are not aware of them or do not immediately suffer from them. If Nines allow themselves to deteriorate into unhealth, they will lose their Basic Desire (union with others) while bringing their

Basic Fear on themselves (separation from those they love) (*PT*, 272). Their very passivity and complacency, their negligence and obstinacy, and their unwillingness to deal with reality inevitably cause conflicts.

Indeed, their unconscious anger toward anyone who tries to make them respond against their will separates them further from others. The irony is that the type that feels so much at peace with the world is often the cause of frustration and conflicts for everyone else. By not taking responsibility for themselves, they compound problems and then must flee the problems they have caused.

Nines must remember that they will never have union with anyone else unless and until they have union with themselves. If they are accommodating to a fault, they will inevitably lose the other because they have never possessed themselves.

Personality Type One:
The Reformer
The Idealistic-Orderly-
Perfectionistic-Intolerant Person

EXPANDED PROFILE

Healthy: Healthy Ones are conscientious, possessing a deep sense of right and wrong and strong moral values. Rational, reasonable, self-disciplined, and moderate. Highly ethical: truth and justice are primary values. Integrity and rectitude make them outstanding moral teachers, personal examples, and witnesses to the truth and other values. Extremely principled, always desiring to be impartial, fair, and objective and willing to sublimate the self for the greater good. Embody the Apollonian ideal of cultivating virtue, achieving excellence and balance. *At their best:* Become extraordinarily wise and discerning, with superb judgment, seeming to know what is (morally) best in all circumstances. Have proper priorities in view, giving them a transcendental perspective. Tolerant of others: the truth will be heard. They give wise counsel and have nobility of vision and purpose.

Average: Average Ones begin to feel a noblesse oblige — that it is up to them to improve everything personally: becoming reformers, crusaders, critics, and high-minded idealists. Promote causes, concerned with working toward an ideal to make things progress as they "should." Become afraid of making a mistake: everything must be consistent with their ideals. Become orderly, neat, methodical, well organized, logical, and detailed, although rigid, impersonal, no-nonsense, and emotionally constricted; they hold their feelings and impulses in check, resulting in an antiseptic, sexually repressed quality. Puritanical, anal (compulsive), fastidious, meticulous, punctual, and pedantic. Thinking is hierarchical and deductive, separating everything into dichotomies of black or white, good or bad, right or wrong. Highly opinionated about everything — correcting people and badgering them to do the right thing as they see it. Critical of self and others: judgmental, impatient, and fault-finding. Perfectionistic, a workaholic and nitpicker, never satisfied with anything less than perfect in self and others. Moralizing, scolding, and indignantly angry toward anyone (or anything) they judge is wrong, in error, messy, or out of place.

Unhealthy: Unhealthy Ones can be self-righteous, intolerant, extremely dogmatic, and inflexible. They alone know The Truth and relentlessly make pronouncements from narrow, forbidding absolutes. Very severe in their judgments; for them to be proved right, others must be proved wrong.

They use sophistry and rationalizations to maintain their "logical" position. Become obsessed about the wrongdoing of others although, ironically, they may do the same thing or worse themselves, hypocritically doing the opposite of what they preach while rationalizing their own contradictory actions or attitudes. If others do not do as they say, they become inhumanly cruel and sadistic, condemning others and seeing to it that they are punished.

Direction of Disintegration: By pursuing an abstract ideal without any human feeling or compassion, Ones finally do something so contradictory that they realize they have failed and so feel profoundly guilty. When they deteriorate to Four, they regress to a state of severe depression, shame, self-reproach, and self-destructiveness, with suicidal thoughts and feelings. At the least, a nervous breakdown or a severe (although relatively short-term) depression is likely.

Direction of Integration: When healthy Ones go to Seven, they accept reality with its necessary imperfections and become more relaxed and productive. They no longer feel compelled to strive constantly to make everything perfect, nor do they feel that they must save the world single-handedly. Life becomes less stressful and grim; they can allow things to unfold in their own way. They become more joyous and more human.

Childhood Origins: Negatively identified with the father or a father figure (*PT*, 279–80). Ones grew up with stern moral prohibitions placed on them. These prohibitions, religious and moral laws and ethical ideals, were internalized in a superego that is quick to make Ones feel guilty if they do not comply with the standards they have been taught. Much of their energy is spent trying to avoid being guilty or in dealing with guilt for their transgressions, in undoing their mistakes, or in making retribution for them.

Basic Fear: Of being condemned (*PT*, 283 and 301).

Basic Desire: To be right (*PT*, 276 and 283).

Secondary Motivations: Ones want to treat others fairly, to strive for the ideal, to improve the world, to control everything so that there will be no mistakes, to be beyond criticism, to justify their position, to be absolutely guiltless, to condemn those who do not live up to their ideals.

Healthy Sense of Self: "I am a reasonable, objective person."

Hidden Complaint: "I am right most of the time, and it would be a better world if people listened to what I tell them."

Key Defense Mechanisms: Repression, reaction formation, displacement.

Characteristic Temptation: An extreme sense of personal moral obligation. Average Ones begin to think that everything falls on them personally to improve. Average Ones feel that if they do not improve something, no one else will. They therefore become increasingly fixated on organizing the environment, correcting and perfecting everything, and on criticizing anyone or anything that does not conform to the ideal as they define it.

Characteristic Vice: Self-righteous anger. The anger of Ones is directed both at themselves for not being perfect (for failing to live up to their ideals) and at others for their failures. As Ones become more unhealthy and self-righteous, their anger is displaced more completely onto others as they make themselves the sole judge of who and what is right and wrong.

Characteristic Virtue: Wisdom, the ability to know how best to achieve their right ends, particularly moral values. It requires great realism and objectivity to set aside their own passions and predilections to discern the best choice to make or the best thing to do.

Saving Grace: Despite how judgmental and perfectionistic average Ones can be, they may still be reasonable enough to prevent themselves from deteriorating into intolerance or self-righteous obsessions. Their healthy capacity for reason and moderation can be the means by which they return to a healthier state.

Suggestions for Personal Growth: See Chapter 8.

Structural Patterns: The keynote is *objectivity*. Ones attempt to be objective, rational, and fair-minded and to be uninfluenced by any personal desire or passion that would interfere with their obligation to the Ideal. Hence, there is a division in their psyches between the objective and the subjective, between thinking and feeling, between what they would sometimes like to do and what they feel they must do. In the outside world, Ones strive for a higher, more perfect state, attempting to improve everything, including the self (though education, discipline, hard work, highmindedness, and so forth). The overall pattern, therefore, is one of constant tension between the objective values they seek to bring to the world and their personal impulses (sexual, aggressive, and personal desires) that tend to erupt if they are not kept under the check of repression and constant self-control.

Inevitable Consequences: Because Ones are rational and logical, of all the personality types they are most concerned about the consequences of their actions. And yet, like everyone else, they can also persuade themselves that things will be different if they make exceptions in their own case. Nevertheless, Ones are not exempt from the consequences of their actions even if the ends toward which they strive are worthwhile. If Ones deteriorate as the result of ego inflation, they will gradually become caught in the grip of their Basic Fear (of being condemned) while losing their Basic Desire (to be right) (*PT*, 301). They fear being condemned but gradually become condemnable because they become inhumanly cruel, condemning others without mercy. They also lose their Basic Desire to be right because neurotic Ones end by contradicting themselves, doing the very things they condemn in others — twisting reason into unreason, order into chaos, righteousness into rank perversion.

Placing some of the features we have seen in this chapter on the Enneagram reveals their patterns more clearly.

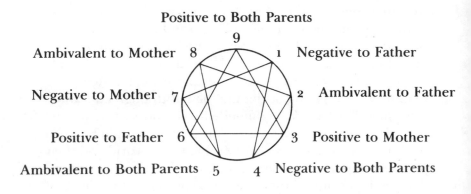

ENNEAGRAM OF CHILDHOOD ORIGINS

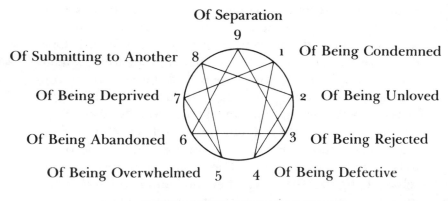

ENNEAGRAM OF BASIC FEARS

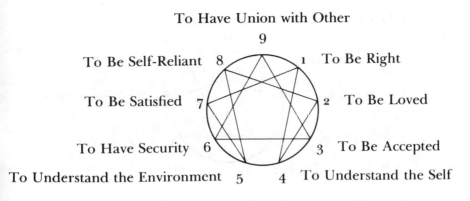

ENNEAGRAM OF BASIC DESIRES

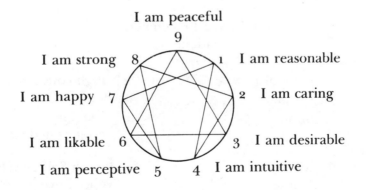

ENNEAGRAM OF THE HEALTHY SENSE OF SELF

ENNEAGRAM OF THE CHARACTERISTIC TEMPTATION

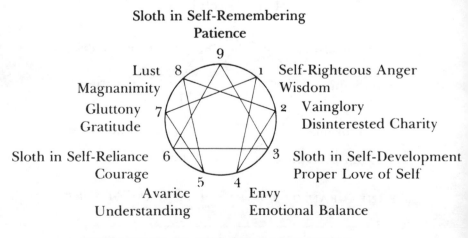

ENNEAGRAM OF THE CHARACTERISTIC
VICES AND VIRTUES

THREE

The Levels of Development

A total description of any person's character structure would involve an enormous amount of information. Included in it would have to be descriptions of the id, the ego, the superego, anxieties, defenses, conscious and unconscious forces, interpersonal relations, significant features of the life history, interests, attitudes, habits, characteristic patterns of handling the world, symptoms (if any), ideals, goals, and many other features. To avoid such extensive labor, for many years analysts sought short-cuts in briefer, more concise evaluations, similar to trait psychology (selfish, ambitious, etc.).

Thus they isolated certain recurrent themes in the life histories of individuals, drew these themes into a consistent constellation (which may or may not be seen as the core of the person), and tried to tie in these themes with the rest of the individual's functioning. Some of the more important characterological descriptions on this basis that are found in the literature can be briefly enumerated.

— Reuben Fine, *A History of Psychoanalysis*, 322

FINE CONTINUES his discussion with brief descriptions of the oral character, the anal character, the phallic-narcissistic character, the hysterical character, the masochistic character, the authoritarian personality, the as-if personality, and others— all of which can be accommodated by the Enneagram, as we will see in Chapter 7, "Psychological Categories."

How the Enneagram helps clarify psychiatric categories was briefly covered in Chapter 14 in *Personality Types*. However, a book devoted entirely to theory will be necessary to do justice to the complexities of this system and to reveal the many different aspects of the theory. In the meantime, we will limit ourselves to one of the most *practical* aspects of the theory— the Levels of Development.

While the core of the Enneagram—the delineation of the nine personality types—has always rung true, many errors had to be corrected before the Enneagram could be really useful in people's lives. For example, the early descriptions of the types in the Jesuit stream of transmission were short (usually not even a page long) and impressionistic—just enough to convey a sense of each type but not enough for an adequate, satisfying description, much less for any deep understanding. The descriptions needed to be filled out a great deal more to account for all the traits of each type.

Moreover, ascertaining precisely which traits belong to each type was an enormous problem, since a "master list" of traits had never been worked out, and the abstract, inner structure of each type had not yet been discovered (or, if it had, it had not been transmitted with the other early material). The Enneagram was, and still is, a young and growing field; those who learned it through the Jesuits were more excited by the essential insights it conveyed and by its psychological and spiritual implications than they were about clarifying whatever was obscure or even contradictory about it.

This chapter is devoted to revealing more about the Levels

of Development, the nine stages within each type, that constitute a Continuum of interrelated traits running from healthy to average to unhealthy states. The Levels of Development are the abstract, inner structure of each type, the conceptual skeleton that is fleshed out with the traits, defenses, interpersonal behaviors, attitudes, and many other complex features.

Like many discoveries, my work on the Levels grew out of a practical need. When I first began to attempt writing descriptions of the personality types, I used a thematic approach, describing each type's behavior in private and at work, its interpersonal relationships, conscious and unconscious attitudes, fears and desires, and so forth. However, I quickly learned that using a thematic exposition would involve a great deal of repetition, and descriptions became long and cumbersome because they lacked an overall structure. There could be no sense of flow and movement from healthy to average to unhealthy states because I had not yet discovered how to organize the material that way. For better or worse, the descriptions seemed to be going around in circles and really going nowhere.

Of course, the thematic approach inadvertently imitates some of the indefiniteness we find in everyday life, although it also suffers from the lack of clarity under which we labor there as well. Ideally, descriptions should not fall into the same traps as human beings but should rise above them. They should clarify human nature, not be as indefinite as people themselves can sometimes be. Finding a way to describe the personality types economically depends on cutting through the confusions of everyday life to discover larger patterns. The Levels of Development are the key to doing this.

After two years of struggling with the problem of organizing hundreds of observations into coherent descriptions, a solution finally occurred to me in the form of the Levels. My understanding of them has grown over the years since I discovered them in 1977, but I am still far from drawing out all their implications.

My working method was to write each trait or observation about the different types onto index cards. Rather than impose an order on them, I decided to see what patterns would emerge if I sorted the cards and allowed what categories there might be to reveal themselves. I started, as I usually do, in the Feeling Triad with personality type Two. After reading through the cards and sorting them into piles of traits that seemed to be related, I finally had eight piles. Sorting the cards for type Three came next, and nine piles emerged; more important, I could also see that they were forming a gradation of some kind. I initially thought that the traits were falling into two groups—healthy and unhealthy (with four healthy piles, one in the middle as a crossover point, and four unhealthy piles).

As I went through the cards of the other types, it gradually became clear that there was also an "average" mid-range of traits. By this time, the traits of the types were also consistently falling into nine piles, and before long it occurred to me that they may well be divided into three groups of three—three piles of healthy, three of average, and three of unhealthy traits. While the preparation for this insight took two years, it took another five years of thought and observation before I was able to work out more details of the Levels of Development, as I began to call them. (And to go further with an important related matter, I was eventually able to work out completely abstract models for each Level that are like blueprints of the psychic activities that happen at each stage. These Psychic Structures have not been published yet, but they are the ultimate conceptual bedrock on which the Levels themselves rest; they provide the rationale for the existence and placement of each trait within each type. The Psychic Structures are the abstract "equations" that can be translated into language—language that can then be expanded into full descriptions.)

As helpful as the discovery of the Levels was, it did not automatically clarify either the types or everything about the Levels themselves. I am still learning more about both, a process that will go on for many more years. The information in this chapter is therefore simpler than a complete exposition of the Levels might be. But since the purpose of this chapter is to be practical and to provide an appreciation of the Levels and how they can be used, it is unnecessary to be either encyclopedic or technical. Understanding the Levels within each type (as well as the symmetries between types) not only is intellectually rewarding but also has immense practical implications, as you will see throughout the remainder of this book.

We will refer to the Levels in virtually all the remaining chapters—in the questionnaire (Chapter 4), in the assessment guides (Chapter 6), in Chapter 5, which clarifies misidentifications made between types, in Chapter 7, which is concerned with the Enneagram and psychiatric types, and so on. As you will see, understanding that there is an inner structure to each type is helpful, but understanding more clearly what that structure is can be very valuable indeed.

The Psychology of the Levels of Development

Each Level can be characterized by a specific psychological and interpersonal process that arises at that point along the Continuum. I have described these processes in *Personality Types* (316–17) but will expand on them here.

You will recall that the Continuum for each personality type looks like this:

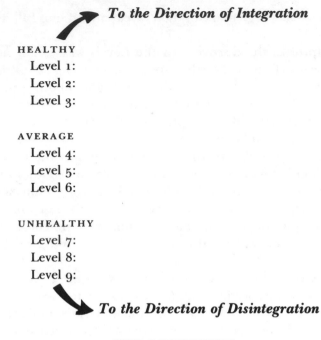

To the Direction of Integration

HEALTHY
Level 1:
Level 2:
Level 3:

AVERAGE
Level 4:
Level 5:
Level 6:

UNHEALTHY
Level 7:
Level 8:
Level 9:

To the Direction of Disintegration

THE CONTINUUM

Although the Levels are unnumbered in *Personality Types*, if you refer to the descriptions you will see that the Levels are clearly delineated by a two- or three-word title that serves as a descriptive signpost for what happens at that stage along the Continuum. Because of space restrictions, I did not supply a master list of the Levels, but readers who wanted to do so could have compiled one and, by analyzing it, could have discovered some of the symmetries and interrelationships for themselves.

The Levels are useful in a number of ways. They describe eighty-one discrete subtypes, as if the nine Levels within each type were static categories. In other words, the personalities of some individuals might be so restricted and narrow that they could be thought of as exemplifying only the traits found at a single Level within their type. Theoretically, each Level can be described both as an integral part of the entire type and as a discrete personality subtype, unique to itself. (Indeed, this is more or less what we find in the psychiatric literature, as we will see in Chapter 7.) The vast majority of people, however, are not static examples of one Level; they move up and down within the Continuum, sometimes spiraling downward through the entire Continuum into neurosis or moving upward toward health and integration. As people shift along the Continuum, different traits and defense mechanisms emerge and combine with existing traits and defenses to form the complex patterns that we see in individuals.

The brief treatment of the eighty-one Levels of Development presented on the following pages allows you to see these patterns more clearly as well as to see how each type fits together as a coherent whole. The descriptive titles are my own and represent the best compromise between technical language and ordinary language to describe what is happening at each stage. For descriptive purposes, the charts list the Levels "downward" from the healthy Levels through the average Levels to the unhealthy Levels, as if the movement were always a progressive deterioration of the person through those stages. However, it is important to understand that movement "up" the Levels is movement toward increasing psychological health and balance (Chapter 8 contains recommendations for personal growth). Movement along the Levels is possible in both directions, and, as we have noted, each of us characteristically oscillates up and down the Levels all the time. But for the sake of economy of description, we will see the Levels "from the top down," as if they always moved in one direction—toward increasing unhealth.

Each type has a complex internal structure, as can be seen from the parallel relationships among the Levels. The internal coherence of each type demonstrates that each is a unity—a whole whose parts fit together with precision and elegance. The internal coherence also makes clear why the traits of each type are not arbitrary: each trait must "fit" within the larger whole that is the type itself.

For example, in type Two, the psychological processes we find at Levels 1, 4, and 7 are parallel. The Disinterested Altruist (at Level 1) deteriorates to The Effusive Friend (at Level 4) and then to The Self-Deceptive Manipulator (at Level 7)—disinterestedness deteriorates to flattery and then to manipulation. Levels 2, 5, and 8 also are parallel. The Caring Person (at Level 2) deteriorates to The Possessive Intimate (at Level 5) and finally to The Coercive Dominator (at Level 8)—empathy deteriorates to possessiveness to coercion. Levels 3, 6, and 9 also are parallel. The Nurturing Helper (at Level 3) becomes The Self-Important "Saint" (at Level 6) and The Psychosomatic Victim (at Level 9)—generosity deteriorates to uninvited self-sacrifice to feeling victimized and taken advantage of by others. These three sets of symmetries do not exhaust the internal correspondences within each type: other kinds of symmetries exist that we will not explore here.

Furthermore, symmetries exist between all of the types. For example, you could compare all the types "horizontally" at the same level to see their differences and similarities.

While the Levels are an analytic way of helping us understand and organize the types, we must keep in mind that they are an artificial construct: real people of course are not so highly structured or predictable. Nevertheless, since they can be represented at this high level of abstraction, the personality types of the Enneagram prove again how remarkably rich in both specificity and sophistication they are.

The following charts contain lists of the Levels of Development of each type along the Continuum as well as a Summary Overview that make the type's internal coherence more explicit.

Continuum for Personality Type Two: The Helper

HEALTHY

Level 1: The Disinterested Altruist	Disinterestedness
Level 2: The Caring Person	Empathy
Level 3: The Nurturing Helper	Generosity

AVERAGE

Level 4: The Effusive Friend	Flattery
Level 5: The Possessive "Intimate"	Possessiveness
Level 6: The Self-Important "Saint"	Self-Sacrifice

UNHEALTHY

Level 7: The Self-Deceptive Manipulator	Manipulation
Level 8: The Coercive Dominator	Coercion
Level 9: The Psychosomatic Victim	Feeling Victimized

Summary Overview: The movement of Two's Continuum can be seen in the following extremely abbreviated way: Twos progressively deteriorate from healthy disinterested altruism, compassionate concern for others, and generosity to average effusive friendliness, overenveloping possessiveness, and self-sacrificial self-importance to unhealthy self-deceptive manipulation, coercive dominance of others, and finally vindicating themselves through psychosomatic suffering (brought on by their suppressed aggressions).

Internal symmetries include those among the healthy Two's disinterestedness (at Level 1), the average Two's flattery (at Level 4), and the unhealthy Two's manipulation (at Level 7). Other symmetries include empathy (at Level 2), possessiveness (at Level 5), and coercion (at Level 8). Generosity (at Level 3) parallels self-sacrifice (at Level 6) and the feeling of victimization (at Level 9).

Continuum for Personality Type Three: The Motivator

HEALTHY
Level 1: The Authentic   Inner-Directedness
Person
Level 2: The Self-Assured   Adaptability
Person
Level 3: The Outstanding   Ambition
Paragon

AVERAGE
Level 4: The Competitive   Competitiveness
Status Seeker
Level 5: The Image-Oriented   Image Projection
Pragmatist
Level 6: The Self-Promoting   Contemptuousness
Narcissist

UNHEALTHY
Level 7: The Exploitative   Opportunism
Opportunist
Level 8: The Malicious   Duplicity
Traitor
Level 9: The Vindictive   Vindictiveness
Psychopath

Summary Overview: The movement of Three's Continuum can be seen in the following extremely abbreviated way: Threes progressively deteriorate from healthy self-accepting authenticity, adaptable self-assurance, and admirable forms of self-development to average competitive status seeking, calculating concern for their image, and self-aggrandizing narcissism to unhealthy exploitative opportunism, malicious deceptiveness, and finally sadistic psychopathic behavior.

Internal symmetries include those among inner-directedness (at Level 1), competitiveness (at Level 4), and opportunism (at Level 7). Other symmetries include adaptability (at Level 2), image projection (at Level 5), and duplicity (at Level 8). A healthy ambition (at Level 3) deteriorates into contemptuousness toward others (at Level 6) and psychopathic vindictiveness (at Level 9).

Continuum for Personality Type Four: The Artist

HEALTHY

Level 1: The Inspired
Creator — Creativity

Level 2: The Self-Aware
Intuitive — Self-Awareness

Level 3: The Self-Revealing
Individual — Individuality

AVERAGE

Level 4: The Imaginative
Artist — Fantasy

Level 5: The Self-Absorbed
Introvert — Self-Consciousness

Level 6: The Self-Indulgent
Aesthete — Exemption

UNHEALTHY

Level 7: The Alienated
Depressive — Self-Inhibition

Level 8: The Emotionally
Tormented Person — Self-Torment

Level 9: The Self-
Destructive Person — Self-Destructiveness

Summary Overview: The movement of Four's Continuum can be seen in the following extremely abbreviated way: Fours progressively deteriorate from healthy self-transcending creativity, self-aware sensitivity, and self-revealing individuality to average fantasizing and aestheticism, introverted withdrawal, and feelings of exemption and self-indulgence to unhealthy self-inhibiting depression, contemptuous self-torment, and finally self-destructive despair.

Internal symmetries include those among healthy creativity (at Level 1), fantasy (at Level 4), and self-inhibition (at Level 7). Other symmetries include those among self-awareness (at Level 2), self-consciousness (at Level 5), and self-torment (at Level 8). Healthy individuality (at Level 3) deteriorates into claims of exemption (at Level 6) and finally into self-destructiveness (at Level 9).

Continuum for Personality Type Five: The Thinker

HEALTHY
Level 1: The Pioneering   Understanding
Visionary
Level 2: The Perceptive   Involvement
Observer
Level 3: The Knowledgeable   Expertise
Expert

AVERAGE
Level 4: The Analytic   Analysis
Specialist
Level 5: The Intensely   Preoccupation
Involved Theorist
Level 6: The Extreme   Reductionism
Reductionist

UNHEALTHY
Level 7: The Isolated   Rejection
Nihilist
Level 8: The Delusional   Distortion
Schizoid
Level 9: The Empty Schizoid   Deranged Behavior

Summary Overview: The movement of Five's Continuum can be seen in the following extremely abbreviated way: Fives progressively deteriorate from healthy comprehensive understanding, insightful observation, and knowledgeable expertise to average analytic dissection, detached speculation, and reductionistic interpretations to unhealthy antagonistic rejection of reality, paranoid distortion, and deranged behavior.

Internal symmetries include those among the healthy Five's profound understanding (at Level 1), intellectual analysis (at Level 4), and rejection of contrary data (at Level 7). Other symmetries include the ability to become involved in thought (at Level 2), preoccupation with abstractions (at Level 5), and distorted perceptions (at Level 8). Healthy expertise (at Level 3) becomes narrowed to extreme reductionism (at Level 6) and finally may deteriorate into delusional ideas that become a source of immense anxiety and mental instability (at Level 9).

Continuum for Personality Type Six: The Loyalist

HEALTHY

Level 1: The Self-Affirming   Self-Affirmation
Person
Level 2: The Engaging Person   Engagement
Level 3: The Committed Loyalist   Cooperation

AVERAGE

Level 4: The Obedient   Obedience
Traditionalist
Level 5: The Ambivalent Person   Evasion
Level 6: The Overcompensating   Defensiveness
Tough Guy

UNHEALTHY

Level 7: The Insecure Person   Inferiority
Level 8: The Overreacting   Overreaction
Hysteric
Level 9: The Self-Defeating   Masochism
Masochist

Summary Overview: The movement of Six's Continuum may be seen in the following extremely abbreviated way: Sixes progressively deteriorate from healthy self-affirming equality with others, engaging appeal, and committed loyalty to an average obedient traditionalism, passive-aggressive ambivalence, and defensive authoritarianism to unhealthy dependent inferiority, irrational overreactions, and finally self-defeating masochism.

Internal symmetries include those among the healthy Six's self-affirmation (at Level 1), obedience to an authority (at Level 4), and inferiority (at Level 7). Other symmetries include the Six's appeal (at Level 2), evasiveness (at Level 5), and overreactions (at Level 8). The cooperation found in the healthy Six (at Level 3) parallels authoritarian defensiveness (at Level 6) and masochistic self-defeat (at Level 9).

Continuum for Personality Type Seven: The Generalist

HEALTHY

Level 1: The Ecstatic Appreciator	Gratitude
Level 2: The Happy Enthusiast	Enthusiasm
Level 3: The Accomplished Generalist	Productiveness

AVERAGE

Level 4: The Experienced Sophisticate	Acquisitiveness
Level 5: The Hyperactive Extrovert	Impulsiveness
Level 6: The Excessive Materialist	Excessiveness

UNHEALTHY

Level 7: The Impulsive Escapist	Dissipation
Level 8: The Manic Compulsive	Compulsiveness
Level 9: The Panic-Stricken "Hysteric"	Hysteria

Summary Overview: The movement of Seven's Continuum may be seen in the following extremely abbreviated way: Sevens progressively deteriorate from healthy appreciative gratitude, responsive enthusiasm, and practical productivity to an average acquisitive sensation seeking, hyperactive extroversion, and materialistic excessiveness to an unhealthy impulsive offensiveness, erratic compulsiveness, and finally hysterical panic.

Internal symmetries include those among the healthy Seven's gratitude (at Level 1), average acquisitiveness for more of everything (at Level 4), and unhealthy dissipated escapism (at Level 7). Other symmetries include those among enthusiasm (at Level 2), impulsiveness (at Level 5), and manic compulsiveness (at Level 8). The healthy productivity (at Level 3) deteriorates into excessive materialism (at Level 6) and panic-stricken hysteria (at Level 9).

Continuum for Personality Type Eight: The Leader

HEALTHY

Level 1: The Magnanimous Hero	Self-Restraint
Level 2: The Self-Confident Person	Self-Confidence
Level 3: The Constructive Leader	Influence

AVERAGE

Level 4: The Enterprising Adventurer	Self-Sufficiency
Level 5: The Dominating Power-Broker	Forcefulness
Level 6: The Confrontational Adversary	Intimidation

UNHEALTHY

Level 7: The Ruthless Tyrant	Ruthlessness
Level 8: The Omnipotent Megalomaniac	Recklessness
Level 9: The Violent Destroyer	Destructiveness

Summary Overview: The movement of Eight's Continuum can be seen in the following extremely abbreviated way: Eights progressively deteriorate from healthy self-restrained magnanimity, self-confident strength, and courageous leadership to an average self-interested adventurousness, forceful expansiveness, and confrontational intimidation to an unhealthy ruthless aggression, reckless megalomania, and finally a vengeful destructiveness.

Internal symmetries include those among the healthy Eight's self-restraint (at Level 1), average self-sufficiency (at Level 4), and unhealthy ruthlessness (at Level 7). Other symmetries are among self-confidence (at Level 2), forcefulness (at Level 5), and recklessness (at Level 8). Constructive, influential leadership (at Level 3) foreshadows intimidation and bullying (at Level 6) and finally may lead to violent destructiveness (at Level 9).

Continuum for Personality Type Nine: The Peacemaker

HEALTHY

Level 1: The Self-Possessed   Autonomy
Person
Level 2: The Receptive   Unself-consciousness
Person
Level 3: The Supportive   Supportiveness
Peacemaker

AVERAGE

Level 4: The Accommodating   Self-Effacement
Role Player
Level 5: The Passively   Passivity
Disengaged Person
Level 6: The Resigned   Fatalism
Fatalist

UNHEALTHY

Level 7: The Neglectful   Neglect
Person
Level 8: The Dissociating   Dissociation
Person
Level 9: The Self-   Self-Abandonment
Abandoning Person

Summary Overview: The movement of Nine's Continuum may be seen in the following abbreviated way: Nines progressively deteriorate from a healthy self-possessed autonomy, receptive unself-consciousness, and reassuring support for others to an average self-effacing accommodation, disconnected passivity, and minimizing resignation to an unhealthy repressed negligence, dissociated disorientation, and finally a self-abandoning fragmentation of consciousness.

Internal symmetries include those among the healthy Nine's autonomy (at Level 1), average self-effacement (at Level 4), and unhealthy negligence (at Level 7). Other symmetries are among their unself-conscious receptivity (at Level 2), passivity (at Level 5), and dissociation and denial (at Level 8). The support that healthy Nines give others (at Level 3) foreshadows a potential for resigned fatalism (at Level 6) and a self-abandoning disregard for reality (at Level 9).

Continuum for Personality Type One: The Reformer

HEALTHY
Level 1: The Wise Realist — Tolerance

Level 2: The Reasonable Person — Reasonableness

Level 3: The Principled Teacher — Objectivity

AVERAGE
Level 4: The Idealistic Reformer — Idealism

Level 5: The Orderly Person — Rigid Logic

Level 6: The Judgmental — Perfectionism
Perfectionist

UNHEALTHY
Level 7: The Intolerant Person — Intolerance

Level 8: The Obsessive Hypocrite — Obsessiveness

Level 9: The Punitive Avenger — Punitiveness

Summary Overview: The movement of One's Continuum can be seen in the following extremely abbreviated way: Ones progressively deteriorate from healthy discerning tolerance, objective rationality, and principled objectivity to an average idealistic reformism, self-controlled orderliness, and judgmental perfectionism to an unhealthy self-righteous intolerance, obsessive compulsiveness, and sadistic punitiveness.

Internal symmetries include the healthy One's wise tolerance (at Level 1), average high-minded idealism (at Level 4), and unhealthy self-righteous intolerance (at Level 7). Other symmetries are among their reasonableness (at Level 2), narrowly rigid logic (at Level 5), and consuming (irrational) obsessions (at Level 8). Their humane objectivity and balance (at Level 3) may deteriorate into a narrow perfectionism (at Level 6) and finally into an inhumane punitiveness (at Level 9).

The Meaning of the Levels
of Development

To provide a fuller explanation of what happens at each Level, the short explanations given in *Personality Types* (316–17) have been expanded here. The descriptions and profiles given in this book and in *Personality Types* fit the following patterns.

IN THE HEALTHY LEVELS

At Level 1: The Level of Liberation. By confronting and surmounting the Basic Fear (which arose in childhood as a result of parental relationships), the person becomes liberated and moves into a state of ego transcendence where he or she begins to actualize the self. Paradoxically, the person also attains his or her Basic Desire and therefore begins to fulfill his or her real needs. Moreover, particular spiritual capacities and virtues emerge, different for each type. This is an ideal state, and the individual is at his or her healthiest, attaining balance and freedom. The person is on the brink of shifting from "personality" to "essence," although he or she has not yet moved in the Direction of Integration. (See Chapter 9, "Personality, Essence, and Spirituality," for more.)

At Level 2: The Level of Psychological Capacity. If the person succumbs to his or her Basic Fear, a Basic Desire arises at this Level to compensate. The person is still healthy, but as a result the ego and its defenses begin to develop in response to anxieties created by succumbing to the Basic Fear. The person's sense of self (see Chapter 2) and "cognitive style" (which can be correlated to Jung's attitudes and functions) manifest themselves at this stage. The Basic Desire is a universal psychological human need, which if acted on rightly provides both what each person needs and a key to transcending the self.

At Level 3: The Level of Social Value. In response to succumbing to secondary (derivative) fears and desires, the person's ego becomes more active, producing a characteristic persona, with its social and interpersonal qualities. The person is still healthy, although less so because both the ego and the persona are protected by defense mechanisms (see Chapter 2). At this Level, we see the healthy social characteristics that the type brings to others. While the personality, ego, and defenses are operative, the person is not seriously imbalanced and is capable of attaining (or regaining) Level 1 functioning by overcoming the Basic Fear and by acting properly on the Basic Desire.

IN THE **AVERAGE** LEVELS

At Level 4: The Level of Imbalance. As a result of the person's succumbing to a significant Characteristic Temptation (see Chapter 2) that violates his or her own best interests and development, the ego is inflated, defenses increased, and imbalances introduced. Imbalances are maintained by drawing on the type's source of psychic energy. This Level marks a descent into the person's psychological "dead end," which, if not resisted, will create increasing intrapsychic and interpersonal conflicts.

At Level 5: The Level of Interpersonal Control. The ego inflates significantly as the person tries to control the environment (especially other people) in characteristic ways. (In the withdrawn types [*PT*, 324], "ego inflation" is negative, marked by the deflation of the persona and a characteristic withdrawal of the person from social interactions.) Defense mechanisms cause interpersonal and intrapsychic conflicts and increasing anxiety if they fail. The traits emerging at this Level are noticeably more negative than any seen prior to this stage. This Level is a turning point in the deterioration of the type since from here downward the traits become more egocentric, defensive, and conflicted.

At Level 6: The Level of Overcompensation. The person begins to overcompensate for conflicts and anxieties brought about by the increasing inflation of the ego as well as by the failure of the behavior seen at Level 5 to provide the person with what he or she has wanted. A characteristic form of self-centeredness emerges (different for each type), as well as overcompensated, extreme forms of behavior, usually found by others to be objectionable (although not neurotic). Conflicts with others arise as the person acts on self-centeredness to maintain ego inflation.

IN THE **UNHEALTHY** LEVELS

At Level 7: The Level of Violation. For various possible reasons, the person's defenses have not worked and serious reactions occur. Each type employs a different survival tactic, an unhealthy "self-protective" response, in a desperate attempt to bolster the ego (now assailed by seriously increased anxiety). This response violates the integrity of the self or that of others (or both), creating serious interpersonal conflicts. This state is severely imbalanced and unhealthy although not fully neurotic yet.

At Level 8: The Level of Delusional Thinking and Compulsive Behavior. As anxiety increases, very serious intrapsychic conflicts occur, and the person attempts to remake reality rather than succumb to anxiety. Thinking and perceiving, feeling and behavior all become severely distorted and unfree; hence, this is a fully neurotic state. The person begins to lose touch with reality (becoming delusional in some way), differently for each type; the resulting behavior can be characterized as "compulsive." Note that the psychological capacity that emerged at Level 2 and became inflated at Level 5 has become delusional by this Level.

At Level 9: The Level of Pathological Destructiveness. This is the neurotic state in which openly destructive behavior is expressed. Having become delusionally out of touch with reality, the person becomes willing to destroy others, the self, or both to spare the self from the massive anxiety produced by facing the consequences of past actions and the need to rebuild his or her life. Different forms of immediate or remote, conscious or unconscious destructiveness (including latent self-destructiveness) manifest themselves, resulting in serious breakdown, violence, or death.

These brief descriptions of the meaning of the Levels still do not do them justice. Nevertheless, with even such a brief explanation, it should be possible to understand the overall rationale of the Levels and therefore to understand the patterns presented by each type. Note that the ego emerges at Level 2, becoming increasingly inflated and destructive by Level 9. Note also that a reverse process happens with personal freedom: the person is most free at Level 1 and becomes increasingly unfree ("compulsive") as he or she deteriorates into neurosis at Level 9. Neurosis is fundamentally unfree, while health is marked by freedom—and further integration is marked by increasing personal freedom.

The characterizations of the Levels can be depicted as follows:

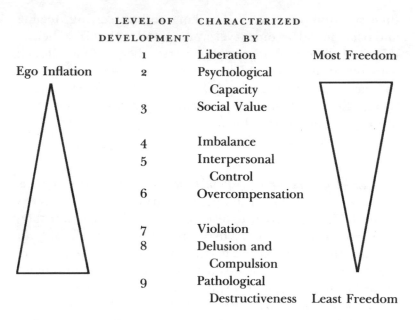

LEVEL OF DEVELOPMENT	CHARACTERIZED BY	
1	Liberation	Most Freedom
2	Psychological Capacity	
3	Social Value	
4	Imbalance	
5	Interpersonal Control	
6	Overcompensation	
7	Violation	
8	Delusion and Compulsion	
9	Pathological Destructiveness	Least Freedom

Ego Inflation

CHARACTERIZING THE LEVELS OF DEVELOPMENT

THE CHARACTERISTICS OF THE LEVELS

A review of *Personality Types* shows that each Level has certain core characteristics. While here they are simplified and presented schematically, it is possible to see how these traits form the major "theme" for each Level; it is also possible to use the following key traits as the basis for comparing each trait "horizontally" from type to type at the same Level of Development.

The core characteristics will be displayed in two ways — as a list of traits and then arranged around an Enneagram.

LEVEL 1   Characterized by: *Liberation*
                 (Self-Transcendence)

Type Two: Disinterestedness: Altruism

Type Three: Self-Acceptance: Genuineness

Type Four: Self-Renewal: Creativity

Type Five: Understanding: Discovery

Type Six: Self-Affirmation: Courage

Type Seven: Assimilation: Gratitude

Type Eight: Self-Restraint: Magnanimity

Type Nine: Self-Possession: Fulfillment

Type One: Discernment: Tolerance

ENNEAGRAM OF LIBERATION

LEVEL 2   Characterized by: *Psychological Capacity*
                     and *Sense of Self*

Type Two: Empathy: "I am caring."

Type Three: Adaptability: "I am desirable."

Type Four: Self-Awareness: "I am intuitive."

Type Five: Observation: "I am perceptive."

Type Six: Emotional Engagement: "I am likable."

Type Seven: Responsiveness: "I am happy."

Type Eight: Self-Assertiveness: "I am strong."

Type Nine: Receptivity: "I am peaceful."

Type One: Rationality: "I am reasonable."

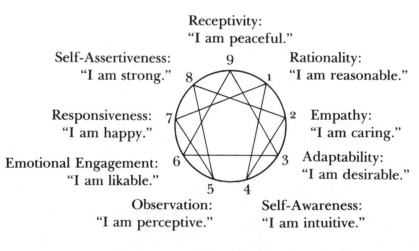

ENNEAGRAM OF PSYCHOLOGICAL CAPACITY

LEVEL 3   Characterized by: *Social Value*
                 (Contribution to Others)

Type Two: Generosity: Service

Type Three: Ambition: Self-Development

Type Four: Individuality: Self-Expression

Type Five: Knowledge: Expertise

Type Six: Commitment: Cooperation

Type Seven: Practicality: Productivity

Type Eight: Authority: Leadership

Type Nine: Stability: Nurturance

Type One: Principles: Objectivity

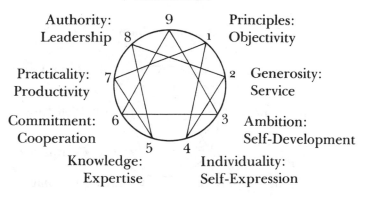

ENNEAGRAM OF SOCIAL VALUE

LEVEL 4   Characterized by: *Imbalance*
                        (Begins with . . .)

Type Two: Thinking oneself only well intentioned
Type Three: Competing with others for superiority
Type Four: Constantly living in the imagination
Type Five: Endlessly analyzing everything
Type Six: Becoming dependent on another
Type Seven: Allowing acquisitiveness to increase
Type Eight: Pursuing only self-interest
Type Nine: Becoming too accommodating
Type One: Constantly feeling personal obligation

ENNEAGRAM OF IMBALANCE

LEVEL 5 Characterized by: *Interpersonal Control* (Cause and Result)

Type Two: Intrusiveness: Possessiveness

Type Three: Calculation: Projecting Images

Type Four: Self-Absorption: Withdrawal

Type Five: Preoccupation: Detachment

Type Six: Ambivalence: Evasiveness

Type Seven: Uninhibitedness: Hyperactivity

Type Eight: Expansiveness: Domination

Type Nine: Disengagement: Passivity

Type One: Emotional Control: Rigid Orderliness

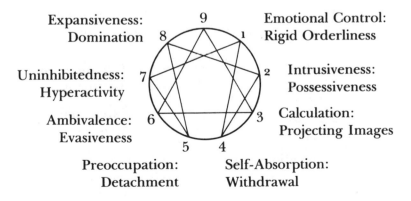

ENNEAGRAM OF INTERPERSONAL CONTROL

LEVEL 6   Characterized by: *Overcompensation*
                 (and Offensive Behavior)

Type Two: Self-Importance: Indispensability

Type Three: Narcissism: Arrogance

Type Four: Self-Pity: Self-Indulgence

Type Five: Contentiousness: Extremism

Type Six: Rebelliousness: Authoritarianism

Type Seven: Insatiability: Excessiveness

Type Eight: Willfulness: Combativeness

Type Nine: Resignation: Fatalism

Type One: Perfectionism: Dogmatism

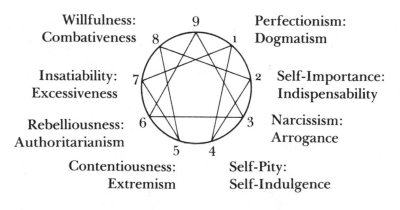

ENNEAGRAM OF OVERCOMPENSATION

LEVEL 7   Characterized by: *Violation* (of Self and
                     Others)

Type Two: Self-Deception: Manipulation of Others

Type Three: Hostility: Exploitation of Others

Type Four: Self-Inhibition: Alienation from Others

Type Five: Rejection: Isolation from Others

Type Six: Self-Disparagement: Dependency on
                     Others

Type Seven: Impulsiveness: Abusiveness Toward
                     Others

Type Eight: Ruthlessness: Violence Toward Others

Type Nine: Repression: Neglectfulness of Others

Type One: Self-Righteousness: Intolerance Toward
                     Others

Repression:
Neglectfulness of Others

Ruthlessness: 9   Self-Righteousness:
Violence toward Others   8 / \ 1   Intolerance toward Others

Impulsiveness: 7   2   Self-Deception:
Abusiveness toward Others   Manipulation of Others

Self-Disparagement: 6   3   Hostility:
Dependency on Others   5   4   Exploitation of Others

Rejection: Self-Inhibition:
Isolation from Others   Alienation from Others

ENNEAGRAM OF VIOLATION

LEVEL 8   Characterized by: *Delusions and*
                   Compulsions (Thinking and
                   Behavior)

Type Two: Entitlement: Coerciveness

Type Three: Malice: Duplicity

Type Four: Self-Hatred: Emotional Torment

Type Five: Paranoia: Phobias

Type Six: Overreaction: Irrational Behavior

Type Seven: Manias: Erratic Behavior

Type Eight: Megalomania: Overextension

Type Nine: Dissociation: Disorientation

Type One: Obsessions: Compulsive Contradictions

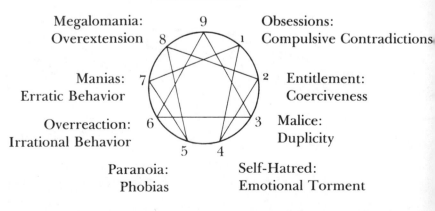

ENNEAGRAM OF DELUSIONS AND COMPULSIONS

LEVEL 9 Characterized by: *Pathological Destructiveness* (Pathology and Result)

Type Two: Conversion Reactions: Psychosomatic Problems

Type Three: Sadism: Psychopathic Behavior

Type Four: Self-Destructiveness: Suicidal Behavior

Type Five: Psychotic States: Deranged Behavior

Type Six: Self-Defeat: Masochistic Behavior

Type Seven: Panic Attacks: Hysterical Behavior

Type Eight: Vengefulness: Antisocial Behavior

Type Nine: Emotional Breakdown: Depersonalized Behavior

Type One: Punitiveness: Retributive Behavior

Emotional Breakdown:
Depersonalized Behavior

Vengefulness: 9   Punitiveness:
Antisocial Behavior   8   1   Retributive Behavior

Panic Attacks: 7   2   Conversion Reactions:
Hysterical Behavior   Psychosomatic Problems

Self-Defeat: 6   3   Sadism:
Masochistic Behavior   5   4   Psychopathic Behavior

Psychotic States: Self-Destructiveness:
Deranged Behavior   Suicidal Behavior

ENNEAGRAM OF PATHOLOGICAL DESTRUCTIVENESS

Assessment

FOUR

Identifying
Your Type:
A Questionnaire

SINCE THE PUBLICATION of *Personality Types,* many people have requested a questionnaire. I hope this one will be helpful to those who are still uncertain about their type and to those who want a questionnaire to help confirm their diagnosis. A questionnaire is certainly among the most efficient methods someone can use to find his or her personality type.

Even after devising a questionnaire, however, I would like to voice my own skepticism about the usefulness of questionnaires in general. To be accurate, questionnaires should be more sophisticated than those usually found in self-help books, especially if they are to be administered by readers themselves. The questionnaire might have to include several hundred items so that a broad range of traits can be tested; sophisticated statistical techniques should be employed to analyze the responses. Taking the test and grading it are time-consuming and can introduce errors; and even in the case of a sophisticated questionnaire administered by trained psychologists, the results can be ambiguous or downright misleading.

Rather than provide a questionnaire in *Personality Types,* I offered an incremental method (29–34). The nine types were introduced first, one word at a time, then by four words, then by a paragraph describing the major traits and dynamics of each within its Triad. Next were the Profiles that began each descriptive chapter with keywords and motivations, then the Overview, and then, finally, the full descriptions themselves. With this method, the descriptions started simply and became increasingly complex—literally going from one word to approximately ten thousand words for each type.

The drawback with this method was that readers were required to choose which description fit them best and to judge whether the descriptions continued to do so as they were expanded. Thus, some degree of prior self-knowledge was necessary for readers to be able to recognize themselves. If someone had absolutely no self-awareness, he or she would be at a loss about where to begin—and even the most accurate diagnosis (by this or any other method) would remain relatively meaningless.

Since self-knowledge is precisely what is missing in many people, some were unable to use this incremental method effectively. The desire to obtain self-knowledge is the reason many people are interested in the Enneagram in the first place; while it might be unrealistic to expect a high degree of self-knowledge from beginners, some degree of it is a prerequisite if there is to be any progress at all. Thus, paradoxically, we need some self-knowledge before we can acquire more of it. Those who have no idea of who they are (or who are completely uninterested in understanding themselves) not only will not make progress, they cannot.

One way out of the problem of ignorance of ourselves is to enlist the aid of friends who can tell us which type they think we are. The old observation that others can see us better than we can see ourselves is often true. Even those who feel confident of their diagnosis can be helped by discussing it with someone who knows them well and who will discuss the description of their type with them frankly.

Those who have some self-understanding but who still remain confused about which type they are should reflect on those two or three types that are the most likely candidates. (You can also consult Chapter 5, "Misidentifications," for comparisons and contrasts between types that you think you might be.)

The Expanded Profiles in this book (and the Profiles in *Personality Types*) are also a kind of "second questionnaire": the two sets of Profiles can be read as if they were questionnaires. To use this approach, go to the Profiles and read them carefully, pausing over each word or phrase and turning it into a question.

Each Profile is, in effect, a long questionnaire with the questions and qualifying statements omitted. Each Profile is a checklist that can be turned into either a question or a descriptive statement that should be potentially true of you all the time. A typical question might be, for instance, "When I am healthy (or average or unhealthy), am I _____?" Someone reading the Profile of the Two (*PT*, 49) could ask, "When I am healthy, am I unselfish? Am I also disinterested? Am I also altruistic? Do I also give unconditional love to others? Am I also empathetic? Am I also compassionate? Am I also caring? Am I also warm? Am I also concerned?" And so forth. The *combination of all of these healthy traits* will apply uniquely to healthy Twos because, of course, any type can occasionally be caring or warm or loving. The essential difference is that healthy Twos are not only caring, warm, and charitable, they are *also* unselfish, disinterested, compassionate, concerned, unconditionally loving, and so forth—virtually at the same time. In varying degrees, healthy Twos possess *all* the healthy traits listed in the Profile and act consistently on them. These traits are "typical" of healthy Twos because they are what make up this particular personality type.

No matter which method you use—the questionnaire, talking with friends, the Profiles, or the descriptions—it is important to allow time for the full descriptions to have an impact on you. Much of the material is complex and subtle, and, even more important, it is difficult to overcome our natural resistance to seeing ourselves clearly. There are elements in each of us that are painful to look at; it takes courage and time to acknowledge and deal with them.

You might also keep a few other general observations in mind as you use this or any questionnaire.

As mentioned in *Personality Types* (34), people often choose the type they would like to be rather than the one they actually are. This is by no means universally true, and perhaps most people identify their personality type correctly right away. (Without controlled research, it is difficult to say.) In any event, understanding our type—and seeing ourselves more objectively—often causes emotional turmoil (at least in the beginning) and presents us with a new set of challenges. Gaining self-knowledge is not always comforting, particularly if we have something to hide—although the more honest we are, the more liberating self-knowledge becomes. After all, if we purposely choose a type that flatters us rather than the one we suspect we really are, whom are we shortchanging? By choosing the wrong type, not only are we not transforming ourselves, we may be deceiving others. And instead of availing ourselves of the insights it has to offer, we will be rendering the Enneagram worthless.

Even so, a related legitimate problem remains: how to know with certainty whether we have correctly chosen our true type. Is the type we have chosen *really* our type? Several "rules of thumb" can be applied.

If the type you have chosen not only stirs up deep feelings but also helps you understand aspects of yourself you have never seen before, then it probably is your type. If your choice leads you to make new connections and see new patterns in yourself and your relationships, then you have probably made an accurate diagnosis. If the type in which you have seen yourself not only upsets you but, more important, encourages and excites you, then you have probably made the correct choice. And if your friends and family concur in your choice, then you are almost certainly on the right path.

However, there is no method to know with total assurance whether the type we have chosen really is our type. We will never find a book in which our personality type has been inscribed or a tattoo of our Enneagram number somewhere on our body. We can be assured of gathering objective evidence only if we see ourselves as we really are. With time and experience, confidence in our diagnosis will increase, although it will always depend on making a judgment based on the best available evidence. Perhaps most individuals can determine their type immediately; others take longer. You may be in either group.

The greatest mistake many people make is that they select a personality type by *taking a few traits out of context* rather than by trying to understand each type as a whole. For example, some Nines think they are Fives because they like to think (ruminate) and they convince themselves that they therefore must be Fives — "the thinking type." Likewise, some Sixes are creative and have artistic talents and therefore think that they must be Fours, and so forth.

Individual traits such as thinking and artistic talent should not be taken as the basis of a diagnosis. As general a trait as "thinking," for instance, must be distinguished from type to type because, of course, every type thinks — and the thinking of Fives and Nines can be contrasted clearly. Taking a trait out of context and making a diagnosis based on that alone is a fundamental error. (We will see many more examples of this kind of misdiagnosis in Chapter 5, "Misidentifications.") The important thing is to discern the whole pattern and the underlying motivations for each type, not to take the individual traits out of context. In time, and with attention, the true patterns will emerge.

The caricatures in *Personality Types* and the new ones in this book should also give you additional impressions of each type. The caricatures embody many traits and, for those who are visually oriented, convey valuable information.

Instructions for the Questionnaire

The questionnaire is *organized according to type* instead of as a list of random statements. All statements for each type are true.

There are twenty statements for each personality type. Approximately the first six reflect the *healthy* traits of the type, the second six reflect the *average* traits, and the third six reflect the *unhealthy* traits. The last two statements reflect average to unhealthy traits.

To determine your type with this questionnaire, you should "agree" or "strongly agree" with fifteen or more of the twenty questions listed. In other words, *most* of the statements should describe you either as you were in the past or as you are in the present or as you could be in the future. Some of the statements may touch only on your potential behavior, although even in these you should be able to see your own *tendencies* clearly.

For example, if you are healthy, you should "agree" or "strongly agree" with the first six statements and generally agree with the next six (average) statements. The unhealthy statements may well not apply to you as you are at present, but they should reflect tendencies that are part of your personality, even if they are not active now.

The most important thing to remember as you take this and all questionnaires is to answer spontaneously, without thinking of extreme circumstances under which the statement might possibly be true of you. The statement should obviously be true or not true, applicable or not, reflect a true tendency or not without your straining to answer the question.

A scoring sheet has been provided on which you can mark the number of "agree" answers for each set of statements, especially if you would like to take the questionnaire for all nine types. Doing so should give you a full profile and should indicate which wing you have, depending on the type on either side of your basic type that you scored higher on.

Also keep in mind that you might have relatively high scores on more than one set of statements because several other questions express attitudes held by that part of you that can be attributed not only to your wing but to the types lying in your Direction of Integration or Disintegration. For instance, someone taking the test might produce the following pattern of answers: agreement with about eighteen of the statements in the person's basic type, with about twelve to fourteen in the wing, and with two to six of the questions in the remaining seven types, with more agreement (five to ten) for those two types in the Directions of Integration and Disintegration from the basic type. In any event, one type should stand out most clearly, and that type is the person's basic type.

However, if someone agrees with virtually all the questions in all the types or, at the other extreme, with none of the questions in any of the types, the problem might be caused either by a faulty understanding of the questions and the need to discriminate between them or by the person's inability or unwillingness to understand and discriminate between them.

Another explanation is possible: many average Nines tend to have a high score for all the types, tending to see themselves everywhere because their sense of self is characteristically un- defined. (For more about distinguishing between Nines and other types, see Chapter 5, "Misidentifications.") Other types may well produce other "typical" overall patterns if resistance is operative. Time and research will tell.

The Questionnaire

PERSONALITY TYPE TWO

1. At my best, I love others unconditionally and do not concern myself with how people repay what I do for them.
2. People would say that I am altruistic and that I really care about the welfare of others.
3. Some people may think of me as a saint, but I know my imperfections and don't think of myself that way.
4. I can be self-sacrificial without calling attention to myself or whatever I have done for other people.
5. I am happy when good things happen to people, and I go out of my way to help others in whatever ways I can.
6. I am a caring person, and my personal feelings for others make me deeply concerned for them.
7. Love is the greatest value in life; without love what would life be?
8. Part of being a good friend is letting others know how much you love them.
9. It's good to be close to people, and I don't feel at all embarrassed to express how I feel, especially by hugging and kissing my friends.
10. I think a lot about my friends and friendships, and I could count five or ten people who are my very close friends.
11. I enjoy having my family and friends around me, and I like it when they come to me for guidance and advice.
12. I am not really possessive of people, although I suppose I do find it difficult to let go of those who are important to me.
13. I suppose it's true that I need to be needed — but doesn't everyone?
14. Maybe I am too good for my own good and should think of myself more instead of caring so much about everyone else.
15. To be perfectly candid, I'm an extremely generous and thoughtful person, and others are lucky to have me in their lives.
16. If I do something for someone, and if I should happen to

mention it to them, it's just to help them be aware of how much I care about them.

17. I don't think I really manipulate others, but even if I occasionally have to, it's to get them to do what is best for them.
18. One of these days my family and friends will have to take care of me the way I have taken care of them.
19. Since I love a lot, it means I suffer a lot, especially since people take me for granted and don't care about my needs very much.
20. The doctors don't know why I'm ill so often, although it seems that I have had more than my share of illness in my life.

PERSONALITY TYPE THREE

1. I accept myself as I am and am honest about my limitations and talents.
2. It is easy to affirm myself as a person because I feel worthwhile and valuable.
3. I come across to others as self-assured and poised, as someone who has a lot of self-esteem.
4. I like myself; I feel valuable and desirable, and I enjoy being who I am.
5. I am ambitious and think that other people should also spend time and effort improving themselves in whatever ways they can.
6. I always distinguish myself from the crowd in some way, and other people see me as an outstanding person, a real "winner."
7. Other people usually don't say it, but I can tell they are often jealous of me for one reason or another.
8. I know I'm competitive—but those who aren't may be losers who just can't face up to the fact.
9. I'm efficient, I know how to get things done, and I don't let someone else's agenda get in my way, especially in my career.
10. There is nothing wrong with wanting to make a good impression on others, even if it means presenting yourself as who you want to be rather than who you are.
11. It is important to know how to project the right kind of image if you want to be successful.
12. People create their own reality, and if they hold themselves back or fail, then that's their choice and they will have to deal with it.

13. When something isn't working for you, the thing to do is to change your tactics and do what it takes to get what you want.
14. What others think about me is important to me, and it really makes me mad when I get a bad "review" from someone.
15. There are "winners" and there are "losers"—and I'm definitely a winner.
16. I am better than most people—smarter, better looking, more successful; I "have my act together"; in many ways, I have it all.
17. I have cut corners now and then to get ahead, but everybody does, so what difference does it make?
18. A lot of people know who I am, although I don't like to get too close to people since they would use me if they could.
19. I've been in several relationships where the other person took it badly when we broke up—but they've got to learn to take responsibility for themselves.
20. If people humiliate me in some way, I can do some pretty mean things to get back at them—and I usually do.

PERSONALITY TYPE FOUR

1. One of my strengths is that I am a sensitive human being, and I make the most of my experiences, even if it hurts.
2. At my best, I am able to create something that seems to come out of nowhere—to be an "inspiration" of some kind.
3. I am almost never wrong when I follow my intuitions.
4. I am deeply convinced that I must be true to myself and, as much as humanly possible, I always try to act authentically.
5. The power of my creativity comes from expressing my deepest feelings in some form, whether personally or artistically.
6. I am aware of what I feel, and I try to be honest with myself about what my feelings are telling me.
7. For better or worse, I have a vivid imagination and am able to create a world of fantasies that is very real to me.
8. I spend a lot of time in long conversations with people and reveries about them in my imagination.
9. I have a poetic sensibility, although, unfortunately, it also usually includes feeling melancholy and emotionally vulnerable.
10. I question myself about everything—my motives and behavior, what I have said to someone, whether or not I will be up to a

certain task—to the point where I can sometimes do little else.

11. Other people may feel that I am not assertive or ambitious enough, but being self-assertive or competitive is just not part of who I am.

12. When someone says something I find upsetting, I can't do anything except turn it over in my mind until I have resolved it.

13. I often feel uncomfortable around people, even my friends, and I am not always sure why; maybe I'm just a loner.

14. When I am feeling vulnerable, I tend to withdraw into my shell to protect myself from being hurt anymore.

15. It's very painful to me, but I can become so angry at people that I can't bring myself even to be in the same room with them, much less to talk with them about what's bothering me.

16. Everyone else seems to be happier than I am; I seem to be emotionally damaged and unable to function very well.

17. I don't seem to be able to "pull myself together"; I don't know where to begin, or, if I do make some progress, it seems it can all be lost in a second.

18. Thank God nobody talks to me the way I reproach myself; some voice inside me says the most cruel, contemptuous things to me.

19. I have thought about suicide: it's a way out I might be forced to take someday.

20. Life is full of pain and loss and sadness—at least my life has been.

PERSONALITY TYPE FIVE

1. I have the capacity to have deep insights into the world around me, and I almost always perceive things that others miss or ignore.

2. Foresight is one of my great capacities: I seem to be able to predict the way things will turn out before they take place.

3. I have always had the ability to concentrate very deeply on my work or whatever I turn my attention to.

4. I have had more than my share of original thoughts and innovative ideas.

5. People come to me to get answers to technical or academic questions because they realize that I know what I am talking about.

6. The life of the mind is the most exciting kind of life.

7. I love the pursuit of knowledge: leave me alone with a book, and I am perfectly happy.
8. Research and scholarship are very appealing to me, and I would like to be a world-class expert in some field one day.
9. I am a rather intense person: I can totally lose myself in my interests because I get so completely immersed in them.
10. I have been made fun of by people who think that I am a little strange; they have called me an "egghead" or "nerd"—and I suppose it's been true enough.
11. My ideas are so complex that it is sometimes difficult for me to express them and difficult for others to understand what I am trying to say.
12. My relationships are frequently rocky because I can overwhelm others with my curiosity, intensity, passion, and desire to understand them in depth.
13. Genius is usually misunderstood, and my theories are sometimes so far ahead of their time that I don't even try to discuss them with anyone.
14. Once or twice I have discovered an extraordinary new insight, a long-sought "key" that explains a great many other things.
15. Political issues fascinate me, especially since I naturally distrust those who have any kind of power over me.
16. The fact is that most people are too stupid to understand what is really going on; in fact, most people are really just too stupid to notice anything.
17. Most religions pander to the infantile, superstitious needs that other people cannot live without.
18. It is safer and easier to live alone; I do not want others to become close to me or to know what I am doing or thinking.
19. Sometimes my thoughts seem to have a life of their own—they keep coming so fast that I find it difficult to slow down my mind or to relax or go to sleep.
20. My most secret thoughts may be strange and frightening, but they express the world as I see it.

PERSONALITY TYPE SIX

1. At my best, I realize that I am the equal of others and that I am as capable as anyone else.
2. People find me appealing and endearing and have told me how lovable I am.

3. Other people usually want to protect me in some way, and I like the feeling of being liked by others.
4. It is important to me to feel secure in my job and relationships.
5. I am very committed to those who are committed to me — my family and friends know they can count on me.
6. I am a reliable, hard worker and have worked hard to build a secure life for myself and my family.
7. I do not mind following orders if I am told to do something by someone in authority or by someone I deeply respect.
8. When it's necessary for me to decide something important, I usually ask the advice of others, or, if that's not possible, I will try to look up the answer in whatever "rules" are applicable.
9. I tend to be indecisive and get anxious when I have decisions to make on my own.
10. I am not always sure about what other people think about me — sometimes I feel they like me, sometimes I feel they don't.
11. My sense of humor throws people off because I say the opposite of what I really mean, so they don't know whether I'm serious or not.
12. I guess I sometimes give people mixed messages — saying yes when I really mean no or going along with what somebody else wants even when I don't want to.
13. Although I usually do what I am told, there are times when I rebel against that, too.
14. I've found that I can "get even" with people by playing tricks on them, like "accidentally" losing their mail or calling them anonymously and then hanging up.
15. It gets me furious when I see others breaking the law and getting away with it.
16. Some part of me really likes it when others get taught a lesson when they step out of line or don't obey the rules like the rest of us.
17. I can be really tough and stubborn when I have to be, although I don't always feel all that tough inside.
18. I can really get down on myself for not being as aggressive and independent as I would like to be, especially if I have let down someone who was counting on me.
19. I tend to be suspicious of some people and feel that they don't like me and are out to get me — or they would if they could.
20. I tend to get tense and overreact when I am really upset or when I am under pressure and things are not going well for me.

PERSONALITY TYPE SEVEN

1. Life is really wonderful, and when I stop and think about it I have so much to be grateful for.
2. When I am at my happiest, I am exhilarated, spontaneous, and full of life—in fact, I am one of the happiest people I know.
3. I get a kick out of things and am enthusiastic about everything because everything seems to give me pleasure.
4. I have a lot of different talents and am one of the most accomplished people I know—really good at a lot of different things.
5. I am also very practical and productive: I have my feet on the ground and know how to get things done.
6. I enjoy going to restaurants, entertaining, traveling, and enjoying myself with my friends.
7. I keep myself amused by having lots of different things to do; after all, you only live once—but, as they say, if you do it right, once is enough.
8. I have strong appetites and I tend to be acquisitive; if I want something, I don't see why I should deny myself.
9. I hate being bored and I enjoy staying on the go as much as possible: my calendar is filled with things to do, and that's the way I like it.
10. It's fun to talk and gossip and joke around and "let it all hang out" even if I sometimes get outrageous or overdo things.
11. I am one of the most uninhibited and outspoken people I know: I say what others wish they had the nerve to say.
12. I don't care if people think I'm "materialistic"—I like beautiful, expensive things, and I want them.
13. I tend to go to extremes—with me it's "feast or famine," although, of course, I "feast" as much as possible.
14. I agree with the statements that "nothing succeeds like excess" and "you can never get enough of a good thing."
15. Inconveniences and other frustrations can make me so mad that sometimes I just feel like screaming until I get what I want—and I usually do!
16. I have a tendency to become "addicted" to different things because once I get used to something, I like it and want to have more of it.
17. It's better to be an escapist than to be depressed and gloomy; I'd rather stay on the go and not look back.
18. Some people may say I'm pushy about getting what I want, but who cares what they think—I go after what I want in life.

19. There have been periods when I was either out of control or I was just about out of control.
20. Sometimes I feel panicky and anxious, but I throw myself into something new, and the anxious feeling goes away.

PERSONALITY TYPE EIGHT

1. I am self-assertive, and I have a lot of self-confidence.
2. I can see opportunities and the way I want things to be, and I can rally others around me to achieve it.
3. I have a lot of "guts"—I'm courageous and have frequently taken on difficult challenges and succeeded in them.
4. People look to me for leadership because I am strong and decisive and can make tough decisions.
5. I like the thrill of danger and adventure; I have often placed myself in tight spots and succeeded despite the odds.
6. I command respect: others look up to me and obey me.
7. I am persuasive, a natural salesperson, and I almost always have some sort of money-making opportunity going for me.
8. I am a deal maker and businessperson, and I make it my business always to come out of a deal better than when I went in.
9. Money is important because money is power; if I have enough money, no one can have any power over me.
10. I am a tough negotiator: I know how to push and how to say no, and I don't back down.
11. People don't dare ignore doing what I tell them since I know how to get what I want.
12. When you get right down to it, it's a matter of survival—them or me—and I am going to be the one who comes out on top.
13. I don't believe in selfless love or "do-good" altruism—that stuff is for sentimental weaklings who can't make it on their own.
14. I don't mind knocking heads when I have to; when you get right down to it, the only thing people really respect is force.
15. You have to make others fear you because they sure as hell won't do what you want because they like you.
16. I'm known as a tough bastard and can make people wish they hadn't tangled with me.
17. At times in the past, my philosophy has been "might makes right"—and I can be pretty ruthless when I have to apply it.
18. The way I've got things fixed, I control everything, and nobody else gets anything unless they play ball with me.

19. I believe in myself: I'm the greatest—I should have been a king or something.
20. If I can't have what I want, I'm going to make sure no one else gets it either.

PERSONALITY TYPE NINE

1. At my best, I can assert myself; yet I am still close to people, particularly my spouse and children.
2. I enjoy creating a warm, supportive atmosphere in which others can flourish and everyone can be happy and loving with each other.
3. People say that I am not judgmental or aggressive, that I'm comfortable and easy to be around.
4. People are basically good, and I trust them and don't question whether they have so-called ulterior motives.
5. I don't think I am a very complicated person: I am optimistic and content with myself and with my life as it is.
6. There is a contemplative and mystical side to me; I love to commune with nature, and I often feel at one with the universe.
7. I want to be close to my family and friends, so I try to go along with whatever they want me to do for them—it seems to make them happy.
8. I suppose I tend to be conservative and old-fashioned in my outlook, especially where my family and other values are concerned.
9. A lot of other people are too critical—they worry too much; but I don't see any point in worrying about most things.
10. I want everything to be pleasant, and I don't like it when people argue or bring up problems or cause upsets.
11. Most problems aren't really such a big deal, and they usually work out for the best eventually anyway.
12. Some people may think that I am forgetful, but there are things I would rather not pay attention to, so I just don't think about them.
13. People really can't change: you just have to accept them as they are.
14. I take life as it comes because things are going to happen as they are going to happen no matter what you do.
15. I don't want to think about myself very much: nothing is going to come of it anyway, so why get upset?

16. I have found that if you ignore problems long enough, they will go away.
17. The past is done, and it's best to get problems behind you as soon as possible.
18. People are sometimes angry at me and I don't understand why—I'm a good person, and I haven't done anything to hurt anyone.
19. Now and then anger or other upsetting feelings of mine seem to come out of the blue, although once I've had my say, that's the end of it.
20. If something terrible happens to me, it is as if everything is suddenly unreal, like a dream, and it really isn't happening to me.

PERSONALITY TYPE ONE

1. I have very good judgment and am extremely prudent: in fact, good judgment is one of my deepest strengths.
2. I have a strong conscience and a clear sense of right and wrong.
3. I tolerate others, their beliefs and actions, even though I don't necessarily agree with them or think that they are right.
4. My conscience leads me to do what I think is best, whether or not it is convenient for me or in my immediate self-interest.
5. I always try to be as fair as possible, especially by not allowing my personal feelings to sway my objectivity.
6. My integrity is very important to me, and I couldn't go to sleep at night if I felt that I had seriously wronged someone.
7. I feel that I should improve whatever I can whenever I see that something is wrong so that the world will be a better place.
8. Unfortunate but true: always striving to attain my ideals can be exhausting.
9. I can sometimes seem to others to be a little unemotional or too cut-and-dried, but they don't know the real me.
10. Being organized is necessary if anything is going to get done and if things are going to be under control.
11. I often feel that if I don't do something, no one else will—and sure enough, I'm usually right.
12. Very few people do things as well or as thoroughly as I do: most people are too lazy and they let themselves off the hook too easily.
13. I don't think I'm that much of a workaholic, but there is so

much that needs my attention that it's difficult to find time to relax.

14. I have opinions about most things, and I think I am right about them—if I didn't, I wouldn't hold the opinions that I have.
15. The fact is, other people would be better off if they would do what I tell them to do more often.
16. Right is right, and wrong is wrong, and I don't see any reason to make exceptions.
17. I don't have to tolerate nonsense, and when people are wrong, I think I have an obligation to set them straight.
18. I am so convinced that I am right about most things in my life that it's virtually impossible that I could be wrong.
19. True, I can get obsessive and rather picky about certain things, but they simply must be done the way they should be—the right way.
20. People who are wrong will get what they deserve—even if I have to see to it myself.

QUESTIONNAIRE SCORING SHEET

PERSONALITY TYPE

	Feeling Triad			*Doing Triad*			*Relating Triad*		
Question	Two	Three	Four	Five	Six	Seven	Eight	Nine	One
20									
19									
18									
17									
16									
15									
14									
13									
12									
11									
10									
9									
8									
7									
6									
5									
4									
3									
2									
1									

FIVE

Misidentifications

WHENEVER I TEACH the Enneagram, I inevitably encounter people who have misidentified their type—Twos who are convinced they are Fours, Nines who think they are Fives, Threes who are persuaded they are Ones, and so on. This chapter has grown out of the need to clarify similarities and differences between the types.

It is time to be more precise about both the similarities and differences so that people will be able to understand them more clearly, and so that teaching about them will be more accurate. After all, deepening self-understanding is the primary aim of the Enneagram, and if people misdiagnose themselves, the Enneagram will do them little good. It will be no more than a fascinating curiosity—or, worse, a way of obtaining insight into others while avoiding insight into themselves.

Even so, it is admittedly easy to misidentify people, and there are good reasons why aspects of virtually all the types can be confused.

First, the Enneagram is complex—and human nature is even more complex. People are extraordinarily varied and ever-changing. Unless we see individuals in different situations over a period of time, it can be difficult to have confidence in the accuracy of our diagnosis.

Second, it is inherently difficult to diagnose others since we must infer their type based on less than complete information about them. In fact, diagnosing personality types accurately is something of an art in itself, although it is actually a skill that anyone can become proficient in, given time and practice. Moreover, the fact that some people misdiagnose themselves or others is to be expected, at least at the present time, considering the state of the art of the Enneagram. There are different interpretations in circulation, some containing serious errors, including misattributions of traits from type to type. This is why it is essential to think critically and independently. If we rely on descriptions that are confused, we will never be sure that our diagnosis is accurate, nor can we hope to get much insight from having "found" our type.

Third, since the Enneagram can accommodate more than 486 subtypes (*PT*, 318), it is inevitable that some of them will be similar. For example, Sixes (at Level 6, The Overcompensating "Tough Guy") resemble Eights (at Level 6, The Confrontational Adversary) in that both are belligerent and authoritarian, although in noticeably different ways, as we will see in this chapter.

Fourth, types are easily confused when they are thought of as narrow entities—as if Nines, for example, were always peaceful and serene. If this is our idea of Nines, then when we encounter someone who is occasionally aggressive, we may automatically conclude that the person cannot be a Nine. While peacefulness and serenity are two of the principal traits of *healthy* Nines, there are also times when Nines can be angry, aggressive, and anxious. However, they virtually always think of themselves as peaceful and return to various forms of peacefulness (for instance, passivity and complacency) as their "home base." And just as important, when Nines are aggressive, angry, or anxious, they manifest these traits in distinctively "Nine-ish" ways. For example, they express anger as a "coolness" toward the person they are angry with—while denying that they are at all angry. Even rather severe out-bursts of aggression can erupt suddenly and subside quickly. To make subtle distinctions such as these, we must learn to discern the overall style and motivations for each type rather than see individual traits in isolation.

Fifth, types may be confused if the *wing* is not taken into consideration. Under certain circumstances, it is possible for a person's wing to be clearer than his or her basic type. By our perception of a person's wing, it is possible, by a process of elimination, to figure out which type the person is. For example, someone may have an element of "Three" about them, although we feel sure that the person is not a Three. This means that the person either has a Three-wing or is a Six or a Nine who has disintegrated or integrated to Three. If, in your estimation, the person is clearly neither highly integrated nor very disintegrated, then he or she probably has a Three-wing, and his or her basic type is either Two or Four. Twos with a Three-wing are rarely dominated by their wing, whereas Fours with a Three-wing might well operate out of their wing since Four is a socially withdrawn type. Thus, in certain social situations, a Four with a Three-wing may seem to be more like a Three than a Four. A tentative di-agnosis of "a Four with a Three-wing" might therefore be in order, to be confirmed by more evidence. The general rule is to be aware of the influence of the wing since this can help to eliminate certain diagnoses while suggesting others.

Sixth, we may confuse some types because our exposure to the full range of all the personality types is limited. It may be that because of our individual experience, we simply do not know many Fives, or Eights, or Twos, or some other type. Until you have correctly identified (and thought about) a wide variety of examples from all the types, it is likely that some of them will remain vague.

Furthermore, even if you do know examples from every type, it is important to keep in mind that *no one manifests all the traits of his or her type.* It is probably exceedingly rare for an individual to have traversed the entire Continuum, and even more unusual (if, indeed, it is even possible) to manifest the full range of the traits at one time. Each of us moves along the Levels of Development around a certain "center of gravity," varying by no more than a few Levels. Or, to put this differently, there is a certain "bandwidth" of Levels within which our own center can be found. (For example, someone might be fundamentally healthy, and the range of his or her behavior might be characterized as being within Level 2 and Level 5, inclusive. Thus, the person would not manifest Level 1 traits or, at the opposite end of the Continuum, traits from Levels 6 downward into the extremes of unhealth.) We simply do not act out the entire range of all the potential traits of our type since to do so would mean that we are simultaneously healthy and unhealthy, balanced and neurotic, integrating and disintegrating—an impossibility.

Since no one manifests the full range of traits at any one time, it is worthwhile to discuss the types (and their many variations) with others. It will be interesting to see what traits others discern in someone you are trying to diagnose and to see if your perceptions agree. When they do not, it will be even more helpful to debate as you search for the best available evidence for a diagnosis. Remember, however, that the most we can do is discern a person's type based on the traits they manifest in their long-term behavior. Observation over a period of time (and under a variety of circumstances) is the best way to come to a sound conclusion.

Seventh, it is helpful to know personally the individuals you want to diagnose, although this is not absolutely necessary. We can diagnose many people at a distance, without direct contact with them—either because they manifest their personalities so clearly or because a great deal of information is available about them, or both.

For example, former President Ronald Reagan seems to be

a personality type Nine. He is genial, unassuming, optimistic, and easygoing; he has also sometimes been detached, passive, inattentive, and forgetful. These and many other traits evidenced in Mr. Reagan's behavior belong to the healthy and average Nine, and so it is reasonable to assume since Mr. Reagan has manifested them so clearly and consistently during his lifetime that he is a Nine. And, of course, while it remains possible that he is not a Nine (and that another type might better explain his personality), given the evidence, the probability is high that Mr. Reagan is a Nine. We can therefore be justified in having some confidence in our diagnosis of him.

The diagnoses of other famous people given in *Personality Types* have been made on the same basis, as educated guesses, based on reading, intuition, and observation over a period of years (*PT*, 43–44). While no claims for infallibility have been made, virtually all of the diagnoses seem to have been accurate and were therefore helpful to give an impression of the range of each type, since people of the same type (particularly those with the same wing) are noticeably similar to each other. For example, based on their behavior as well as what has been written about them, former President Richard Nixon and Marilyn Monroe both seem to be Sixes, although with a Five-wing and a Seven-wing, respectively. Both Nixon and Monroe were deeply insecure and self-defeating and, in different ways, brought disaster on themselves. Both had "paranoid" episodes, although Nixon's paranoia seems to have been deeper and more pervasive than that of Monroe. Biographers, journalists, political analysts, and others can make similar long-distance diagnoses of other politicians and public figures, provided they do so based on as much evidence as possible.

Eighth, one of the most important ways to distinguish similar traits of different types is to try to discern the different *motivations* behind their behavior. Different types can act in virtually identical ways although their motives are quite different. For instance, every type gets angry, but the anger of Ones is differently expressed from that of every other type and also has different causes. It is essential to try to be aware of underlying motives rather than deal solely with the more superficial behavior.

Ninth, the longer you are familiar with the Enneagram and the more you practice using it, the more perceptive you can become. In the last analysis, however, learning how to diagnose people depends on knowing how to match the traits of individuals with those of the personality types. Thus, two areas must be learned: first, which traits go with which types, and second, how to recognize those traits in individuals. Even though there are hundreds of traits for each type (and scores of subtle distinctions that must be made), the first area is easier to learn than the second. It is admittedly very difficult to perceive the true behavior, attitudes, and motivations of others, especially since they often do not recognize those things in themselves, much less want them recognized by anyone else. As difficult as it is to become more perceptive, however, it is a skill that is certainly worth acquiring since so much in life is enriched by it.

Even after we have taken into consideration all the difficulties that stem from misinformation or misunderstanding—as well as from the inherent difficulty of the undertaking itself— the fact is that there are legitimate similarities among the personality types. It is precisely these similarities that contribute to misdiagnoses and confusion.

The following comparisons and contrasts are based both on similarities between types and between Levels from one type to another. Thus, some familiarity with the Levels of Development is necessary (*PT*, 41–42, 313–18, and Chapter 3 in this book). Unless stated otherwise, the comparisons and contrasts made in this chapter are between *average* people of each type.

The order of the discussions begins with type One and ascends numerically.

Misidentifying Ones and Other Types

ONES AND THREES

Average Ones and average Threes are sometimes mistaken because both types are efficient and highly organized. If an isolated behavior is the only thing being considered (chairing a business meeting or planning a vacation, for instance), their organizational abilities are similar—hence the confusion between them. The two types are very different, however, particularly in their motivations.

Average Ones are idealists, striving for perfection and order in every area of their lives, especially their emotional lives, in an effort to control both themselves and their environment so that errors and failures of all sorts will not be introduced. Inner-motivated by strong consciences, they are organized and efficient so as not to waste time and other resources or allow themselves to be in a position for their consciences to rebuke them for being imperfect, for not trying hard enough, or for being guilty of some form of selfishness.

Average Threes, by contrast, are efficient pragmatists, not idealists. Unless they are very healthy, Threes are not inner-motivated nor do they have strong consciences, although a fear of humiliation may act as an internal regulator on their behavior. Average Threes are interested in success, prestige, and advancing their careers, and the efficiency we see in them is a way of attaining those goals. Because emotional depth and a full range of emotions remain undeveloped, average Threes are rarely emotionally disturbed for long by anything (although they may become momentarily depressed by setbacks), nor are they generally ever distracted by their feelings. They are able to invest most of their energy into achieving their goals and in staying focused on them single-mindedly.

Both types can be cool and impersonal, although they are usually polite and well mannered. With average Ones, we get the impression of deeper feelings being held in check or sublimated elsewhere, say into social reform. Even though Ones do not ordinarily allow their passions to be expressed, their emotions remain potentially available should the self-control Ones typically exercise be lifted. (Their most prevalent negative emotions are righteous anger, indignation, and guilt.) In average Threes, however, the impression of aloofness and of emotional coldness is an indicator of the absence of deep feeling, although average Threes are able to give the impression of having emotions by projecting charm and "personality." However, the chameleonlike quality of these states is discernible in the abruptness and ease with which Threes can change their "feelings" from situation to situation and from person to person. (Their most prevalent negative emotions are hostility and a snickering contempt for others.)

In addition, Ones are trying to be perfect, while Threes feel that they (more or less) already are. In effect, Ones say, "Listen to me — I know the right way to live," whereas Threes say, "Be like me — I know how to succeed." Ones offer themselves as examples of those who are striving for perfection, particularly moral perfection; Threes offer themselves as exemplars of individual perfection, particularly personal desirability, as those who "have it all."

These two types are similar because both types are "thinking" types — the One corresponds to Jung's extroverted thinking type (*PT*, 277–78), who attempts to be objective and impersonal, while the Three's thinking is goal-oriented and pragmatic, similar in orientation to the extroverted thinking of the average One, although, technically, there is no Jungian correlation. Both types have in mind some sort of goal they want to achieve. The difference is that Ones attempt to discover which objective means will best lead to the desired ideal, whereas Threes are pragmatists who work backward to find the most efficient means to achieve their goal. Morality and idealism very rarely enter the picture for Threes, whereas those qualities are central to Ones. The differences between these types can be seen by comparing Adlai Stevenson (a One) with Gary Hart (a Three) or Jane Fonda (a One) and Jane Pauley (a Three).

ONES AND FOURS

See Fours and Ones.

ONES AND FIVES

Both Ones and Fives correspond to Jungian thinking types —the One to the extroverted thinking type (*PT*, 277–78) and the Five to the introverted thinking type, or to what I suggest might better be termed the "subjective" thinking type (*PT*, 137). Although many significant differences exist in form and style between these two types, they differ most markedly in the One's capacity for judgment and the Five's relative lack of judgment.

Judgment is not as centrally important to Fives. They think to understand how the world works on an abstract, theoretical level; thus, Fives tend to be detached from the practical world and intensely involved with complex mental constructs. And while healthy Fives observe and evaluate information, average Fives, as they become more deeply enthralled by their own thought processes and more deeply immersed in their own theories, lose their capacity to make accurate judgments about the truth, significance, or accuracy of their theories. They gradually care less about an idea's objective rightness than about how their ideas seem to explain other thoughts that arise from their thinking. By contrast, Ones employ thinking so that they can relate more perfectly to the world: they make rules and legislate practical changes for the progress and improvement of all. Ones are not as detached from the world as Fives are: although they may be cool and impersonal, somewhat Olympian and condescending, Ones are keenly interested in applying their principles to daily life.

Thus, Ones and Fives are opposites in the way they judge and evaluate reality. Ones judge situations from idealistic standards based on what they think should be the case. Fives judge things from theoretical standards, based on what they think or already have discovered. Ones are deductive, operating from principles to specific applications; Fives are inductive, operating from given data to form more sweeping theories. Both are philosophical and love knowledge: Ones as a means of perfecting the world, Fives as a way of discovering more about the world. Ones tend to be teachers and moralists, not analysts and scientists like Fives. The difference between these types can be seen by comparing George Bernard Shaw (a One) and Isaac Newton (a Five) or Margaret Thatcher (a One) and Susan Sontag (a Five).

ONES AND SIXES

See Sixes and Ones.

ONES AND EIGHTS

Both Ones and Eights are in the Relating Triad, both have strong wills, both want to get their way, and both types can aggressively order people around to do so. However, Ones exert pressure on others to do the right thing (as they see it) from the standpoint of a moral imperative—because it is the "right thing" to do. Eights, on the other hand, rely on personal forcefulness, intimidation, and the (implicit or explicit) threat of retribution and violence to get others to do what they want, without any reference to right and wrong, principles or morality. In short, Ones have strong and active consciences and can become angry when others do not follow their lead, whereas Eights defy their consciences and become more aggressive to get their way.

The greatest misunderstanding between these two types involves the Eight's so-called concern with justice, according to the traditional teaching of the Enneagram. Strictly speaking, only Ones are concerned with justice; Eights rarely are. Justice is an extremely important principle to Ones—not merely to healthy Ones but also to average and even unhealthy Ones. Ones at all Levels of Development refer to justice and think that they seek justice (no matter how skewed their neurotic interpretation of it may become). They strive after justice and want to rectify injustices wherever they find them because, among other reasons, to do otherwise would make them feel guilty, an emotion almost completely absent in Eights.

. Justice is not at all a concern for average to unhealthy Eights: on the contrary, Eights can be flagrantly unjust toward others without the slightest hint of guilt or remorse. Only the very healthiest Eights may acquire an appreciation of justice and the need for the just treatment of others. But even for healthy Eights, usually their sense of justice is an extension of their ego and of their role as protectors and providers for others. When Eights care about justice, it is usually expressed in a concern that those in their care (or under their power and authority) be treated fairly. The cowboy marshal protecting the town against criminals and the union chief negotiating a just wage for the rank and file are examples of this more restricted concern for justice.

The confusion between Eights and Ones probably also stems

from the fact that some Ones may misidentify themselves as Eights since they would like to have the authority and influence of Eights. They may also recognize that they have aggressive impulses and misidentify themselves as an "aggressive" type, although they are really compliant to their ideals; the Eight is the true aggressive type *par excellence.* On the other hand, Eights almost never misidentify themselves as Ones, viewing Ones as lily-livered and bloodless—moral only because they are too weak to be strong. Contrasting Ones such as Pope John Paul II and Ralph Nader with Eights such as Lee Iacocca and Franklin Delano Roosevelt gives a vivid sense of their differences.

Misidentifying Twos and Other Types

TWOS AND SIXES

This misidentification may be made by Twos who diagnose themselves as Sixes, perhaps because they find the description of the Two in *Personality Types* too emotionally upsetting. They would rather admit to being insecure and paranoid than being domineering and having unacknowledged claims about themselves. On the other hand, others may sometimes also mistake these types because of some genuinely similar traits.

Both are warm and engaging and want to be liked—although, more precisely, Sixes want to have the approval and protection of others, whereas Twos want to be loved and to be important to others. Both ingratiate themselves with people, although Sixes do so by being playful and silly, by bantering and teasing those they want to elicit an emotional (protective) response from. Average Twos also ingratiate themselves, but more from an implied position of superiority —they are warm and friendly, although the implication is that they are offering their love and friendship, their approval and advice, rather than that they are seeking it from you, at least at first. Other people are supposed to be flattered by the Two's attention, whereas other people find the Six's interest in them endearing and only sometimes flattering. In short, the feeling-tone of both types is completely different: Sixes warily invite selected others into their lives, whereas Twos throw out the net of their feelings with more abandon and see whom they can sweep into the fold.

Both types are emotional, corresponding to the Jungian feeling types—the Two is the extroverted feeling type (*PT*, 51–52), and the Six, the introverted feeling type (*PT*, 166). Twos "wear their hearts on their sleeves" and are openly warm and demonstrative about how they feel toward others. Sixes, by contrast, are often ambivalent about their feelings, frequently sending ambiguous, mixed signals to other people. As they deteriorate, average to unhealthy Twos become increasingly covert in their dealings with people, ultimately becoming manipulative while concealing their true motives even from themselves. By contrast, average to unhealthy Sixes become wildly reactive (overreacting) and consciously confused about their feelings, ultimately becoming masochistic (and only possibly manipulative) by making threats against themselves. For example, they might say, "Don't leave me! I'll commit suicide!" With Sixes, the manipulation is in the open; with Twos, it rarely is.

Not only do both types have the Jungian feeling function in common, but both types are oriented to their fathers, according to my theory of their Childhood Origins. Twos develop as a result of being ambivalently oriented to their fathers, while Sixes develop as a result of being positively related to their fathers. (As a psychological generalization, the father's role is to tell us what the world is like, while the mother's role is to tell us who we are). If this is so, the Two's father told the child that the world will reward him or her if the child does things for others—although this means always being good. The Six's father told the child that the world will protect him or her if the child is obedient and dutiful—although the child must find a good protector, someone who will really take care of him or her. Both "life scripts" present the children with potential rewards and punishments as well as sources of security and insecurity.

Indeed, Sixes are consciously assailed by anxiety, indecision, and doubts—and they look to others (especially some kind of authority) to settle these problems for them. Twos are also sometimes anxious, of course, as all human beings are; however, they are not indecisive or assailed with doubts, nor do Twos consult an authority figure for answers. On the contrary, as they grow in self-importance, average Twos usually make themselves into authority figures, gurus, or religious leaders within their spheres of influence. In short, average to unhealthy Twos want to control others to get the love they want, whereas average to unhealthy Sixes want to be controlled by others to get the love they want. At the end of the Continuum, the differences can be seen most starkly between the unhealthy Two's psychosomatic suffering and the unhealthy Six's self-defeating masochism. Both suffer, but for different reasons. Contrast Twos such as Bill Cosby and Sammy Davis, Jr., with Sixes such as Johnny Carson and Jay Leno.

TWOS AND SEVENS

These types are frequently mistaken because both are emotional and histrionic, although the emotions of Sevens are more labile (changing quickly) and less deep than the feelings of Twos. Average Twos are friendly and effusive, even gushy and dramatic, although they take pains to express their warm, personal appreciation of other people. They are deeply feeling (one of the types in the Feeling Triad), and their feelings are intimately connected with their sense of self, their behavior, and their interactions with others.

Average Sevens are also histrionic in that they dramatize their emotions flamboyantly, although their emotions are usually short-lived and wide-ranging—from elation to delight to giddiness to flightiness to highly negative displays of anger, frustration, vituperation, and rage at others. (Unless they are very unhealthy, Twos do not express their anger at others as openly, nor do they ever display the range of emotions—or such a dazzling variety of them—as Sevens.)

Although both types are gregarious and enjoy being with people, their interpersonal styles are noticeably different. The Two is the more interpersonal, genuinely friendly and warm, and interested in others—someone who would like to be the heart and soul of a family or community, the best friend or confidant everyone comes to for attention, advice, and approval. Twos want to be significant to others and on intimate terms with them, although sometimes they go too far, meddling too much and being too solicitous to make sure they are needed.

By contrast, Sevens do not get as involved in other people's lives. Sevens do not see themselves as the center of a community or family, but as members of a free-floating party of sensation seekers whose own enjoyment is enhanced by being with others. Because Sevens do not like to eat or drink alone, or go to the theater alone, or go on vacation alone, they are not necessarily great lovers of people—their activities are simply more enjoyable when others are around to contribute to the excitement and stimulation they seek. To provide themselves with the company of others, Sevens may pay for the pleasure, buying tickets for poorer friends, inviting them to dinner or the country house, and so forth. Sevens may thus exhibit a certain kind of generosity, although their motives may well have less to do with helping needier friends than with making sure that they themselves have a good time by having others around.

While average Twos want others to need them, average Sevens do not want to be needed by anyone: just the reverse, they have little patience for anyone who is dependent on them since dependents become a drain on their resources. And while average Twos are possessive of others because they feel they have invested a lot of time and emotional energy in their friends and do not want to see them drift away, average Sevens tend to be possessive of people primarily to the extent that they need others for their convenience or to heighten their enjoyment. Sevens can drop people without a second thought, especially if someone more exciting comes along (and the newest acquaintance is by definition always more exciting since this person has the advantage of newness).

Despite their many genuine differences, however, these two types are often rather compatible because Sevens are unconsciously looking for a mother figure to make up for the maternal nurturance they fear they have not gotten — and Twos offer this to Sevens in the form of affection, attention, and encouragement. It is gratifying for average Twos to shower attention on someone who responds to them, and no type is more responsive than Sevens. (Sevens are usually vivacious, witty, and fun; they also usually have money and are socially well connected, thus making an average Seven a desirable friend or spouse for the Two.) The problem is that while average Sevens are only too happy to take whatever love and attention Twos provide, they may not give Twos enough appreciation and gratitude in return to satisfy Twos' emotional needs.

It is probable that more Sevens misidentify themselves as Twos than vice versa. The differences between Leo Buscaglia and Ann Landers (Twos) and Leonard Bernstein and Joan Rivers (Sevens) may clarify these two types.

TWOS AND EIGHTS

It is not difficult to see how Twos and Eights can be confused, although there is a world of difference between them. Some average Twos realize that they are forceful and dominating, two of the significant traits of Eights. A particularly aggressive Two may find himself or herself in a work-related role that requires leadership and discipline. For these and other reasons, it is possible for some Twos to misidentify themselves as Eights. (The difference even on these points, however, is that average Twos do not dominate others and their environment to extend their personal power. Twos do indeed dominate others, although indirectly: they may be overbearing and controlling, although always under the guise of being concerned for others, behavior that is completely foreign to average Eights.) Twos and Eights are nevertheless similar in the deep feelings and passion they bring to their relationships, although the expression of their feelings and the effects they have on others are quite different.

It is worth noting that both types are ambivalent to one of their parents: Twos are ambivalent to their fathers (*PT*, 54), while Eights are ambivalent to their mothers (*PT*, 223–24). This ambivalence probably predisposes both types to have stormy relationships and, should conflicts occur, to express their intense passions in interpersonal conflicts (Eights) or in manipulation (Twos).

The probable source of the confusion is that both types have strong wills and egos and a tendency to dominate others. Eights are openly aggressive, forceful, egocentric, and concerned about their self-interest, particularly their financial self-interest. Twos can also be aggressive, forceful, self-satisfied, egocentric, and so forth, although covertly, under an increasingly thin veneer of love. Their oft-stated concern for others allows unhealthy Twos to manipulate people to get the responses they want. By contrast, Eights intimidate people openly; when they are frustrated, they push harder to get what they want, possibly becoming violent. When Twos are frustrated, they try to make others feel guilty, especially by dramatizing the suffering they feel. In the end, of course, as Twos become more unhealthy, they increasingly resemble unhealthy Eights since Eight is the Two's Direction of Disintegration. Contrasting Twos such as Mother Theresa and Barbara Bush with Eights such as Indira Gandhi and Bea Arthur will yield more insight into these two types.

TWOS AND NINES

Confusion between Twos and Nines is the result of the wishful thinking of people of one type who would like to be another. In this case, it is usually average Nines who mistakenly think that they are Twos; it is rare for average Twos to make the reverse misidentification.

Some average Nines (particularly women) would like to be Twos because Two is the "loving" type, and since these Nines also see themselves as loving, they feel that they must therefore be Twos. But of course, the capacity to love is not restricted to Twos, and other types (including Nines) are equally capable of loving others. As with other general traits that are common to all the types (such as aggression and anxiety), love is expressed differently from type to type and must be distinguished.

In fact, the way Twos and Nines love others is quite different. Nines are unself-conscious, with little sense of their own identities apart from their identifications with others. They are self-effacing and accommodating, quite content to support others emotionally without looking for a great deal of attention or appreciation in return. (Of course, while Nines want to feel that their love is returned, they are patient about it and can be satisfied with fewer responses than Twos.) Nines want to merge with others and have union with them — even at the risk of living through someone else. Average Nines tend to idealize others and fall in love with a romantic, idealized version of the person rather than the person as he or she actually is. Average Twos, on the other hand, have an acute sense of other people—especially their needs and weaknesses—and may consciously or unconsciously play on them.

Unlike average Nines, average Twos have a very sharp sense of their own identities. Although highly empathetic, they do not merge with others, nor are they particularly self-effacing or accommodating. Rather than being unselfconscious, they are highly aware of their feelings and virtues and are not hesitant to talk about them.

At their best, healthy Twos can be as unselfish and humble as healthy Nines, but by the average Levels there is quite a marked difference: Twos need to be needed, they want to be important in the lives of others, and they want people to come to them for approval, guidance, and advice. Average Twos are always in danger of subtly encouraging people to become dependent on them, and they tend to do things for people so that others will reinforce their sense of themselves as all-good and loving. By contrast to average Nines (who usually react very little, if at all, when they get into conflicts with others), average Twos have no hesitation about telling people how selfish they are or informing them in no uncertain terms how much others are indebted to them. In short, as they become more unhealthy, the egos of Twos inflate and become more self-important and aggressive, whereas the egos of Nines become more self-effacing and diffused.

There is almost no tendency in Nines to manipulate others or to make them feel guilty for not responding as they would like. (Healthy Nines are more patient and humble—traits Twos could learn from them.) By contrast, healthy Twos are willing to get down to the nitty-gritty and help out in difficult situations. They have a staying power that Nines lack. Moreover, the help that healthy Twos give has a direct, personal focus: it is a response to *you* and your needs. In general, Twos will walk that extra mile with you, whereas while Nines sincerely wish you well, they generally offer more comfort and reassurance than practical help. (The particularity of the love of healthy Twos is something that Nines could learn.) The similarities and differences between these two types may be seen by contrasting Eleanor Roosevelt and Lillian Carter (Twos) with Lady Bird Johnson and Rose Kennedy (Nines).

Misidentifying Threes and Other Types

THREES AND ONES

See Ones and Threes.

THREES AND FIVES

The principal reason these two very different types are confused is that some average Threes (especially if they are intelligent) would like to see themselves as "thinkers." Since I have characterized personality type Five as a whole by that designation, average Threes may choose it rather than the type they actually are. This misidentification is made almost exclusively by Threes since Fives are not likely to think that they are Threes. Average Threes are constantly searching for an acceptable image to project, and being a thinker (intellectual, brilliant, and original) is a flattering one, at least if only these traits are considered.

Some Threes may well be thinkers and have original ideas; they may excel academically and be brilliant students. But these traits alone are not sufficient to be a Five. Once again, the root of the misidentification lies in focusing on one or two traits rather than considering the type as a whole, including its central motivations.

There are many significant dissimilarities between these two types. The kind of thinking they engage in is very different: Fives are analytic and extraordinarily involved in abstract ideas for the sake of acquiring knowledge, virtually as an end in itself. The pursuit and possession of knowledge enthralls Fives, and not only do their researches need have no practical results for them to be intellectually satisfying, average Fives are just as likely never to seek fame or fortune for their discoveries. Fives follow their ideas wherever they take them, with no end in view other than to discover how the world works—or, at most, to have a theory validated. Average Fives will stay with a project for years until they exhaust their subject or themselves, or both.

Threes, in contrast, are not usually involved in subjects for their own sake: they change their interests and careers rapidly if the success and recognition they seek elude them. Moreover, average Threes pursue their intellectual work with personal goals in mind (either consciously or unconsciously): to impress others, to be famous, to be known as best in their field, to be acclaimed as a genius, to beat a rival at a discovery, and so forth. The essential consideration is that their intellectual work is frequently undertaken to achieve goals that deal more with success and garnering recognition than with the love of knowledge and the excitement of intellectual discovery. Competitive and status-seeking elements are always operative. Average Threes tend to promote themselves and to talk about their brilliant achievements, whereas average Fives tend to be secretive and reticent about their work and discoveries. Furthermore, the pragmatic thinking of average Threes calculates how to achieve goals in the most efficient manner, something completely alien to impractical, curiosity-driven Fives.

In addition, Threes are highly sociable, often physically

attractive and well groomed, and they know how to present themselves favorably. Fives are usually loners and often are not physically attractive: their appearance means less to them than pursuing their intellectual interests until the problems are solved and the work is done. Average Threes are highly aware of what others think about them, whereas average Fives care little about anyone else's good opinion. Average Threes want to be considered sexually and socially desirable and will conform to and set social standards. Fives are often strange, eccentric, and isolated from others—not at all concerned about conforming to social standards. Contrast the personalities of Threes such as Michael Tilson Thomas and Truman Capote with those of Fives such as Glenn Gould and Ezra Pound.

THREES AND SEVENS

Both Threes and Sevens are aggressive types (*PT*, 324, 329–30) and both are interested in enjoying different aspects of success. Both types pursue the acquisition of wealth and status symbols, but with significant differences: Sevens because their sense of self is maintained by possessing things, Threes because status symbols reinforce their feeling of superiority and hence their sense of self.

Sevens love the material world and want to acquire a variety of exciting experiences because having a steady stream of sensations makes them feel alive. They are sensation seekers whose sense of self is maintained and reinforced by heightening their experience of the world, irrespective of anyone else's knowledge of their acquisitions. For them what is important is the stimulation that the pursuit and acquisition of experiences and things gives them, whether or not anyone else is part of the picture. For example, taking a first-class cruise on an ocean liner is a source of pleasure for Sevens, whether or not anyone else knows that they are doing so. By contrast, unless everyone knows that they are going on an expensive trip and are made to feel envious about it, the experience has far less value for average Threes.

The similarity between Threes and Sevens can be most confusing in the average Levels when Sevens become faddish trendsetters who want to experience whatever is new and exciting right away. (Average Sevens want the excitement of being the first at the hottest place, whereas average Threes are trendy in that they create new status symbols of various kinds for the exclusivity of being one of the "in crowd.") Thus, both types become snobs, with Sevens looking down on others because of the expensive things they have that others do not, and Threes looking down on people because they are able to exclude others from associating with them while still tantalizing them to want to do so.

The differences, however, are very great. The underlying motive for average Sevens is to provide themselves with a continuous stream of stimulation from the environment, particularly from material things. By contrast, the principal underlying motive for average Threes is to rise above others competitively in whatever ways they can—socially, sexually, in status symbols and careers, or simply in their own minds. For Threes, expensive possessions advertise to others that they have arrived socially and that they are desirable—someone others must pay attention to. For example, money allows Threes to hire a governess for their children so they can pursue their careers and so that they can let everyone know that they are successful enough to afford a governess. By contrast, Sevens may engage a governess so that they can travel and not be tied down by having to raise their children themselves.

One of the fundamental reasons why Sevens and Threes are confused in the traditional Enneagram teaching is that *unhealthy* Sevens in a manic phase have grandiose delusions similar to the grandiose feelings of self-esteem we find in narcissistic Threes. The difference is that Sevens are grandiose about their ability to achieve things: they have great expectations about their activities and plans for the future. When they become manic, everything seems possible for them. By contrast, average Threes are grandiose about their self-worth: narcissistic, exhibitionistic, arrogant, and contemptuous of others.

It is likely that these two very different types have been confused because both seem to be narcissistic—that is, inflated with self-love or self-regard. However, average Sevens are not really narcissistic; they may be selfish, self-centered, greedy, insensitive, and so forth, but they do not have an inflated sense of self-worth. Instead, Sevens inflate their desires, appetites, plans, and the glut of their possessions.

Furthermore, by the time that Sevens become grandiose, they are neurotic (at Level 8) and delusionally trying to escape from reality, whereas grandiose Threes are still within the average Levels of Development (at Level 6) and are overcompensating for their fear of failure. The crucial difference is that, beneath their grandiose plans, manic Sevens are intensely insecure and in a flight from anxiety, whereas narcissistically grandiose Threes are not insecure and are fleeing from failure or from being humiliated in any way.

Last, one of the simplest ways to distinguish these two types is by marking the difference in their overall emotional tone and style. Average Threes are cool, in control, projecting the impression that they are perfectly together, with no emotional or personal problems. So convinced of their superiority, they become shameless braggarts and showoffs, arrogantly looking down on others. By contrast, Sevens have many more rough edges, rarely seeming as perfect or as coolly self-contained as Threes. For better or worse, Sevens do not censor themselves and can be funny, outspoken, vulgar, ill mannered, and outrageous—allowing far less polished behavior and attitudes to be displayed for public view. Contrast Sevens such as Richard Simmons and Morton Downey, Jr., with Threes such as Tom Cruise and Bryant Gumbel.

THREES AND EIGHTS

Threes and Eights are both aggressive (*PT*, 324, 329–30), although the confusion between them centers on the competition found in average Threes and a similar competitiveness in average Eights.

In general terms, both Eights and Threes are ambitious and competitive: both types want to rise above others. The difference is that average Eights are self-assertive and want others to give them their way immediately so they do not have to waste time and energy fighting with people — not that they are afraid to do so. Eights compete for material and sexual dominance, less over purely social or status issues. For instance, Eights usually do not spend a lot of time comparing themselves with others, and certainly never to the degree that Threes do. For the same reason that Threes confuse themselves with Sevens or Fives (because they are looking for a flattering identity), it is far more likely that Threes identify themselves as Eights rather than vice versa.

Despite some superficial similarities, the differences are profound: Eights are leaders, deal makers, and power brokers who want to make the world conform to their personal vision. They want to have a large impact, to build and accomplish great things, possibly something that will live as a testament to the greatness of their audacity and will. Strong and implacable, they can be ruthless when something or someone gets in their way. They have large egos, and achieving some form of glory is important to them. Money is both a form of power and a means to amass more of it. Achieving personal power is the dominating drive in Eights, and there is nothing ambiguous, much less furtive or duplicitous, about them.

By contrast, power is not the key motive of Threes; achieving success and prestige and basking in the admiring attention of others is. (For their part, Eights do not care about popularity; they do not care about the goodwill of others, so long as they get their way.) If Eights are natural leaders, Threes are natural managers and technicians. If Eights do not fear failure as such, Threes fear failure deeply because they see it as a personal humiliation, a potential occasion for being rejected, their deepest fear. Eights, however, see failure as an opportunity to learn something and come back stronger. If Eights are too busy achieving their purposes to worry about public opinion, Threes live and die on the opinions of others and desperately want to be in demand socially. If average Eights are combative and intimidating and can "take the heat," despite a certain bravado, average Threes will back down or be driven to deviousness: they cannot take pressure for long or exposure for a moment. In short, even average Eights are the "genuine article," whereas average Threes are an imitation of it. Contrast Eights such as Telly Savalas and John Wayne with Threes such as Sylvester Stallone and Burt Reynolds.

Misidentifying Fours and Other Types

FOURS AND ONES

Since Fours and Ones are so different, it might seem strange that they can be confused. The confusion seems to arise when a One (who may have disintegrated to Four at some time in the past) begins to think that he or she is a Four. Invariably, Ones who misidentify themselves as Fours focus almost exclusively on the traits of the unhealthy Four and not on the type as a whole. Because they were once depressed and guilt-ridden and felt worthless and subject to excruciating self-contempt and self-hatred (and even felt suicidal), Ones convince themselves that they must be Fours. Their confusion would clear if they were to see both themselves and the Four as a whole. Furthermore, the wings in both cases are completely different: someone having a Two-wing or a Nine-wing, for example, simply could not be a Four.

Despite these differences, there are similarities. Both tend to be perfectionistic and dissatisfied with things as they are: Ones with the world as it is, Fours with themselves as they are. While average Ones are perfectionists about almost everything, average Fours are perfectionists mainly about their creative work since their work is such an important symbol of themselves. Both types are angry: average Ones are frequently critical and irritable; average Fours are hypersensitive and consequently may also be irritable, although they tend to withdraw to sort out their feelings and lick their wounds. Average Ones do not withdraw from people. On the contrary, they press themselves and their opinions on others with increasing urgency as they become more angry at what they see as the irresponsibility of others.

It is also possible for an occasional healthy Four to be mistaken for a One; such a misidentification would, however, be a compliment to the Four since it indicates that he or she has integrated to One and is living with purpose beyond the self. Fortunately for them, some Fours actually do integrate and begin to manifest the reason, moderation, and attraction to objective values of healthy Ones. Furthermore, some Fours may well be teachers and in a teaching situation be called on to move beyond their feelings and interior states. But a Four who has genuinely integrated to One is still a Four — and besides having either a Three-wing or a Five-wing, other important characteristics not found in a One will continue to be present in the Four's overall personality. Contrast a Four such as Virginia Woolf and a One such as Shana Alexander or a Four such as Ivo Pogorelich and a One such as Maurizio Pollini for more insight into these types.

FOURS AND SIXES

See Sixes and Fours.

FOURS AND SEVENS

Fours and Sevens are vastly different, and except for a superficial similarity at Level 6 of both types, it would be difficult to see how anyone familiar with both could misidentify them for long.

It seems, however, that the basis for mistaking them is that both types tend to be excessive—Sevens go to extremes in the external, material world with the lavishness and number of possessions and experiences they acquire. Highly materialistic, Sevens tend to become jaded and hardened, insensitive and demanding, selfish and uncaring about others. At Level 6, I have characterized them as The Excessive Materialist.

Fours at the same Level (The Self-Indulgent Aesthete) are also excessive and go to extremes, although emotional extremes. Emotionally self-indulgent, average Fours go for the big emotional charge in their fantasy lives, allowing themselves to feel and imagine anything, no matter how ultimately unrealistic or emotionally debilitating it might be. They wallow in their feelings and fantasies, squeezing the last breath of life from them to reinforce their sense of self. Thus the Fours' self-indulgences are more internal and private, centered on the emotional world they inhabit. Outwardly, their emotional excess is expressed in an increasing preciosity and impracticality, an effete, overripe decadence and sensuality that is the main point of similarity between the two types. While both types may become decadent and sensual, Sevens do so to dissipate themselves and thus flee from anxiety. By contrast, Fours embrace sensuality, luxuriating in sex or drink or drugs to heighten their emotions and to deaden the pain of their self-consciousness.

Both types share a love of fine, expensive things, although here too there are differences. Fours make do with fewer material things, cherishing beautiful objects for the sake of their beauty and the feelings that beauty awakens in them. A stone picked up on the beach or a twig with a single bud can quicken their aesthetic feelings and satisfy them. By contrast, while average Sevens want to possess beautiful objects, they become increasingly unappreciative and insensitive to the beauty or value of those objects. They become more and more acquisitive not because they enjoy things for themselves but because possessing things provides a sense of security. And even more fundamentally, what excites Sevens is the stimulation they feel when they desire something new. The stimulation of their appetites reinforces their sense of self, although once they have actually acquired what they want, they usually lose interest in the acquisition. The pair of shoes that they were "dying" to have joins the racks with dozens of others; the fur coat they were drooling over for weeks suddenly becomes "that old thing" as they turn their attention to acquiring something else. In short, average Sevens tend to be acquisitive materialists, while average Fours tend to be languishing aesthetes — very different types. Compare the styles of Chopin (a Four) and of Liberace (a Seven) and those of Ingmar Bergman (a Four) and Steven Spielberg (a Seven) to understand the difference.

FOURS AND NINES

In another instance of one type wishing to be another, some average Nines think that they are Fours because they have artistic talents and creative inclinations of one kind or another. As in the case of love not being the sole domain of Twos, artistic capacity is not the sole province of Fours. Other types can be, and often are, artists.

Even so, the artistry of Fours is much more personal and self-revealing than that of Nines. The art of Nines often expresses idealized, mythological, and archetypal worlds — usually the real world glossed into something fantastic and wondrous. Nines are often gifted storytellers in which "and they all lived happily ever after" is assured. (There are no unhappy endings in the Nine's world of make-believe.) By contrast, the art of Fours is generally more personal and realistic, the expression of their (and of everyone's) deep longing for love, wholeness, and meaning. Fours often deal in the tragic, finding redemption in self-transcendence; Nines deal in the commonplace, finding comfort in ordinary lives and simple situations.

The principal reason these types may be confused is that they are both withdrawn types (*PT*, 324, 329). Fours withdraw from others so that they can protect themselves and give themselves time to deal with their emotions. Nines, on the other hand, are withdrawn in the sense that they remove their attention from people or situations that threaten them, disengaging themselves emotionally so that they will not be anxious or upset. They cut off their identification with others (or never identify with them in the first place), identifying instead with a private idealized version of reality. Average to unhealthy Nines tune out any unpleasantness by dissociating from whatever upsets them, whereas Fours do just the opposite, brooding over their anxieties in an attempt to come to terms with them. Fours are certainly not detached from their emotions — just the reverse, they are keenly aware of them, perhaps too much so.

Both types can therefore be shy, absent-minded, confused, and detached from the real world. The difference is that Nines are detached both from the external world and from their emotions, whereas Fours withdraw from whatever has caused them pain. (In the end, that may add up to quite a lot.) Nines see the world through rose-colored glasses, and their view of it is comforting, whereas Fours see the world from a garret window as outsiders and are not comforted: everyone else seems to be living a happier, more normal life. Contrast the personalities of Mahler (a Four) and Aaron Copland (a Nine), Saul Steinberg (a Four) and Norman Rockwell (a Nine).

Misidentifying Fives and Other Types

FIVES AND ONES

See Ones and Fives.

FIVES AND THREES

See Threes and Fives.

FIVES AND NINES

A detailed comparison and contrast between Fives and Nines is warranted because so many Nines mistakenly think that they are Fives; typically, the misidentification almost never happens the other way around. Particularly if they are well educated and intelligent, average male Nines tend to think that they are Fives. (As noted in the discussion of Twos, average female Nines tend to think that they are Twos.)

Of all the personality types, Nines have the most difficulty identifying which type they are because their sense of self is undefined. Average Nines have little sense of who they are apart from those they have identified with; hence, they are usually at a loss to know where to begin to find their type. (As we have seen, either they think they are Fives or Twos or they see a little of themselves in all the types and make no further effort at identifying themselves. If they have no guidance, Nines in this predicament usually shrug their shoulders and give up on the Enneagram and, more important, on acquiring self-knowledge.)

Even relatively healthy Nines still have a somewhat diffused sense of self because it is based on their capacity to be receptive to others — and to be unself-conscious. Moreover, average Nines have problems identifying their type because doing so arouses anxiety, something completely anathema to them. Whatever disturbs their peace of mind is ignored or met with a blind eye. They avoid introspection in favor of entertaining comforting notions about themselves, whatever they may be. Maintaining an undefined understanding of themselves, and thus maintaining their emotional comfort, is more important to average Nines than acquiring deeper insights.

None of this is true of Fives, and the two types are opposites in many ways. Nines are gentle, easygoing, patient, receptive, and accommodating, whereas Fives are intense, strong-minded, argumentative, contentious, and highly resistant to the influence of others. Nines like people and trust them; perhaps at times they are too trusting. By contrast, average Fives are suspicious of people and are anything but trusting, perhaps at times too cynical and resistant. Both types are among the three withdrawn types of the Enneagram, and (as we have seen with Fours and Nines), there are genuine similarities between them, although only superficial ones (*PT*, 324, 329).

Despite their similarities, the main point of confusion for Nines arises around the notion of "thinking." Nines think they are Fives because they think they have profound ideas: therefore, they must be Fives.

Part of the problem stems from the fact that individuals of both types can be highly intelligent, although as a group Fives are probably the most intelligent of the nine personality types. (When Nines are highly intelligent, they can be as brilliant as

Fives, although their intellectual prowess is compartmental-
ized. They are brilliant at work but unfocused and inattentive
everywhere else, whereas Fives are focused and attentive
everywhere all the time.) Although intelligence can be manifested in different ways, being intelligent does not make Nines
intellectuals, just as thinking does not make them thinkers.
As we have seen, the pattern as a whole (and the motivations)
must be taken into consideration, not one or two traits in
isolation. Since all the types think in one way or another,
thinking alone, with no further distinction, is not a sufficient
basis for a personality diagnosis.

The fundamental difference between the thinking of Nines
and that of Fives is that Nines are impressionistic, involved
with generalities, imaginative ruminations, and fanciful situations. Nines typically do not concern themselves with details, nor are they usually good at following up once they have
acted. By contrast, the thinking of Fives is highly focused,
penetrating, and almost microscopic in the narrowness of
its frame of reference. Fives love details, losing themselves
in research, scholarship, and complex intellectual pursuits.
They think in depth, concentrating so much that they block
out other perceptions (eventually to their detriment). By
contrast, even brilliant Nines tend to have problems concentrating; they also tend to lose interest quickly and to allow their attention to drift off when they become bored or
anxious.

Nines tend to spin grand, sweeping, idealistic solutions to
problems, while Fives tend to speculate on problems, then on
the problems that their problems have raised, then on those
problems, ad infinitum. Nines may be gifted storytellers, able
to communicate simply and effectively to others, even to children. Fives usually communicate to only a few or keep their
ideas entirely to themselves. (Moreover, their ideas may be
so complicated that they are difficult to communicate to all
but other specialists.) Nines usually do not consider the con-

sequences of their actions; Fives are extremely interested in predicting the consequences of every action. The Nines idealize the world and create imaginary worlds in which good always triumphs over evil; Fives analyze the real world and create horrifying scenarios in which evil usually triumphs over good or exists in tension with it. Nines simplify; Fives complexify. Nines look to the past; Fives to the future. Nines are fantasists; Fives are theorists. Nines are disengaged; Fives are detached. Nines are utopians; Fives are nihilists. Nines are optimists; Fives are pessimists. Nines are open; Fives are resistant. Nines are nonthreatening and nonjudgmental; Fives are defensive and contentious. Nines are at peace; Fives are in tension. Nines end in dissociation, Fives in paranoia.

Comparisons and contrasts such as these could be multiplied almost indefinitely because, while these two types are such opposites, they are also paradoxically similar. What they have in common is the tendency to ask "What if?" questions. The difference is in their response: Nines tend to ruminate on their fantasies, while Fives attempt to see if their ideas could come true. The Nine's ideas usually involve a single insight that, while true enough, is often impractical and goes nowhere. For instance, a Nine may think that the way to world peace is "for everyone to love one another." While this is doubtlessly true, the problem not addressed is how to get everyone to love one another. A Five wondering about the same problem would write a treatise on world peace after doing exhaustive historical research, eventually erecting a grand theory of peace. (The Five's ideas may also come to nothing, but at least they are pursued, and practical results may eventually come of them.) To give another example, a Nine might wonder what it is like to fly and make up a story about it. A Five might wonder how to fly and invent an airplane or do research on birds or design a rocket.

In short, Nines have an active fantasy life and think that they have deep thoughts. Sometimes they do, of course, although the thinking of intelligent, well-educated Nines tends to be in the direction of simplifying reality and cutting through abstruse thickets to get at the kernel of truth beneath. Nines tend to see things the way they want them to be; they reinterpret reality to make it more comforting and less threatening, simpler and less daunting. By contrast, the thinking of Fives is complex. By attempting to arrive at a grand unifying theory that encompasses and explains everything, average Fives end up involved in increasing complications and abstractions. Their thought is focused on specifics, often highly technical and concerned with foresight and the consequences of acting one way rather than another. But at an extreme, Fives risk seeing reality not as it is but as a projection of their preoccupations and fears. They distort their perceptions of reality so that reality seems more negative and threatening than it actually is.

Nines feel at ease in the world, and their style of thinking reflects their unconscious desire to merge with the world. Fives are afraid of being overwhelmed by the world, and their intellectual efforts are an unconscious defense against the world, an attempt to master it intellectually. There is a world of difference between these two types since they see the world so differently. Compare Charles Darwin (a Five) and Walt Disney (a Nine), Albert Einstein (a Five) and Jim Henson (a Nine) to understand the similarities and differences between these two types more clearly.

Misidentifying Sixes and Other Types

SIXES AND ONES

Both Sixes and Ones are among the compliant types of the Enneagram. As noted in *Personality Types* (324, 329), Ones are compliant to the demands of their superegos and their ideals, while Sixes are compliant to the demands of their superegos and other people, especially authority figures. While Sixes may rarely mistake themselves for Ones or Ones misidentify themselves as Sixes, other people may be confused by some superficial similarities between them. (And, in fact, a Six with a Five-wing will more likely be confused with a One than a Six with a Seven-wing because of the seriousness and intensity that the Five-wing brings to the Six's overall personality.)

When it does arise, the confusion seems to stem from an authoritarian, legalistic streak in both types: Sixes at Level 6 are The Overcompensating Tough Guy and Ones at the same Level are The Judgmental Perfectionist. Both types do not hesitate to tell others what to do, although in different ways and for different reasons. Ones moralize and scold, lecturing others in the name of an ideal, such as truth, justice, or perfection. Ones do not hesitate to order others around, telling them what they should be doing so that things will be done more perfectly.

Sixes also give orders—and see to it that the law is enforced—because they are angered and threatened by the disobedience of others. Sixes identify with an authority (or authority figures) and internalize the values that the authority has taught them. Having identified with what they have been taught, Sixes can be aggressive toward anyone who does not accept the same values they do. The indifference of others to their beliefs may infuriate Sixes as much as outright disobedience does. Given the right circumstances, Sixes can be as aggressive and mean-spirited, petty and vindictive as punitive Ones can be.

These two types are easy to distinguish, however, by noting the overall emotional tone of each type. Average Sixes are anxious, indecisive, ambivalent, and, above all, reactive. They find it difficult to relate to others with self-confidence as equals, tending instead either to become too obedient and dependent or to go to the opposite extreme and become rebellious and defiant; if they are stuck in the middle, they become ambivalent, vacillating endlessly.

These traits are almost completely absent in average Ones. Their overall emotional tone is one of self-controlled coolness, impersonal efficiency, orderliness, and propriety. Ones are emphatically not indecisive: they know their own minds and have opinions about everything, which they are more than willing to express to others. Average Ones are so tightly self-controlled as to not be aware of their tensions, while average Sixes struggle with considerable anxious tension. Righteous anger and moral indignation are the principal negative emotions in Ones, whereas fearfulness and anxiety are the principal negative feelings in Sixes. Moreover, while average Ones can be sarcastic and verbally abusive, they are almost never physically violent, whereas average Sixes not only can be belligerent but can sometimes erupt into physical violence.

Their vast differences notwithstanding, what these two types have in common is the tendency to feel guilty when they do something contrary either to their ideals (Ones) or to the mandates of their authority figures (Sixes). Guilt feelings owing to strong consciences and the tendency to strike out either at themselves or at others (or both) are the main points of similarity between them. Compare the personalities of George

Bush (a Six) and Mario Cuomo (a One), Meryl Streep (a One) and Marilyn Monroe (a Six) for examples of the similarities and differences between these two types.

SIXES AND TWOS

See Twos and Sixes.

SIXES AND FOURS

While there are real similarities between the two types, there are even more differences. The principal difference is that Sixes are usually extremely appealing and relate well to people; they have the ability to unconsciously engage the emotions of others so that others will like them and form secure relationships with them. Fours, in contrast, do not relate primarily to people but to their own inner emotional states. Fours take it for granted that they are alone in life and find it difficult to form bonds with others — something that comes easily to Sixes. The psychic structures of the two types are also very different: Fours are true introverts, while Sixes are a blend of introversion and extroversion — true ambiverts who possess qualities of both orientations.

Confusion arises between these types principally on the part of Sixes who think that they are Fours, for two main reasons. First, some Sixes identify with the negative side of the Four (depression, inferiority, self-doubt, and hopelessness, for example) and think they must be Fours because they recognize similar traits in themselves. The difference lies in the motivations for these traits. For example, while all the types can become depressed, Fours do so because they are disappointed with themselves for having lost some opportunity to actualize themselves. They become depressed when they realize that in their search for self they have gone down a blind alley and now must pay the price. Unhealthy, depressed Fours are essentially angry at themselves for bringing this on themselves or for allowing it to happen.

By contrast, Sixes become depressed when they fear that they have done something to make their authority figure mad at them. Their depression is a response to their self-disparagement; it comes from the fear that the authority is angry at them and will punish them. Thus, the depression of Sixes is exogenous (coming from the outside) and can be relieved by a word of reassurance from the authority. This is not the case with Fours, whose depression is endogenous (coming from the inside), a response to their self-accusations.

Second, I have characterized the Four as The Artist, and some Sixes who are artistic think that they therefore must be Fours. However, as noted above in the discussion of Fours and Nines, artistic talent is not the sole domain of Fours, so it is entirely possible for Sixes to be artists of one kind or another. Even so, there are important differences in the creative work produced by these two types.

In general, Sixes tend to be performing artists, while Fours tend to be original creators. Sixes are more likely to be actors or musicians than poets and playwrights, more likely to perform the words or music of someone else than to create it themselves. Even those Sixes who are creative tend to be traditionalists, creating within firmly established rules and styles, or they go to an extreme and become rebellious, reacting against traditionalism — such as rock stars and experimental novelists who purposely defy traditional forms. In either case, both tradition and reactions against it are an important aspect of their art. The themes typically found in the art of Sixes have to do with belonging, security, family, politics, country, and common values.

Creative Fours, by contrast, are individualists who go their own way to explore their feelings and other subjective personal states. The artistic products of Fours are much less involved either with following a tradition or with reacting against it. Fours are less apt to use political or communal experiences as the subject matter for their work, choosing instead the movements of their own souls, their personal revelations, the darkness and light they discover in themselves as they become immersed in the creative process. By listening to their inner voices, even average Fours may speak to the universal person or fail to communicate to anyone, at least to their contemporaries. They may be ahead of their time not because they are trying to be rebellious or avant garde but because they develop their own forms to express their personal point of view. What is important to Fours is not tradition but personal truth. Tradition is no more than a backdrop against which Fours play out their own personal dramas. Compare and contrast the personalities of Rudolf Nureyev and Peter Ilich Tchaikovsky (Fours) with those of Mikhail Baryshnikov and Johannes Brahms (Sixes) to understand more about the similarities and differences.

SIXES AND EIGHTS

Both Sixes and Eights are aggressive, although only the Eight is an entirely aggressive personality. Sixes react both to their fears and to other people and constantly oscillate from one state to another, from Level to Level. They are ambivalent and passive-aggressive, evasive, and contradictory. In contrast, Eights have solid egos and formidable wills; they keep pushing others until they get what they want. There is little softness in Eights and even less tendency to comply with the wishes of anyone else. They have no desire to be liked or to ingratiate themselves with others. Rather than look to others for protection, Eights offer protection (patronage) in return for hard work and loyalty.

As different as these two types are, they are nevertheless similar at Level 6 — but only at this Level. At this stage both

Sixes (The Overcompensating Tough Guy) and Eights (The Confrontational Adversary) show similar aggressive traits— belligerence, defiance, a willingness to intimidate others, a quick and threatening temper, the threat of violence, hatred of others, and so forth. However, Eights arrive at this stage as a result of constantly escalating their pressure on others to get what they want until they have become highly confrontational and combative. Sixes arrive at this state from a very different route—in reaction to their vacillation and dependency. Sixes become aggressive because they do not want to be pushed around anymore; Eights become aggressive to push others even more.

The essential difference is that Sixes eventually will yield and their defenses will crumble if enough pressure is applied to them, whereas opposition to Eights only encourages them to remain defiant and to meet their adversary with renewed aggression.

Both types at this Level can be dangerous; ironically, Sixes are probably more dangerous at this stage than Eights since they are anxious and may strike out at someone impulsively or irrationally. On the other hand, average Eights are more rational: they take the odds of success into account at every move. If and when they finally do become violent, however, Eights are more dangerous than Sixes because they are more ruthless, and the momentum of their inflated egos makes them feel that they can and must press onward until their enemies are utterly destroyed. Eights eventually become megalomaniacs (and may be destroyed after they have destroyed others). By contrast, unhealthy Sixes eventually become self-defeating (and may be destroyed by their own fear). Compare G. Gordon Liddy and Mike Tyson (Sixes) with Henry Kissinger and Muhammad Ali (Eights) to understand more about the similarities and differences between these types.

Misidentifying Sevens and Other Types

SEVENS AND TWOS

See Twos and Sevens.

SEVENS AND THREES

See Threes and Sevens.

SEVENS AND FOURS

See Fours and Sevens.

SEVENS AND NINES

Sevens and Nines might seem difficult to confuse since average Sevens are the hyperactive extroverts of the Enneagram, while average Nines are obviously passive and complacent and live at a much lower energy level than Sevens.

The main reason they can sometimes be confused is that both types can be extremely busy and both are usually rather ebullient and happy. Furthermore, the defense mechanisms of both types are similar: both have repressed their inner worlds—Nines to maintain their identification with an idealized other, Sevens to avoid cutting themselves off from sources of external stimulation.

The points of similarity are reflected in their psychic structures—both are sensation types in the Jungian model, Sevens corresponding to the extroverted and Nines to the introverted sensation type (*PT*, 193 and 250). While it is clear from even a superficial acquaintance with Sevens that they are highly extroverted and orient themselves to the world via sensation, what is unclear is that Nines are introverted. What is even more unclear is the nature of the sensation that they introvert on. This is why the inner world of Nines is so obscure and difficult to describe (and why others have not understood this type's proper correlation to the Jungian category).

A deeper understanding of Nine's psyche comes from realizing that the Nine orients itself to the world by introverting on the sensation of possessing union with another — by introjecting another and then idealizing that introjection. To put this in simpler terms, Nines' sense of self comes from the emotion they feel when they sense their identification with another person, much as a pregnant woman introverts with thoughts of love for her unborn child. By talking to the child in her womb, she gains a sense of herself as a mother. In a similar way, Nines commune with their inner sensations (identifications), maintaining their sense of self by living through an identification with another person. Hence they correspond to the Jungian introverted sensation type.

This introversion accounts for the inner life of Nines, which is largely out of view, protected in the inner sanctum of their psyches so that it cannot be easily disturbed or changed. It is in their dealings with the outside world that Nines can resemble Sevens.

Average Sevens are hyperactive, busy with too many things superficially. They dabble around to amuse themselves and to stave off boredom and anxiety. Similarly, Nines are highly intolerant of anxiety, and they stay busy to avoid it, using errands and hobbies to occupy their minds in undemanding, nonthreatening ways. They want to avoid conflict or overexcitement; by contrast, Sevens love excitement. Sevens become demanding and excessive and crassly materialistic as they deteriorate, while Nines become more passive, indifferent, and unresponsive as they become more unhealthy. Sevens want to be stimulated, whereas Nines want to avoid anything that would overly stimulate, much less upset, them. The essential difference is that average Nines do not want to be emotionally involved in their activities (since these can threaten their identifications), whereas Sevens want to have an increasingly high emotional charge from their activities (since they have few subjective identifications).

Furthermore, Nines do not seek the same kind of happiness that Sevens do (euphoria and elation). Instead, they wish to maintain a state of placid contentment, of being neither too excited nor in discomfort. Indeed, if they could, they would be completely free of excessive stimulation of any kind. The Nine's desire to avoid becoming deeply involved with anything lest it arouse too high a response is the polar opposite of what we find in the average Seven. As we have seen, like all opposites, these two types can nevertheless be alike in many ways. Consider the differences between John F. Kennedy (a Seven) and Ronald Reagan (a Nine) or between Bette Midler (a Seven) and Ingrid Bergman (a Nine) for further insight into these two types.

Misidentifying Eights and Other Types

EIGHTS AND ONES

See Ones and Eights.

EIGHTS AND TWOS

See Twos and Eights.

EIGHTS AND THREES

See Threes and Eights.

EIGHTS AND SIXES

See Sixes and Eights.

Misidentifying Nines and Other Types

NINES AND TWOS

See Twos and Nines.

NINES AND FOURS

See Fours and Nines.

NINES AND FIVES

See Fives and Nines.

NINES AND SEVENS

See Sevens and Nines.

Assessment Guides

THIS CHAPTER will give you an opportunity to develop your skills as you apply the Enneagram both for self-discovery and for understanding others more perceptively.

These "workbook" pages have been included so you can record observations as you use the Enneagram in your daily life. This chapter might best be thought of simply as a convenient place to write down your reflections; the space provided will enable you to respond to whatever depth and extent you wish.

A variety of assessment guides for self-examination have been included here; of course, you should feel free to add others or to modify them depending on your needs. The object of these exercises is to help you begin or continue the lifelong habit of self-understanding.

These exercise pages do not have to be filled out in any particular order, nor do they have to be fully completed. To save space, you might want to work in pencil and to restrict your comments to single words and short phrases rather than long responses. If your collection of observations and insights grows beyond the space provided here, you might consider recording your notes on index cards or by some other appropriate method. For example, a separate "personality types journal" might be a good place to record longer observations.

Your Basic Personality Type

Use this page for making additional notes about your personality type.

HEALTHY: _____

_____

_____

_____

_____

_____

AVERAGE: _____

_____

_____

_____

_____

_____

UNHEALTHY: _____

_____

_____

_____

_____

_____

Your Wing

Sometimes when we get stuck in our development, our wing can nudge us out of our situation.

As you reflect on your wing, try to pay particular attention to whether it conflicts with your basic type or complements it. Also be aware of whether your wing is moving in its Direction of Integration or of Disintegration (*PT*, 307).

Your Direction of Integration

What aspects of the type in your Direction of Integration do
you find in yourself?

Your Direction of Disintegration

What aspects of the type in your Direction of Disintegration do you find in yourself?

_____

_____

_____

_____

_____

_____

_____

_____

_____

_____

_____

_____

_____

_____

_____

_____

_____

_____

Seeing Yourself in Each Personality Type

Each of us can acquire the use of the healthy potentials of all the types of the Enneagram (*PT*, 40). No matter what basic personality type you are, you also have elements of every other type. Becoming aware of these facets of yourself can be illuminating since it not only helps you see yourself more clearly but also helps you become more knowledgeable about the traits associated with the other types.

MY TWONESS: MY THREENESS: MY FOURNESS:

_____   _____   _____

_____   _____   _____

_____   _____   _____

_____   _____   _____

MY FIVENESS: MY SIXNESS: MY SEVENNESS:

_____   _____   _____

_____   _____   _____

_____   _____   _____

MY EIGHTNESS: MY NINENESS: MY ONENESS:

_____   _____   _____

_____   _____   _____

_____   _____   _____

_____   _____   _____

Childhood I:
The Positive Aspects of Our Parents

Each of us has had a mother and a father, and there are aspects of their personalities that we have liked. Use this page to sketch those traits of your mother and your father that you like—the characteristics that you admire and want to emulate. Do not attempt to be complete or too analytic here; use half-sentences and keywords, jotting down memories and observations as they come to mind.

I like about my mother (and her type): _____

_____

_____

_____

_____

_____

_____

I like about my father (and his type): _____

_____

_____

_____

_____

_____

Childhood II:
The Negative Aspects of Our Parents

It is inevitable that there are aspects of our parents that we dislike and disapprove of. Use this page to sketch those traits of your mother and your father that you feel are shortcomings, the characteristics that you wish they could change or could have changed. As with the previous exercise, do not attempt to be complete or too analytic. Use half-sentences and keywords, jotting down memories and observations as they come to mind.

I dislike about my mother (and her type): _____

_____

_____

_____

_____

_____

_____

I dislike about my father (and his type): _____

_____

_____

_____

_____

_____

_____

Childhood III:
Unresolved Issues

Which issues from childhood seem to come up continually in your adult life? For instance, if your father was harshly critical, do you automatically feel harshly criticized when someone says anything even mildly critical to you? If you had unresolved sibling rivalries, do you find yourself relating to people as if you were competing with your own brothers and sisters for the attention and love of others? Which childhood issues are still unresolved in your present life?

Your Habitual Desires

It is instructive to become aware of your habitual desires. Are you driven by the desire for power? To be loved? To be independent? To be right? To prove something to yourself? To be admired by others? And so forth. What are you basically seeking in life and from other people? While your motives are often mixed and are by no means easy to sort out, having insight into your desires goes a long way to getting in control of your behavior.

HEALTHY: _____

_____

_____

_____

_____

AVERAGE: _____

_____

_____

_____

_____

UNHEALTHY: _____

_____

_____

_____

_____

Your Habitual Fears

The negative side of motivation—what you fear—causes anxiety and unease both with yourself and with others. Do you fear not being in control? Being alone? Being bored? Being unwanted? Failing or being humiliated? Your own aggression or other feelings? As with your habitual desires, your fears are mixed and complex, but with time you should begin to get insight into the roots of your most common fears.

HEALTHY: _____

_____

_____

_____

_____

AVERAGE: _____

_____

_____

_____

_____

_____

UNHEALTHY: _____

_____

_____

_____

_____

Your Habitual Conflicts

When you get into conflicts with others or with yourself, what issues seem to come up time and again? Without necessarily judging who was right or wrong, what is it about yourself that has seemed to initiate conflicts or to perpetuate them?

_____

_____

_____

_____

_____

_____

_____

_____

_____

_____

_____

_____

_____

_____

_____

_____

_____

_____

_____

Making a Decision

When attempting to make an important decision in your life, it is helpful to be conscious of how you usually react to new situations and challenges. (If you have done the previous exercises about your habitual fears and desires, you will be able to see how they affect your decision making.) Try identifying those healthy, average, and unhealthy traits that either help or hinder you to make decisions easily and productively.

HEALTHY: _____

_____

_____

_____

_____

_____

AVERAGE: _____

_____

_____

_____

_____

_____

UNHEALTHY: _____

_____

_____

_____

_____

_____

What You Like Most About
the Other Types

Regardless of which type you are, you probably admire certain aspects of the other types — although not necessarily the healthy traits of each type. Reflect on which traits you find particularly admirable, inspiring, or for whatever reason desirable to *you* in some way.

ABOUT   ABOUT   ABOUT
  TYPE TWO: TYPE THREE: TYPE FOUR:

_____   _____   _____

_____   _____   _____

_____   _____   _____

_____   _____   _____

ABOUT   ABOUT   ABOUT
  TYPE FIVE: TYPE SIX: TYPE SEVEN:

_____   _____   _____

_____   _____   _____

_____   _____   _____

_____   _____   _____

ABOUT   ABOUT   ABOUT
  TYPE EIGHT: TYPE NINE: TYPE ONE:

_____   _____   _____

_____   _____   _____

_____   _____   _____

_____   _____   _____

What You Like Least About the Other Types

Each of the types has negative aspects that not only annoy you and cause conflicts but also strike deep chords in your own psyche. Negative traits in others often bring out the worst in us. Which negative traits do you find most disturbing and objectionable about each type?

ABOUT TYPE TWO:	ABOUT TYPE THREE:	ABOUT TYPE FOUR:
_____	_____	_____
_____	_____	_____
_____	_____	_____
_____	_____	_____

ABOUT TYPE FIVE:	ABOUT TYPE SIX:	ABOUT TYPE SEVEN:
_____	_____	_____
_____	_____	_____
_____	_____	_____
_____	_____	_____

ABOUT TYPE EIGHT:	ABOUT TYPE NINE:	ABOUT TYPE ONE:
_____	_____	_____
_____	_____	_____
_____	_____	_____
_____	_____	_____

Close Friends, Favorite People

Each of us has had close friends, or we have known people
we would have liked to have as friends. What is it about them
that you find appealing and admirable? List their names and
one or two of their most significant traits. See if common
patterns emerge. Also see if one or two personality types
attract you more than others or give you more problems than
others.

TYPE TWO: TYPE THREE: TYPE FOUR:

_____   _____   _____

_____   _____   _____

_____   _____   _____

_____   _____   _____

TYPE FIVE: TYPE SIX: TYPE SEVEN:

_____   _____   _____

_____   _____   _____

_____   _____   _____

_____   _____   _____

TYPE EIGHT: TYPE NINE: TYPE ONE:

_____   _____   _____

_____   _____   _____

_____   _____   _____

_____   _____   _____

Extra Workbook Space I

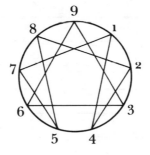

Extra Workbook Space II

Extra Workbook Space III

Type Two *The Helper*			
Type Three *The Motivator*			
Type Four *The Artist*			
Type Five *The Thinker*			
Type Six *The Loyalist*			
Type Seven *The Generalist*			
Type Eight *The Leader*			
Type Nine *The Peacemaker*			
Type One *The Reformer*			

New Connections,
New Directions

SEVEN

Psychological
Categories

THE ENNEAGRAM reaches out in many directions because it
is a symbol of that most elusive and complex thing, human
nature. Wherever human beings express themselves, the Enneagram can be used to further our understanding. Because
it is a symbol of the psyche, it touches on everything that has
been created by the psyche. It connects to many widely different fields because it reflects how we humans connect to
ourselves, to others, and to the world around us. Like human
nature, the Enneagram encompasses a great deal.

Using the Enneagram is both exciting and somewhat over-
whelming: it takes us beyond psychology into so many other
areas of human endeavor. It is ancient yet modern; personal
yet universal; esoteric and mystical yet scientific and objective;
psychological in scope yet religious in overtone; clear and
simple to understand yet ever strange and mysterious. The
following illustration indicates some of the Enneagram's connections with other bodies of knowledge.

Space in this book, as well as my own limited time and
abilities, does not allow these connections to be developed any
further here. Nevertheless, the cross-fertilization of the many
different ideas stimulated by the Enneagram will continue as
the Enneagram becomes more widely known. Naturally, there

From the Western Tradition		*From the Eastern Tradition*
Academic Psychology		Early Greek Philosophy
Freud and Followers		Pythagoreans and Gnostics
Jung and Followers		Middle Eastern Cultures
Karen Horney, Maslow,		Islam
& Cultural Psychology		Sufism
Quantitative Psychology		Gurdjieff and The Work
Questionnaire and Test Validation		Ichazo and Arica
Therapeutic Methods		Mythology
Interpersonal Relations		Astrology
Personnel, Management, Advertising,		Numerology
and Other Practical Applications		Cabala
Theology and Religious Studies		Symbolism
Spiritual Direction and Counseling		Chakras
Political Science, Journalism		Meditation Techniques
Cultural Criticism, Sociology		Philosophy, Transpersonal Psychology

THE UNIVERSALITY OF THE ENNEAGRAM

is no telling where these connections will lead — although any discoveries will be enriching not only for those directly involved but ultimately for everyone.

In this chapter we examine how the Enneagram corresponds with the personality disorders catalogued in *The Diagnostic and Statistical Manual of Mental Disorders*, revised third edition (*DSM*-III[R]), the primary reference work for mental health professionals. Demonstrating in detail the correlations between the Enneagram and the work of Freud, Jung, Karen Horney, Erich Fromm, Abraham Maslow, Timothy Leary, Theodore Millon, Myers-Briggs, and other typologies will also be valuable, to name only a few areas for future work.

The Enneagram and the *DSM*-III(R)

One of the most amazing aspects of the Enneagram is how well it corresponds with other typologies, particularly those devised by psychiatry and psychology. The fact that it does so is one of the most persuasive indications that the Enneagram is probably scientifically valid. In a sense, modern psychology unintentionally validates the Enneagram—and even more extraordinary, the ancient Enneagram validates *and corrects* some of modern psychology's findings.

It is also fascinating that psychology has been intuitively moving toward a dynamic typology like the Enneagram. From different theoretical points of view, psychologists have been inching toward a comprehensive, systematic understanding (and a clearer presentation) of "character types," although it has taken a while for academic psychology to overcome its bias against types and typologies. Insights that those familiar with the Enneagram take for granted have become exciting new discoveries for psychologists.

Two brief quotations from a leading psychiatrist involved with the formulation of the *DSM*-III(R) indicates that psychiatry has been moving toward something like the Enneagram.

> There is [the] implicit and reasonable assumption that traits and their disordered counterparts [the personality disorders] exist on continua, which means that the distinction [between normal traits and personality disorders] is inherently arbitrary. Recognition of the universality of character types and the importance of documenting them is, I think, the single most important accomplishment of DSM-III. (John G. Gunderson, M.D., in Frosch, ed., *Current Perspectives on Personality Disorders*, 20–21)

> I believe the main virtue of DSM-III is that its multiaxial format will allow better study of the relationships between personality and symptoms and that—if not in DSM-IV, then in some future diagnostic text—we may eventually be ready to place the personality disorders . . . arranged as outgrowths or extensions of these various personality types. (34)

Fortunately, it will not be necessary to wait for "some future diagnostic text" to correlate personality types and personality disorders since much of this work has already been done here and in *Personality Types*. The Enneagram is a "multiaxial" typology that can accommodate all the personality disorders and neurotic disorders presented in the *DSM*-III(R).

Furthermore, my work on the Continuum of nine Levels of Development proves the "reasonable assumption" that "traits and their disordered counterparts [the personality disorders] exist on continua." Many of the discoveries that contemporary psychologists working in the vanguard of their field anticipate have already been made with the Enneagram. What remains is to demonstrate the correspondences between it and the *DSM*-III (and other typologies) and to communicate the potential of the Enneagram to psychologists in language they can accept and use.

Before we compare each of the Enneagram's personality types with the personality disorders described by the *DSM*-III(R), let us first define "traits" and "personality disorders."

> Personality *traits* are enduring patterns of perceiving, relating to, and thinking about the environment and oneself, and are exhibited in a wide range of important social and personal contexts. It is only when *personality traits* are inflexible and maladaptive and cause either significant functional impairment or subjective distress that they constitute *Personality Disorders*. (*DSM*-III[R], 335)

In lay terms, personality traits (such as anger, shyness, excitability, and empathy, for example) are the building blocks of our personalities. Traits constitute the larger patterns that make up much of our individual and interpersonal life. However, if our normal traits turn "inflexible and maladaptive" —if they become negative and destructive to ourselves or others or both—they become the basis for personality disorders.

Since the personality types of the Enneagram include the healthy and average Levels of Development, they encompass more than the personality disorders described by the *DSM*-

III(R), which focus only on the pathological end of the Continuum.

In correlating the Enneagram with the *DSM*-III(R) I have discovered that the personality disorders correspond to only certain Levels of each type, not to an entire type. Two or more disorders often appear within each type, although at different Levels. Traits start to become "inflexible and maladaptive" beginning at Level 5, and these increasingly disordered traits cause significant conflicts as they deteriorate into the traits that emerge in the unhealthy Levels. Hence, more than one personality disorder can (and often does) correspond to one of the Enneagram personality types because the personality disorders are based on maladaptive traits as they appear at only one Level of Development.

For example, a single personality disorder may appear at Level 5, another at Level 7, and yet another at Level 9—all within the same personality type of the Enneagram. While the *DSM*-III(R) would regard these as three different (although related) personality disorders, from our point of view we can see that these three disorders are parts of a larger whole, parts of a single personality type that has become unhealthy.

We can also see that there are different gradations and patterns within the neurotic process itself: a person with a personality disorder at Level 5 would be less unhealthy than someone who has a personality disorder at Level 8. In some cases, the same person may later deteriorate from a Level 5 disorder to a Level 8 disorder, and in other cases closely related disorders could exist at the same time in the same person—for instance, someone might have disorders corresponding to Levels 7 and 8 as well as disorders that are attributable to their wing. Thus, understanding that the personality disorders are part of a larger whole—a personality type at different Levels of Development—will provide a much clearer idea of the status and direction of patients' pathologies and will help simplify the psychiatric "differential diagnoses" that are often intuitively made to fit individual cases.

Understanding the personality disorders with greater clarity will help therapists be more insightful about their patients' past difficulties, present condition, and future prognosis. It will help psychologists design better therapies for the different disordered personality types as well as interact more effectively in group therapy with people of many different types. In short, understanding the interrelatedness of the various personality disorders will help therapists have a much clearer understanding of their patients—something that can only be to the good.

This section is necessarily more technical than the average reader may need or want. Nevertheless, it is essential to demonstrate that the Enneagram types and the psychiatric disorders correlate, for two reasons. The first reason is to help establish the Enneagram's intellectual credentials so that it will gain wider acceptance with mental health professionals and the educated general public. It must be shown that the Enneagram does not contradict the established findings of psychiatry; in fact, we will see the reverse: by helping us understand the psychiatric categories more clearly, the Enneagram improves on them.

Second, correlating the Enneagram and the personality disorders acts as a much-needed corrective for some of the misinformation in circulation about the personality types themselves. A number of incorrect correlations have been made in dissertations and books about the Enneagram; while these correlations may be of interest primarily to Enneagram teachers and writers, they should also be of interest to everyone who believes in the validity and usefulness of the Enneagram.

The issue of "which types go with which disorders" is important because the disorders (and subsequent neuroses) are the result of average traits that have deteriorated into "inflexible and maladaptive" traits. If a teacher or author mistakes which disorders correlate with which type, it is also highly likely that he or she will misattribute the traits from which the disorders emerge. To put this another way, just as apples do not grow on lemon trees, each disorder is not arbitrary: it is part of *the entire pattern of traits* that make up a type as a whole. If the disorders are mistakenly assigned to the types, something is seriously wrong. Many misattributions of traits are evidence that the person making the misattributions does not have a sufficiently clear idea of the personality type in question or the disorder or both.

In this section, the nine Levels of Development are given for each personality type along with the corresponding personality disorders that appear at each Level. Because of space limitations, generally only one excerpt from the dominant personality disorder of the *DSM*-III(R) has been included for each type to indicate how the systems correspond. For additional information, refer to the *DSM*-III(R) itself, using the page references provided in parentheses.

Interested readers may also want to turn to *Personality Types* at the corresponding Level to see how the psychiatric categories correlate to the descriptions I have given. For instance, the *DSM*-III(R) Passive Aggressive Personality Disorder is listed under personality type Six. In the section describing The Ambivalent Person (*PT*, 175–77) are references to the passive-aggressive traits of the average Six. Both my description and the psychiatric text will illuminate and supplement each other. Rather than comment here on each *DSM*-III(R) excerpt individually, I have added short interlinear comments in brackets as well as page references to *Personality Types*.

Personality Type Two: The Helper

LEVELS OF DEVELOPMENT
Level 1: The Disinterested Altruist
Level 2: The Caring Person
Level 3: The Nurturing Helper

Level 4: The Effusive Friend	Histrionic Personality Disorder (348)
Level 5: The Possessive Intimate	
Level 6: The Self-Important "Saint"	Somatization Disorder (261)
Level 7: The Self-Deceptive Manipulator	Hypochondriasis (259)
Level 8: The Coercive Dominator	
Level 9: The Psychosomatic Victim	Conversion Disorder, Hysterical Neurosis (257)

Histrionic Personality Disorder (Type Two Beginning at Level 4)

The essential feature of this disorder is a pervasive pattern of excessive emotionality and attention-seeking, beginning by early adulthood and present in a variety of contexts. In other classifications this category is termed Hysterical Personality.

People with this disorder constantly seek or demand reassurance, approval, or praise from others and are uncomfortable in situations in which they are not the center of attention. They characteristically display rapidly shifting and shallow expression of emotions. [Twos and Sevens are often confused; see Chapter 5 for their similarities and differences.] Their behavior is overly reactive and intensely expressed; minor stimuli give rise to emotional excitability. Emotions are often expressed with inappropriate exaggeration, for example, the person may appear much more sad, angry, or delighted than would seem to be warranted [*PT*, 60–61, 65, 68]. (*DSM*-III[R], 348) [For example, Twos complain excessively about their health or other worries to elicit attention and sympathy from others.]

Somatization Disorder (Type Two Beginning at Level 6)

The essential features of this disorder are recurrent and multiple somatic complaints, of several years' duration, for which medical attention has been sought, but that apparently are not due to any physical disorder. . . .

Complaints are often presented in a dramatic, vague, or exaggerated way, or are part of a complicated medical history in which many physical diagnoses have been considered. Those affected frequently receive medical care from a number of physicians, sometimes simultaneously. . . . Complaints invariably involve the following organ systems or types of symptoms: conversion or pseudoneurologic symptoms (e.g., paralysis, blindness), gastrointestinal discomfort (e.g., abdominal pain), female reproductive difficulties (e.g., painful menstruation), psychosexual problems (e.g., sexual indifference), pain (e.g., back pain), and cardiopulmonary symptoms (e.g., dizziness) [*PT*, 63, 70–71].

Associated features. . . . Histrionic Personality Disorder [type Seven] and, more rarely, Antisocial Personality Disorder [type Eight] are often also present. (*DSM*-III[R], 261–62) [Note that the Antisocial Personality Disorder corresponds to the Eight, the type in the Two's Direction of Disintegration.]

Personality Type Three: The Motivator

LEVELS OF DEVELOPMENT

Level 1: The Authentic Person
Level 2: The Self-Assured Person
Level 3: The Outstanding Paragon

Level 4: The Competitive Status-Seeker
Level 5: The Image-Oriented Pragmatist
Level 6: The Self-Promoting Narcissist   Narcissistic Personality Disorder (349)

Level 7: The Exploitative Opportunist
Level 8: The Malicious Traitor   Sadistic Personality Disorder (369)
Level 9: The Vindictive Psychopath

Narcissistic Personality Disorder (Type Three Beginning at Level 6)

The essential feature of this disorder is a pervasive pattern of grandiosity (in fantasy or behavior) [PT, 93–94], hypersensitivity to the evaluation of others [PT, 81], and lack of empathy that begins by early adulthood and is present in a variety of contexts [PT, 95].

People with this disorder have a grandiose sense of self-importance. They tend to exaggerate their accomplishments and talents, and expect to be noticed as "special" even without appropriate achievement... [PT, 92–94].

These people are preoccupied with fantasies of unlimited success, power, brilliance, beauty, or ideal love, and with chronic feelings of envy for those whom they perceive as being more successful than they are [PT, 97]. Although these fantasies frequently substitute for realistic activity, when such goals are actually pursued, it is often with a driven, pleasureless quality and an ambition that cannot be satisfied [which is why Threes seem to be workaholics although, strictly speaking, they are not].

Self-esteem is almost invariably fragile; the person may be preoccupied with how well he or she is doing and how well he or she is regarded by others [PT, 90]. This often takes the form of an almost exhibitionistic need for constant attention and admiration [PT, 93]. The person may constantly fish for compliments, often with great charm. In response to criticism, he or she may react with rage, shame, or humiliation, but mask these feelings with an aura of cool indifference.

Interpersonal relationships are invariably disturbed [PT, 95–96]. A lack of empathy (inability to recognize and experience how others feel) is common.... A sense of entitlement, an unreasonable expectation of especially favorable treatment, is usually present.... Interpersonal exploitativeness, in which others are taken advantage of in order to achieve one's ends, or for self-aggrandizement, is common [PT, 95]. Friendships are often made only after the person considers how he or she can profit from them [PT, 88]. In romantic relationships, the partner is often treated as an object to be used to bolster the person's self-esteem....

Associated features.... Depressed mood is extremely common [especially in Threes with a Four-wing, although they get over them quickly; moods may be up and down, superficially like a manic-depressive, although the problem here is with narcissism, not anxiety].... Feelings may be faked in order to impress others. (DSM-III[R], 349–50) [See Chapter 5 for more about the narcissistic personality (Three) and the traits displayed by the average to unhealthy Seven.]

Personality Type Four: The Artist

LEVELS OF DEVELOPMENT
Level 1: The Inspired Creator
Level 2: The Self-Aware Intuitive
Level 3: The Self-Revealing Individual

Level 4: The Imaginative Artist
Level 5: The Self-Absorbed Introvert   Avoidant
                                              Personality
                                              Disorder (351)
Level 6: The Self-Indulgent Aesthete

Level 7: The Alienated Depressive
Level 8: The Emotionally Tormented   Major Depressive
         Person   Episode (218)
Level 9: The Self-Destructive Person

Avoidant Personality Disorder (Type Four Beginning at Level 5)

The essential feature of this disorder is a pervasive pattern of social discomfort [due to self-consciousness] [*PT*, 119], fear of negative evaluation, and timidity [shyness and self-doubt], beginning by early adulthood and present in a variety of contexts.

Most people are somewhat concerned about how others assess them, but those with this disorder are easily hurt by criticism and are devastated by the slightest hint of disapproval [the Four's hypersensitivity to criticism or to any form of aggression from others] [*PT*, 119–20]. They generally are unwilling to enter into relationships unless given an unusually strong guarantee of uncritical acceptance. . . .

Social or occupational activities that involve significant interpersonal contact tend to be avoided [average Fours withdraw from others and remain reserved and private "outsiders" rather than risk further damage to their self-esteem]. For example, a promotion that will increase social demands may be refused. In social situations, these people are reticent because of a fear of saying something inappropriate or foolish, or of being unable to answer a question. They fear being embarrassed by blushing, crying, or showing signs of anxiety before other people.

Generalized timidity [self-doubt resulting in self-inhibitions] produces resistance to doing anything that will deviate from the person's normal routine [*PT*, 122]. . . .

Unlike people with Schizoid Personality Disorder, who are socially isolated, but have no desire for social relations, those with Avoidant Personality Disorder yearn for affection and acceptance [*PT*, 119]. They are distressed by their lack of ability to relate comfortably to others. . . .

People with Avoidant Personality Disorder may sometimes appear dependent, since once they have been able to form a relationship, they tend to be very clinging and fearful of losing it. (*DSM*-III[R], 351–52) [Loss of a loved one is particularly devastating for Fours since they have difficulty establishing and maintaining long-term relationships; also note that a certain dependency foreshadows movement in the Direction of Disintegration to the coercive dependency found in the unhealthy Two (*PT*, 127–28).]

Personality Type Five: The Thinker

LEVELS OF DEVELOPMENT
Level 1: The Pioneering Visionary
Level 2: The Perceptive Observer
Level 3: The Knowledgeable Expert

Level 4: The Analytic Specialist
Level 5: The Intensely Involved
       Theorist
Level 6: The Extreme Reductionist   Schizotypal Personality
                                            Disorder (340)

Level 7: The Isolated Nihilist
Level 8: The Delusional Paranoid   Delusional (Paranoid)
                                            Disorder (199)
Level 9: The Empty Schizoid   Schizophrenia (187)

Schizotypal Personality Disorder (Type Five Beginning at Level 6)

The essential feature of this disorder is a pervasive pattern of peculiarities of ideation, appearance, and behavior and deficits in interpersonal relatedness . . . that are not severe enough to meet the criteria for Schizophrenia [*PT*, 155].

The disturbance in the content of thought may include paranoid ideation, suspiciousness, ideas of reference, odd beliefs, and magical thinking that is inconsistent with subcultural norms and influences the person's behavior [*PT*, 153]. . . . Often speech shows marked peculiarities, but never to the point of loosening of associations or incoherence. Speech may be impoverished, digressive, vague, or inappropriately abstract [*PT*, 147–48]. Concepts may be expressed unclearly or oddly, or words may be used in an unusual way. People with this disorder often appear odd and eccentric in behavior and appearance [*PT*, 151]. For example, they are often unkempt, display unusual mannerisms, and talk to themselves.

Interpersonal relatedness is invariably impaired in these people [*PT*, 149]. They display inappropriate or constricted affect, appearing silly and aloof and rarely reciprocating gestures or facial expressions, such as smiling or nodding. They have no close friends or confidants (or only one) [*PT*, 151] . . . and are extremely anxious in social situations involving unfamiliar people. (*DSM*-III[R], 340–41)

Personality Type Six: The Loyalist

LEVELS OF DEVELOPMENT
Level 1: The Self-Affirming Person
Level 2: The Engaging Person
Level 3: The Committed Loyalist

Level 4: The Obedient Traditionalist	
Level 5: The Passive-Aggressive Person	Passive Aggressive Personality Disorder (356)
Level 6: The Overcompensating Tough Guy	
Level 7: The Insecure Person	Dependent Personality Disorder (353)
Level 8: The Overreacting Hysteric	
Level 9: The Self-Defeating Masochist	Self-Defeating Personality Disorder (371)

Passive Aggressive Personality Disorder (Type Six Beginning at Level 5)

The essential feature of this disorder is a pervasive pattern of passive resistance to demands for adequate social and occupational performance. . . . The resistance is expressed indirectly rather than directly [PT, 177], and results in pervasive and persistent social and occupational ineffectiveness even when more self-assertive and effective behavior is possible. [Sixes could act more assertively if they wanted to, and they do at Level 6, when they overcompensate.] The name of this disorder is based on the assumption that such people are passively expressing covert aggression.

People with this disorder habitually resent and oppose demands to increase or maintain a given level of functioning [by oppositional and obstructionistic behavior]. This occurs most clearly in work situations, but is also evident in social functioning. The resistance is expressed indirectly through such maneuvers as procrastination, dawdling, stubbornness, intentional inefficiency, and "forgetfulness." These people obstruct the efforts of others by failing to do their share of the work. [Notice that the resistance is intentional and therefore conscious, in distinction to the passive negligence found in average Nines.] . . .

These people become sulky, irritable, or argumentative when asked to do something they do not want to do [Sixes easily feel "pressured" into doing things against their will, especially when they are ambivalent or under increasing tension]. They often protest [defensively, as well as whine and complain] to others about how unreasonable the demands being made on them are, and resent useful suggestions from others concerning how to be more productive. As a result of their resentment of demands, they unreasonably criticize or scorn the people in authority who are making the demands [PT, 178].

Associated features. Often people with this disorder are dependent and lack self-confidence. Typically, they are pessimistic about the future [PT, 180–81], but have no realization that their behavior is responsible for their difficulties. (*DSM*-III[R], 356–57) [PT, 183]

Personality Type Seven: The Generalist

LEVELS OF DEVELOPMENT
Level 1: The Ecstatic Appreciator
Level 2: The Happy Enthusiast
Level 3: The Accomplished Generalist

Level 4: The Experienced Sophisticate

Level 5: The Hyperactive Extrovert

Level 6: The Excessive Materialist

Level 7: The Impulsive Escapist

Level 8: The Manic Compulsive

Level 9: The Panic-Stricken Hysteric

Histrionic Personality Disorder (348)

Hypomanic Episode (218)

Manic Episode (214)

Histrionic Personality Disorder (Type Seven Beginning at Level 5)

The essential feature of this disorder is a pervasive pattern of excessive emotionality and attention-seeking, beginning by early adulthood and present in a variety of contexts. In other classifications this category is termed Hysterical Personality. [Sevens have much of the following in common with Twos; see Chapter 5 for the differences between these two types.]

People with this disorder . . . characteristically display rapidly shifting and shallow expression of emotions [the feelings of Twos, by contrast, are deeper and more genuine than those of Sevens]. Their behavior is overly reactive and intensely expressed; minor stimuli give rise to emotional excitability [*PT*, 197]. Emotions are often expressed with inappropriate exaggeration, for example, the person may appear much more sad, angry, or delighted than would seem to be warranted [*PT*, 203]. People with this disorder tend to be very self-centered with little or no tolerance for the frustration of delayed gratification [*PT*, 205]. Their actions are directed to obtaining immediate satisfaction.

These people are typically attractive and seductive, often to the point of looking flamboyant and acting inappropriately [*PT*, 208]. They are typically overly concerned with physical attractiveness [*PT*, 206]. In addition, their style of speech tends to be expressionistic and lacking in detail. For example, a person may describe his vacation as "Just fantastic!" without being able to be more specific [*PT*, 203].

Associated features. People with this disorder are lively and dramatic and are always drawing attention to themselves. They are prone to exaggeration in their interpersonal relations and often act out a role such as that of "victim" or "princess" without being aware of it. They crave novelty, stimulation, and excitement and quickly become bored with normal routine [*PT*, 204]. Others frequently perceive them as superficially charming and appealing, but lacking genuineness [of substance]. They are often quick to form friendships, but once a relationship is established, can become egocentric and inconsiderate [*PT*, 206–7]. They may constantly demand reassurance because of feelings of helplessness and dependency [especially a 7w6]. . . .

Differential diagnosis. . . . People with *Narcissistic Personality Disorder* are similarly excessively self-centered, but are usually preoccupied with a grandiose sense of self and with intense envy. [This is one of the main differences between a Three and a Seven, for example.] (*DSM*-III[R], 348–49)

Manic Episode (Type Seven Beginning at Level 8)

The essential feature of a Manic Episode is a distinct period during which the predominant mood is either elevated, expansive, or irritable [*PT*, 208], and there are associated symptoms of the Manic Syndrome. . . . The associated symptoms include inflated self-esteem or grandiosity (which may be delusional [*PT*, 209]), decreased need for sleep, pressure of speech, flight of ideas, distractibility, increased involvement in goal-directed activity, psychomotor agitation, and excessive involvement in pleasurable activities which have a high potential for painful consequences that the person often does not recognize [*PT*, 210]. . . .

The elevated mood may be described as euphoric, unusually good, cheerful, or high. . . . The expansive quality of the mood disturbance is characterized by unceasing and unselective enthusiasm for interacting with people and seeking involvement with other aspects of the environment [*PT*, 209]. . . .

Manic speech is typically loud, rapid, and difficult to interrupt. Often it is full of jokes, puns, plays on words, and amusing irrelevancies. It may become theatrical, with dramatic mannerisms and singing. . . . If the person's mood is more irritable than expansive, his or her speech may be marked by complaints, hostile comments, and angry tirades [*PT*, 208]. . . .

The increase in goal-directed activity often involves excessive planning of, and participation in, multiple activities (e.g., sexual, occupational, political, religious). Almost invariably there is increased sociability. . . . The person does not recognize the intrusive, domineering, and demanding nature of these interactions [*PT*, 209–10]. Frequently, expansiveness, unwarranted optimism, grandiosity, and lack of judgment lead to such activities as buying sprees, reckless driving, foolish business investments, and sexual behavior unusual for the person. (*DSM*-III[R], 214–15)

Personality Type Eight: The Leader

LEVELS OF DEVELOPMENT
  Level 1: The Magnanimous Hero
  Level 2: The Self-Confident Person
  Level 3: The Constructive Leader

  Level 4: The Enterprising Adventurer
  Level 5: The Dominating Power-Broker
  Level 6: The Confrontational Adversary

  Level 7: The Ruthless Tyrant   Antisocial
                                               Personality
                                               Disorder (342)
  Level 8: The Omnipotent
              Megalomaniac
  Level 9: The Violent Destroyer

Antisocial Personality Disorder (Type Eight Beginning at Level 7)

The essential feature of this disorder is a pattern of irresponsible and antisocial behavior beginning in childhood or early adolescence and continuing into adulthood. . . .

Lying, stealing, truancy, vandalism, initiating fights, running away from home, and physical cruelty are typical childhood signs. In adulthood the antisocial pattern continues, and may include failure to honor financial obligations [reneging on promises], to function as a responsible parent or to plan ahead, and an inability to sustain consistent work behavior. These people fail to conform to social norms [*PT*, 220] and repeatedly perform antisocial acts that are grounds for arrest, such as destroying property, harassing others, stealing, and having an illegal occupation [*PT*, 235; typically hoodlums, gangsters, mobsters, and drug pushers may well form the majority of this type].

People with Antisocial Personality Disorder tend to be irritable and aggressive and to get repeatedly into physical fights and assaults, including spouse- or child-beating [*PT*, 236]. Reckless behavior without regard to personal safety is common, as indicated by frequently driving while intoxicated or getting speeding tickets [*PT*, 229 and 238]. Typically, these people are promiscuous [*PT*, 231]. . . . Finally, they generally have no remorse about the effects of their behavior on others [*PT*, 236]; they may even feel justified in having hurt or mistreated others. (*DSM*-III[R], 342–44)

Personality Type Nine: The Peacemaker

LEVELS OF DEVELOPMENT
Level 1: The Self-Possessed Person
Level 2: The Receptive Person
Level 3: The Supportive Peacemaker

Level 4: The Accommodating   Dependent Personality
Role-Player   Disorder (353)
Level 5: The Passively Disengaged
Person
Level 6: The Resigned Fatalist

Level 7: The Neglectful Person
Level 8: The Dissociating Person   Schizoid Personality
Disorder (339)
Level 9: The Self-Abandoning Person

Dependent Personality Disorder (Type Nine Beginning at Level 4)

The essential feature of this disorder is a pervasive pattern of dependent and submissive behavior. . . . [Much of this is in common with the Six: both types are dependent and submissive, although in different ways and for different reasons.]

People with this disorder are unable to make everyday decisions without an excessive amount of advice and reassurance from others, and will even allow others to make most of their important decisions. For example, an adult with this disorder will typically assume a passive role [*PT*, 261] and allow his or her spouse to decide where they should live, what kind of job he or she should have, and with which neighbors they should be friendly [Sixes, by contrast, react for and against those they are dependent on and are rarely "passive" or completely dependent, as Nines tend to be. The dependency of Sixes is based on their need for reassurance against anxiety, whereas the passive dependency and lack of interest in decision making is based on the desire of Nines that things not change and that they never be upset]. . . .

This excessive dependence on others leads to difficulty in initiating projects or doing things on one's own [*PT*, 248 and 264]. People with this disorder tend to feel uncomfortable or helpless when alone, and will go to great lengths to avoid being alone.

They are devastated when close relationships end, and tend to be preoccupied with fears of being abandoned [*PT*, 265–66].

These people are easily hurt by criticism and disapproval, and tend to subordinate themselves to others [the Nine's self-effacement and excessive accommodation to others, for example, rather than risking conflicts with others], agreeing with people even when they believe them to be wrong, for fear of being rejected. (*DSM*-III[R], 353–54) [*PT*, 268]

Schizoid Personality Disorder (Type Nine Beginning at Level 8)

The essential feature of this disorder is a pervasive pattern of indifference to social relationships and a restricted range of emotional experience and expression [*PT*, 264]. . . .

People with this disorder neither desire nor enjoy close relationships, including being part of a family [owing to the profound fatalism, depression, and indifference that unhealthy Nines gradually fall prey to]. They prefer to be "loners," and have no close friends or confidants (or only one) other than first-degree relatives. They almost always choose solitary activities and indicate little if any desire to have sexual experiences with another person. Such people are indifferent to the praise and criticism of others [*PT*, 259]. They claim that they rarely experience strong emotions such as anger or joy, and in fact display a constricted affect [*PT*, 260]. They appear cold and aloof. [Average to unhealthy Nines are increasingly disengaged emotionally and dissociated from reality.]

Associated features. People with this disorder are often unable to express aggressiveness or hostility [*PT*, 264; this is one of the differences between Fives and Nines, for instance]. They may seem vague about their goals, indecisive in their actions, self-absorbed, and absentminded [*PT*, 260]. Because of a lack of social skills or desire for sexual experiences, males with this disorder are usually incapable of dating and rarely marry. Females may passively accept courtship and marry. (*DSM*-III[R], 339–40)

Personality Type One: The Reformer

LEVELS OF DEVELOPMENT
Level 1: The Wise Realist
Level 2: The Reasonable Person
Level 3: The Principled Teacher

Level 4: The Idealistic Reformer
Level 5: The Orderly Person
Level 6: The Judgmental   Obsessive Compulsive
        Perfectionist   Personality Disorder (354)

Level 7: The Intolerant Person
Level 8: The Obsessive Hypocrite Obsessive Compulsive
                                  Disorder (245)
Level 9: The Punitive Avenger

Obsessive Compulsive Personality Disorder (Type One Beginning at Level 6)

The essential feature of this disorder is a pervasive pattern of perfectionism and inflexibility [PT, 289–91]. . . .

These people constantly strive for perfection, but this adherence to their own overly strict and often unattainable standards frequently interferes with actual completion of tasks and projects. No matter how good an accomplishment, it often does not seem "good enough" [PT, 291]. Preoccupation with rules, efficiency, trivial details, procedures or form interferes with the ability to take a broad view of things [PT, 287]. . . .

Work and productivity are prized to the exclusion of pleasure and interpersonal relationships [PT, 288]. Often there is preoccupation with logic and intellect and intolerance of affective behavior in others [PT, 291]. When pleasure is considered, it is something to be planned and worked for. . . .

Decision making is . . . protracted, perhaps because of an inordinate fear of making a mistake. . . .

People with this disorder tend to be excessively conscientious, moralistic, scrupulous, and judgmental of self and others [PT, 292] — for example, considering it "sinful" for a neighbor to leave her child's bicycle out in the rain.

People with this disorder are stingy with their emotions and material possessions. They tend not to express their feelings, and rarely give compliments or gifts. Everyday relationships have a conventional, formal, and serious quality. Others often perceive these people as stilted or "stiff" [PT, 288].

Associated features. . . . These people have an unusually strong need to be in control [PT, 287]. (DSM-III[R], 354–55)

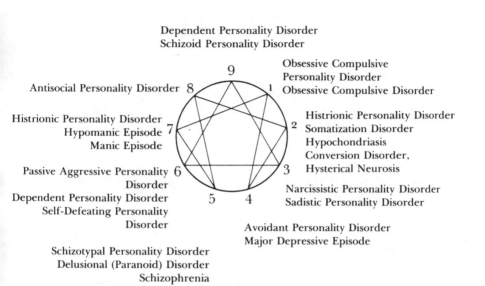

Dependent Personality Disorder
Schizoid Personality Disorder

Obsessive Compulsive
Personality Disorder
Obsessive Compulsive Disorder

Antisocial Personality Disorder 8

Histrionic Personality Disorder
Hypomanic Episode 7
Manic Episode

Histrionic Personality Disorder
Somatization Disorder
Hypochondriasis
Conversion Disorder,
Hysterical Neurosis

Passive Aggressive Personality 6
Disorder
Dependent Personality Disorder
Self-Defeating Personality
Disorder

Narcissistic Personality Disorder
Sadistic Personality Disorder

Avoidant Personality Disorder
Major Depressive Episode

Schizotypal Personality Disorder
Delusional (Paranoid) Disorder
Schizophrenia

THE ENNEAGRAM AND THE *DSM*-III DISORDERS

EIGHT

Recommendations

MANY PEOPLE HAVE REQUESTED specific suggestions about how to use the Enneagram for their growth and development.

Naturally, no general recommendations can apply to all individual cases, so you must personalize these suggestions just as you must personalize the descriptions themselves. These recommendations are not a substitute for self-knowledge and are, at best, a means of "priming the pump" for personal growth. They are merely another source of insight; for real change to occur, you will always need self-discipline and perseverance. A set of recommendations will not in itself cause improvements in anyone's life.

These suggestions are not exhaustive, nor are they meant to be. But the recommendations may help focus your attention on typical problems so that you can begin to do something about them. They may also be helpful in Enneagram study groups, in therapy, or as the basis for discussion with family and friends about yourself and your type.

In a sense, sets of recommendations should be unnecessary since reading the descriptions should suggest dozens of areas that can be used as starting points for change and growth. If, for instance, you are a Six and read that "authoritarian Sixes are extremely prejudiced in the defense of their own group, reacting with a siege mentality to all outsiders, whom they look on with suspicion as potential enemies" (*PT*, 178), you should attempt to discover how authoritarian you are, whether you react against others with a "siege mentality," if you are suspicious, and so on. Used in this way, virtually every paragraph of *Personality Types* can be not only a source of insight into ourselves but, by implication, a source of recommendations about what to do to change. In a word, we should stop our negative behavior and act more positively.

But, of course, knowing our problems is not the same thing as doing anything about changing them. Indeed, it may well be that many people do not consider that their negative behavior is a problem at all. Without insight and proper judgment, they cannot possibly do anything about changing themselves. And even if we have already come to know ourselves, probably much remains to be done.

> Books can provide valuable information and advice, they can give us new insights, they can encourage. But knowledge alone is not enough to change us. If it were, the most knowledgeable people would be the best people, and we know from our own experience that this is not so. Knowledge would be virtue, and it is not. Knowing more about ourselves is but a means toward the goal of being happy and leading a good life, but the possession of knowledge alone cannot bestow virtue, happiness, or fulfillment on us. Books cannot provide answers to all the problems which confront us or impart the courage necessary if we are to persevere in our search. For these things, we must look both within and beyond ourselves. (*PT*, 10)

Whether or not we grow as persons depends on our having insight into what needs to be changed as well as having the motivation to change. Wanting to change takes courage because it necessarily involves stirring up—and consciously dealing with—anxiety. Changing ourselves is never easy, and we can use all the help we can get. If this chapter is simply a first step in the right direction, then, as limited as it is, it will be valuable.

The Process of Change

Before turning to the recommendations for personal growth, you might consider how you can go about the process of changing yourself. First, an exercise may be helpful.

When you catch yourself falling into negative patterns of thought or behavior, you can do a version of Gurdjieff's "stop" exercise. Gurdjieff watched his students going about their various activities and made them aware of their habitual actions by suddenly ordering them to stop whatever they were doing and to freeze in whatever position they were in until he told them to continue what they had been doing.

You can do a similar exercise by ordering yourself to stop whenever you are thinking or doing what you have come to understand is unhealthy. For example, if you realize that your negative thoughts about yourself drain your energy and undermine your self-esteem, then whenever you become aware that you are thinking negatively, order yourself to stop the thought. After you have understood why you have had the thought, you should not necessarily analyze it further, nor should you excoriate yourself for having self-accusations in the first place. You must simply stop supporting the thought and allow your mind to free itself from the negativity by paying attention to what is happening in the moment.

This "stop exercise" helps people become more aware of subconscious thought patterns—the thoughts to which we habitually return to maintain our sense of self. Because we are not fully conscious and in control of ourselves, we have perpetuated mental routines that occupy our minds with wasteful negativity without being aware that we are doing so.

In fact, it is surprising how many of our thoughts are negative—angry, hateful, resentful—as reflected in what Gurdjieff called the "chief feature" of our type. In the more

precise terminology of *Personality Types,* our negative thoughts
are a reflection not only of the Characteristic Vice of our type
but also of the Level(s) of Development at which we live. While
it is worth becoming aware of our characteristic negative
thoughts, perhaps even more important is to realize how frequently they occur. Once we become conscious of them, we
will discover that a great deal of our time and energy is spent
either in negative thoughts or in dealing with their aftermath.
We will also begin to understand that we will never be able
to change ourselves unless we learn to control our negative
thinking. However, change is possible because, if we deny
negative thoughts the attention they require, they will gradually lose their power over us.

This exercise will also begin to break the habit of identifying
with our thoughts and feelings — or with any of our other
ego states. It is important to make this distinction and to stop
identifying with our transient states. *We* are not the same as
our thoughts and feelings (which change almost from moment to moment).

Second, to change ourselves, *we must be motivated:* we must
want to change. Generally speaking, most people do not want
to change anything in their lives until they absolutely must.
Most of us have found a tolerable balance between happiness
and unhappiness, peace and anxiety, the desire for change
and the desire to remain the same. We all have a certain
amount of psychic inertia — a tendency to remain as we are.
Unfortunately, however, by resisting change we may deteriorate rather seriously before we exert ourselves to do anything about it.

From one point of view, however, inertia and resistance
protect us so that we will not waste time and energy changing
constantly. It would be wasteful to react to every circumstance
with a corresponding change; a certain self-possession must
guide us and help us resist changing needlessly. The problem

is that we tend to resist change long past the point when it is necessary and, in fact, overdue. We cling to old habits for fear of seeing ourselves differently, of leaving behind old attitudes and defenses, and of causing shifts in our relationships. Change means that something new is going to happen—that we are moving into unknown territory—and this arouses anxiety (*PT*, 348). Moreover, risk is involved: the change we seek may not turn out well; our efforts may backfire. Without wisdom and a clear vision of which changes to make and which to reject, we may end worse off than before.

But we also have an even deeper inhibition regarding change because we fear being really free. If we really were to change and outgrow those bad habits that have held us back for so long, what would we do with our new freedom? If we really could be in charge of ourselves, what kind of person would we choose to be?

While we are in bondage to our bad habits, this sort of question almost never arises, but, paradoxically, as we become more healthy, our growing freedom begins to be not only our greatest reward but the source of our greatest fear about continuing to grow. With every step we take toward further integration, our freedom increases until we are faced with the ultimate challenge of choosing to be really free, to accept a full, cooperative role in our own creation.

It may be that many people begin on the path of growth and intuit where their growing freedom is leading them—into spiritual realms and larger responsibilities that will take them far beyond their ordinary states—and they become afraid. It would be more comfortable if they could loosen the chains of habit and negativity just a little (since they suffer under them) while not throwing them off altogether. To be free is, for most of us, more threatening than to not be free at all.

Third, motivation to change takes two forms: we can be positively motivated by our desires because we desire what we judge is a "good" for ourselves or negatively motivated by our fears because we want to avoid the anxiety aroused by them. We should enlist both fear and desire to help us change.

On the negative side, it is helpful to foresee the consequences of our actions if we continue to live and act as we have been. If foresight produces a strong enough impression, it may be sufficiently frightening to induce change. This is why the descriptions of the unhealthy Levels of each type are upsetting. Suffering can be a great teacher; it certainly gets our attention. The descriptions are intended to point out the inescapable fact that neurosis is destructive, both of ourselves and of others.

Whether or not we are conscious of them, the laws of the psyche work themselves out as they must. As we have already seen in Chapter 2, in the Inevitable Consequences for each type (and in *Personality Types* at the end of each description in the short section called Some Final Thoughts), the inescapable consequences of inflating the ego is that we lose what we most desire while bringing on ourselves the very thing we most fear. This process happens automatically as we deteriorate through the Levels of Development toward unhealth. The sure prospect of it and the clear vision of what will happen if we persist in going this way should be chilling enough to scare us into changing ourselves.

The negative side of motivation is not enough, however. We may well understand that something is wrong and that we are in danger, but we may not see a way out of our predicament. For example, if an animal is chasing us in a cage, it is not enough to know that it is a lion—we also have to know where the door to the cage is and that we can escape. It is not enough to be frightened by seeing our neurotic tendencies; we must also realize that there is a better way to live and that our healthy desires are pointing us in a direction toward a good that will fulfill us.

It is here that this interpretation of the Enneagram helps identify the strengths we must cultivate by showing us the positive qualities of our personality type. But it goes further, by pointing out our Direction of Integration and the many strengths that become available to us when we move in that direction from type to type in an upward spiral of growth. An understanding of the healthy possibilities for each type should excite us onward at least as much as an understanding of neurosis should frighten us away.

Thus, the Enneagram is useful in three ways: first, by helping us to identify our strengths and weaknesses; second, by helping us to know with clarity what it will cost in the long run if we inflate our ego and move away from genuine growth; and third, by helping us to know with assurance that there is a more positive way to live.

Above all, one fact is certain: we change. Either we move forward or we move backward, but it is not possible to stay the same. If our change is to be toward growth, we must learn to desire what is truly right for us and have the courage not to succumb to our fears. Knowing ourselves so that we will know what will be truly good for us is our surest guide.

Recommendations for Personality Type Two

1. Ask yourself what others really need and then help them attain it. If you give people what they really need — not what they necessarily want or what you think will please them — not only will you be genuinely helpful, but by focusing on real needs you will avoid getting caught in conflicts either with others or with yourself.
2. Let the quality of your goodness and the unselfishness of your service attract people to you or not, as the case may be. Be appreciative of genuine talents and encourage

real strengths. Be generous and openhanded without concern for a return. If you are really good, others will surely notice and seek you out. No amount of wheedling will really secure a place for you in anyone's life if you maneuver to get there.

3. Try to become more conscious of your ulterior motives, your tendency to control others, your aggressions and tart tongue, and whatever other negative elements may be present in your personality. These communicate themselves to others and are the very traits that frustrate your desire to be close to people.

4. Resist the temptation to call attention to yourself and your good works. After you have done something for others, do not remind them about it. Let it be: either they will remember your kindness themselves and thank you in their own way or they will not. Your calling attention to what you have done for them only puts people on the spot and makes them feel uneasy. It will not satisfy anyone or improve your relationships.

5. Do not always be "doing" for people and above all do not try to get people to love you by giving them either gifts or undeserved praise. On the other hand, do not pointedly withdraw your service when others do not respond to you as you would like. Do not make what you do for others depend on how they respond to you. Help others when they ask for it, especially helping them to become more capable of functioning on their own.

6. It is tempting to make new friends and to want to enjoy their company. While it is exciting to feel the flush of a new love, your service to those who already depend on you may suffer. Moreover, your primary commitments (to spouse and children, for example) must be honored first before you spend time cultivating new relationships.

7. It will be helpful for you to work behind the scenes more,

doing things for the good of others, without their even realizing it. Always remember that it is a privilege to play a part in the lives of others, not something that you can rightfully claim as your due.

8. Do not be possessive of your friends; share them with others just as they have shared themselves with you. Remember: if the love among you is genuine, there will be enough to go around for everyone. Genuine love is the only commodity that can be given away endlessly without ever running out.

9. Try to become more aware of how mixed your real motives might be: often they are fine, of course, although sometimes your own needs and ego are behind much of what you do for others. Be sure that your motives for helping others are as pure and disinterested as possible. It is also important not to hide behind alleged good intentions if you know that your intentions really are not completely good. Remember, you will ultimately be judged not by what you say your intentions are but by what you actually do.

10. To love others selflessly is an extraordinary achievement — one of human nature's very highest powers. If you have achieved the ability to love others unselfishly, you are already an extraordinary individual. If you develop your great capacity to care about others, you will never go far wrong — in fact, you will do a great deal of good in life. Others are probably already seeking you out because you possess what everyone wants: the ability to love and appreciate others for who they are.

Recommendations for Personality Type Three

1. Develop charity and cooperation in your relationships. Refrain from giving in to the temptation to put others down, to exclude others from social situations, or to give people the feeling that they are inferior to you. Take their feelings and needs into consideration. When you do so, you will become a more loving person, a more faithful friend—and a much more desirable individual.
2. It is essential to be truthful. Be honest with others about your accomplishments without bragging or exaggerating in any way. Likewise, resist the temptation to impress others or inflate your importance. You will impress people more deeply by being genuine than by bragging about your successes and accomplishments.
3. Be trustworthy. Make an effort to keep secrets and confidences and resist any desire to use them for your own advantage. Watch out for any tendency to be duplicitous or to play people falsely in any way.
4. Develop a social conscience. As part of a social world, you owe your community much in return for what it gives you. Be aware of your tendency to feel entitled to get what you want at the expense of others. An unhealthy quality of your type is the tendency to use others and to take advantage of situations. Be willing to give as much as you get, perhaps more.
5. In their desire to be accepted by others, some average Threes conform so much to expectations that they can justly be called "clones" rather than be regarded as the superior individuals they see themselves as being. Develop yourself by resisting doing what is acceptable just

to be accepted. Act on your own best talents and develop your own attitudes and values.

6. Support and encourage others. Instead of looking for attention and admiration yourself, give your attention and admiration to others, especially when they deserve it. Paradoxically, you will feel better about yourself when you learn to appreciate others. Your relationships will be happier and more satisfying if they are not based on competition but on cooperation. You will become even more desirable as a friend when you give as much attention and affirmation as you receive.

7. You have great energy and a good sense of humor, are good at organizing events, and create excitement, usually simply by your presence and high spirits. Use these qualities for the welfare of the groups you belong to and for individual members of it, making sure that they are developing themselves and their best capacities.

8. Unfortunately, Threes tend to become enraged when they feel that others are slighting them in some way. An inflated sense of self-worth is at the root of their problems in many of their relationships. If this applies to you, be aware of how inflated your expectation of acclaim might be. If people find merit in whatever you have accomplished, they will let you know about it. And if people do not praise you as much as you would like, it is possible that your achievement is not as grand as you think. Beware of inflating your evaluation of what you do and of expecting that others' praise be as extravagant as you would like.

9. If unchecked, the tendency to compete with others eventually leads to increasing hostility and contempt for them. These tendencies are at the root of many of your conflicts and the cause of many of your frustrations. You would be a more genuine success in every area of your life if you could eliminate these negative feelings.

10. As is true of all the types, Threes have spiritual capacities and must develop themselves into the best persons they can be. Many of your strengths already lie in this direction, so follow them. Do not become distracted by comparing yourself with anyone else or by fretting about anyone else's success. When you focus your attention and abilities on doing worthwhile work (especially when it benefits others), you are well on your way to being your best, and comparisons with anyone else become completely beside the point. In short: become your best self—and do not worry about anyone else.

Recommendations for Personality Type Four

1. Do not pay so much attention to your feelings; they are not a true source of support for you, as you probably already know. Remember this advice: "From our present perspective, we can also see that one of the most important mistakes Fours make is to equate themselves with their feelings. The fallacy is that to understand themselves they must understand their feelings, particularly their negative ones, before acting. Fours do not see that the self is not the same as its feelings or that the presence of negative feelings does not preclude the presence of good in themselves" (*PT*, 133). Always remember that your feelings are telling you something about yourself as you are at this particular moment, not necessarily more than that.

2. Avoid putting off things until you are "in the right mood." Commit yourself to productive, meaningful work that will contribute to your good and that of others, no matter how small the contribution may be. Working consistently

in the real world will create a context in which you can discover yourself and your talents. (Actually, you are happiest when you are working—that is, activating your potentials and realizing yourself.) You will not "find yourself" in a vacuum or while waiting for inspiration to strike, so connect—and stay connected—with the real world.

3. Self-esteem and self-confidence will develop only from having positive experiences, whether or not you believe that you are ready to have them. Therefore, put yourself in the way of good. Commit yourself to something that will be good for you. You may never feel that you are ready to take on a challenge of some sort, that you always need more time. (Fours typically never feel that they are sufficiently "together," but they must nevertheless have the courage to stop putting off their lives.) Even if you start small, commit yourself to doing something that will bring out the best in you.

4. A wholesome self-discipline takes many forms, from sleeping regular hours to working regularly to exercising regularly, and has a cumulative, strengthening effect. Since it comes from yourself, a healthy self-discipline is not contrary to your freedom or individuality. On the other hand, sensuality, excessive sexual experiences, alcohol, drugs, sleep, or fantasizing have a debilitating effect on you, as you already know. Therefore, practice healthy self-discipline and stay with it.

5. Avoid lengthy conversations in your imagination, particularly if they are negative, resentful, or even excessively romantic. These conversations are essentially unreal and at best only rehearsals for action—although, as you know, you almost never say or do what you imagine you will. Instead of spending time imagining your life and relationships, begin to live them.

6. Talk openly with someone you trust. This need not be a therapist, although it might be. You need both to express your feelings spontaneously and to have someone react honestly. You may well discover that you are not as different or as much of an outsider as you sometimes feel you are. Paradoxically, one of the surest ways of "finding yourself" is by being in a relationship with someone else.

7. Community service of some kind will make you less self-conscious and give you a better perspective on yourself. There are good things in you that you have kept hidden, possibly even from yourself. Find out what they are by getting involved in practical service.

8. Do not succumb to self-pity or to complaining about your parents, thoughts of your unhappy childhood, your unfulfilled past, your failed relationships, and how no one understands you. Someone would likely understand you if you made a real effort to communicate. (One of your type's unhealthy claims is that you have been damaged by your upbringing and are therefore exempt from having realistic expectations of any sort placed on you.) Use your self-knowledge to be aware of the true effects of your negative attitudes. Do not undermine your self-esteem: doing so will only make things worse for yourself.

9. Do not take everything so personally—do not be touchy or hypersensitive, always thinking that every remark is aimed at you. And even if one occasionally is, do not go over it in your mind. After all, a critical or hostile remark does *not* reflect the whole truth about you. In a sense, you have to be more critical of the remarks of others and less critical of yourself. This may also involve learning to defend yourself better, to speak up more spontaneously, and to not allow yourself to be taken advantage of by others.

10. You are a better friend to others than you are to yourself.

You tend to say and do things to yourself that you would never dream of saying or doing to anyone else. You are more hostile to yourself than to others, more contemptuous, and less interested in your own true welfare than you should be. In fact, it is easy for you to take more interest in someone else's life than in your own. Cliché though it is, become a friend to yourself. Stand up for yourself and give yourself a chance.

Recommendations for Personality Type Five

1. You want to understand the environment, but your understanding becomes distorted if you impose preconceptions on reality rather than observe it. Therefore, analyze less and observe more. Use your gift for observation rather than occupying your mind with fantastic theories and endless speculations.

2. You tend to be extremely intense and so high-strung that you find it difficult to relax and unwind. Make an effort to learn to calm down in a healthy way, without drugs or alcohol. Exercising or using biofeedback techniques will help channel some of your tremendous nervous energy. Meditation, jogging, yoga, and dancing are especially helpful for your type.

3. You see many possibilities but often do not know how to choose among them or judge which is more or less important. Even in average Fives, a sense of perspective is missing, and with it the ability to make accurate judgments. Taking the advice of someone whose judgment you trust will probably be difficult for you but well worth doing since it will not only guide your own judg-

ments but help you trust someone else, also a difficulty for your type.

4. Do not jump to conclusions. Some Fives tend to form opinions based on relatively little evidence. Or, as new information comes in, they do not modify their conclusions to account for it, and their ideas remain biased by the evidence they first accepted. Beware of this tendency since it creates problems in many different situations, not the least of which is in your relationships. Or, to put this recommendation another way — keep an open mind and try your best to give people a second chance, especially as you get more information about them.

5. Fives tend to find it difficult to trust people, to open up to them emotionally, or to make themselves accessible in various ways. Their awareness of potential problems in relationships may tend to create a self-fulfilling prophecy. It is important to remember that having conflicts with others is not unusual and that the healthy thing is to work them out rather than reject attachments with people by withdrawing into isolation. Having one or two intimate friends whom you trust enough to have conflicts with will enrich your life greatly.

6. Try to be more cooperative with others and less a loner. Although it goes against the grain, it will be instructive for you to learn to be supportive and nurturing to people. And, where possible, yield to others graciously without feeling that you have been beaten intellectually or have been put into a vulnerable position.

7. Some Fives tend to make others feel ill at ease. Because they are so intensely involved in what interests them and find their ideas so fascinating, they tend to forget the social niceties that help others be comfortable with them. If this applies to you, remember that your very brilliance may be intimidating to many (indeed, it is probably some-

thing you are proud of and use to distance yourself from people). Rather than being encouraged to share your interests, others can be put off unnecessarily.

8. You tend to look down on those who you think are less intelligent than you. However, even if other people are not as intelligent, this does not automatically mean that they are stupid or their ideas worthless. Try to be more accepting of their intellectual limitations without being cynical or harsh in your judgments. Also remember that there are different kinds of intelligence and that even if your intellectual gifts are superior to those of others, it does not give you the right to be condescending or abrasive to anyone else. Use your gifts for others, not against them.

9. If others begin to avoid you or react to you antagonistically, consider the possibility that you—rather than they—have begun the antagonisms. Examine yourself to discover what you may have contributed to your interpersonal conflicts.

10. You have an enormous capacity for understanding. Think of ways to develop your compassion for others, to understand what they are going through from their point of view. By using your insight into people with compassion and caring, your own more gentle feelings will emerge to soften your hard edges. You will become more trusting, relaxed, and happier if you identify with other people rather than standing back and observing them analytically. Do not use only your head—use more of your heart: it will make you a more rounded person.

Recommendations for Personality Type Six

1. Remember that there is nothing unusual about being anxious since everyone is anxious—and much more often than you might think. Learn to use your anxiety, to explore it, and to come to terms with it. Work creatively with your tensions without turning to excessive amounts of alcohol (or other drugs) to allay anxiety. Within reasonable limits, anxiety can be energizing, a kind of tonic that can help make you more productive and aware of what you are doing.

2. Try not to be defensive and testy. You get edgy when you are upset or angry, and you have a tendency to turn on people and blame others for things you have done or brought on yourself. When you get in a bad mood, resist the tendency to whine and to think negatively—and, ultimately, to self-destruct. Realize that often you are your own worst enemy and may harm yourself more than anyone else does.

3. Sixes tend to overreact when they are under stress and feeling anxious. Learn to identify what makes you overreact. Also realize that almost none of the things you feared so much has actually come true, unless you have been self-defeating and have brought them on yourself. (Even if things are as bad as you think, you can find a way to make good come of them if you want to.)

4. Work on becoming more trusting. There are doubtless several people in your life you can turn to who care about you and who are trustworthy. If not, go out of your way to find someone trustworthy and allow yourself to get close to that person. This will mean risking rejection and stirring up some of your deepest fears, but the risk is

worth taking. You have a gift for getting people to like you, but you are unsure of yourself and may be afraid of making a commitment to them. Therefore, come down clearly on one side or the other of the fence in your relationships. Let people know how you feel about them.

5. Others probably think better of you than you realize, and few people are really out to get you. In fact, your fears tell you more about your attitudes toward others than they indicate about others' attitudes toward you.

6. Accept responsibility more gracefully and maturely. People respect those who take responsibility for their actions, especially if they have made a mistake. If you try to avoid responsibility, you may succeed only in alienating others and in undermining the respect they have for you.

7. You want to feel secure, but this will never be possible unless you are secure with yourself. Sixes easily get into patterns of negative thinking and perpetuate them by anxiety and worry. You need to focus on becoming more self-affirming—developing a realistic belief in yourself and your own abilities. If you do not believe in yourself, other people probably will not either. The challenge is, of course, to give yourself good reasons for believing in yourself lest your self-belief be little more than overcompensation for your fears.

8. Do not worship authority or hide behind an "I was only following orders" attitude. Ingratiating yourself to those in authority will get you nowhere in the long run with anyone really worth associating with. If someone is looking for a team player who will do anything he or she is told, it should not be you. That kind of person will very likely betray you as soon as you are expendable. And remember that if you cooperate in this kind of behavior, you will end with less security and self-respect than you had hoped to find.

9. What bothers other people and undermines your relationships is giving others mixed signals, ambiguous signs of your real attitudes and desires. Be fair with others and tell them what is on your mind lest you appear wishy-washy, indecisive, or defensive. Any of these alternatives causes conflicts and tensions in your relationships.

10. It is courageous for Sixes to speak up, particularly to those in authority — to the boss, for instance, or to someone whose help and goodwill they need. It is very difficult for Sixes to risk criticism and rejection, but sometimes they have no alternative. When you do speak up, however, do not go to the other extreme and become belligerent or antagonistic. It is difficult for you to keep your emotions in balance, but it is a sign of real maturity when you do so.

Recommendations for Personality Type Seven

1. Do not allow yourself to be impulsive. Rather, get in the habit of observing your impulses rather than giving in to them. This means letting most of your impulses pass and becoming a better judge of which ones are worth acting on. The more you restrain yourself from acting on impulse, the more you will be in control of yourself and will discover that you are better able to focus on what is really good for you.

2. Learn to listen to other people. They are often interesting, and you may learn things that will open new doors for you. Also learn to appreciate silence and solitude: you do not have to distract yourself (and protect yourself from anxiety) with constant noise from the television or

the stereo. By learning to live with less external stimulation, you will learn to trust yourself. You will be happier than you expect because you will be satisfied with whatever you do, even if it is less than you have been doing.

3. You do not have to have everything this very moment. That tempting new acquisition will most likely still be available tomorrow (this is certainly true of food, alcohol, and other common gratifications—that ice cream cone, for instance). Most good opportunities will come back again—and you will be in a better position to discern which opportunities really are best for you.

4. Always choose quality over quantity, especially in your experiences. The ability to have experiences of quality can be learned only by giving your full attention to what you do. If you avidly consume your experiences without assimilating them, you undermine the possibility of ever being satisfied.

5. Make sure that what you want will really be good for you in the long run. As the saying goes, watch what you pray for since your prayers may be answered. In the same vein, think about the long-term consequences of what you want since you may get it only to find that it becomes a source of unhappiness.

6. Happiness usually comes indirectly, as a by-product of giving yourself to something worthwhile. Happiness occurs when we are doing other things properly. When their priorities are right, people become happy without seeking happiness as their primary goal. Therefore, do not make being happy your main goal in life since it will lead you down the wrong path, toward being demanding and self-centered.

7. Beware of your tendency to get out of control. It is easy for you to do so because you are naturally enthusiastic about everything. You have a great deal of energy and

strong appetites. Your type's deepest fear is of being deprived, but by not denying yourself some things you will inevitably be deprived not only of the happiness you seek but of many other things besides.

8. You can be very funny and entertaining. Your sense of humor, wit, and flamboyance are a source of pleasure for you and others. However, watch what you say. Avoid any tendency to be rude or to say more than you mean for effect or to get a reaction from others. You may well hurt people and damage your relationships just for the sake of getting off a quip or for having the last word. It is not worth ruining friendships and hurting people just to get a laugh.

9. Find ways of giving rather than getting. The saying that "it is better to give than to receive" is worth considering. Material possessions will never fully satisfy you for a number of reasons: you can, by definition, never have all you want, and even if you could, how is it possible for a thing to fulfill a person? Persons are not things, so material objects will never satisfy your deepest needs. The only "thing" that can really satisfy a person is a relationship with another person. If your attraction to the material world gets in the way of this deeper source of satisfaction, you are going in the wrong direction.

10. One of your highest psychological and spiritual capacities is for joy and for feeling intense gratitude for all that you have. Remember to take time to be grateful and to allow yourself to be enthralled by existence: your sense of wonder at the beauty and preciousness of life will lead you into unexpected realms. Prepare to be surprised.

Recommendations for Personality Type Eight

1. It goes against the grain, but act with self-restraint. You show true power when you forbear from striking out at others, even when you could. Your real power lies in your ability to inspire and uplift people. You are at your best when you take charge and help everyone through a crisis. Few will take advantage of you when you are merciful, and you will do more to secure the loyalty and devotion of others by showing mercy than you ever could by displays of raw power.

2. You are not the only person in the world. Others have the same rights as you, and their needs and rights cannot be ignored, much less violated. If you do ignore them, it is inevitable that people not only will fear you (as you often wish) but will also lose respect for you and, in the end, hate you. If you treat people unfairly, you have reason to fear that they will redress the wrongs you have done.

3. It is difficult for Eights, but learn to yield to others, at least occasionally. Often, little is really at stake, and you can allow others to have their way without fear of sacrificing your power or your real needs. The desire to dominate everyone all the time is a sign that your ego is beginning to inflate—a danger signal that more serious conflicts with others are inevitable.

4. Eights typically want to be self-reliant and depend on no one. But, ironically, they depend on many people. For example, you may think that you are not dependent on your employees because they depend on you for their jobs. You could dismiss them at any time and hire other workers. Everyone is expendable in your little kingdom

—except you. But the fact is that you are dependent on others to carry out your orders, especially if your business concerns grow beyond what you can manage alone. But if you drive away everyone associated with you, you will eventually be forced to employ the most obsequious and untrustworthy operatives to carry out your orders. When you do, you will have reason to question their loyalty and to fear your continued dominance. The fact is that whether in your business world or your domestic life, your self-sufficiency is largely an illusion.

5. Eights typically overvalue money as a source of power. Having wealth allows them to do whatever they want, to feel important, to be feared and obeyed. But the old cliché that "money does not buy happiness" remains true because those who are attracted to you for your money do not love you for yourself, nor do you love or respect them. While this may be the Faustian bargain you have made, you will nevertheless have to pay the price that whatever wealth you have will inevitably be at a cost to you. It remains to be seen how dear that price will be.

6. Learn to serve a higher purpose than your self-interest. Family and relationships provide a means of doing this in the lives of most people. Giving and receiving the love of a spouse and of children is the higher purpose that helps most people transcend themselves to find meaning in their lives. But if everything is reduced to serving your self-interest, the possibility of self-transcendence is eliminated—and with it the possibility of deep happiness, spiritual growth, and many other values. Maintaining a grossly inflated ego is the only way many Eights have of staving off meaninglessness—a meaninglessness, however, that they themselves have created.

7. If God exists, there is someone else you must submit to, and submission to another is one of the most difficult things for Eights to accept. If you do not believe in God,

is your nonbelief based on genuine intellectual convictions or merely on the fact that you do not want to give up your ego and the things you enjoy? A great deal may depend on your answer to this question.

8. If you have been ruthless or caused pain and injury to others, if you have used people for your pleasure or profit (in short, if you are guilty of any of the typical offenses of average to unhealthy Eights), then you have reason to turn your life around while you still can. A life lived on the lowest level of human functioning—at the level of the beast—results in an end similar to that suffered by other animals, an ultimately meaningless existence and a lonely death.

9. One of your greatest potentials is your ability to create opportunities for others. When Eights use their power to create hope and prosperity for everyone, they are respected and remembered for being the benefactors they truly are. Therefore, if you are in a position of power and have great resources at your disposal, and if you use them magnanimously, you will have no one to fear. Rather than make enemies, you will make fervent allies. Rather than question the loyalty of others, you can count on it with assurance. And even if you are ever taken advantage of by someone, the greatness of what you may have accomplished can never be taken away or forgotten. Indeed, others will see to it that it is not. If you look out for other people's needs, they will look out for yours.

10. Think of the harm you can do to others; then think of the good. By which do you wish to be remembered?

Recommendations for Personality Type Nine

1. It is worth examining your type's tendency to go along with others, doing what they want to keep the peace and be nice. Will constantly acquiescing to the wishes of others provide the kind of relationships that will really satisfy you? Remember, it is impossible to love others if you are not truly present to them. This means that you have to be yourself, that you (paradoxically) have to be independent so that you can really be there for others when they need you.

2. Exert yourself. Force yourself to pay attention to what is going on. Do not drift off or tune out people or daydream. Work on focusing your attention to become an active participant in the world around you. Try to become more mentally and emotionally responsive.

3. Recognize that you also have aggressions, anxieties, and other feelings that you must deal with. Negative feelings and impulses are a part of you and they affect you emotionally and physically whether or not you acknowledge them. Furthermore, your negative emotions are often expressed inadvertently and get in the way of the peace and harmony you want in your relationships. It is best to get things out in the open first, at least by allowing yourself to become aware of your feelings.

4. Although this will be very painful for you, if your marriage has ended in divorce or if you are having problems with your children, you must honestly examine how you have contributed to these problems. Examining troubled relationships will be extremely difficult because the people involved have been close to your heart. The feelings

you have for others endow you with much of your identity and self-esteem. But if you really love others, you can do no less than examine the role you have played in whatever conflicts that have arisen. In the last analysis, the choice is simple: you must sacrifice your peace of mind (in the short run) for the satisfaction of genuine relationships (in the long run).

5. Exercise frequently to become more aware of your body and emotions. (Some Nines run around doing errands and think that they are getting enough exercise.) Regular exercise is a healthy form of self-discipline and will increase your awareness of your feelings and other sensations. Developing body awareness will help teach you to concentrate and focus your attention in other areas of your life as well. Exercise is also a good way to get in touch with and express some aggressions.

6. Repressing your feelings will lead to somatization reactions—unexplained headaches, backaches, nausea, and other bodily ailments. Sudden migraines, crying spells, panic attacks, and fear of going out in public (agoraphobia) are examples of physiological and psychological problems caused by repressed emotions. It will be difficult to seek help for these if you need to, but it may be necessary. Do not be afraid. Your life will be richer and you will be more truly at peace if you do.

7. Do not use tranquilizers, except at times of great crisis. They may spare you from anxiety, but at the cost of dulling the very awareness and ability to cope that you are trying to develop. Using tranquilizers is, for Nines, like "bringing coals to Newcastle"—not something you really need, only something you think you need to spare yourself discomfort. Coping with crises not only will increase your self-esteem but will be a real sign to others that you are truly a strong person and that they will be

able to look to you for support at times of crisis in their lives.

8. To the degree that they are repressed as individuals, one of the greatest tragedies for Nines is that they may come to the end of their lives and realize that they have never really lived. It is as if their lives have happened to some-one else: they have never really lived them themselves. They may realize (if only faintly) that they were "asleep" most of the time. Do not live like this. Accept your life and learn to feel the magnitude of what it is to be alive. It can be frightening, but being aware that we are alive is one of the things that separates us from the animals. If you give up your consciousness, you give up much of your life.

9. Trust yourself to ventilate your fears and anxieties with your spouse and friends. (Standing up to others and ex-pressing feelings is threatening to many of the personality types, so you are not alone.) Have confidence that you will not damage your relationships by expressing your-self. Think of the comfort of knowing that your rela-tionships are solid, that your family and friends will respond to you, and that you can be yourself and grow as an individual. This is a basis for genuine reassurance and comfort.

10. One of your greatest assets is your receptivity to people: others feel calm, safe, and accepted around you. But they will love you and seek you out even more if they also feel that you understand them and are attentive to their needs. Listen to people carefully and get to know them as they really are. The love you have for them—and they for you—will be that much more real and that much more valuable.

Recommendations for Personality Type One

1. Learn to relax. Take some time for yourself, without feeling that everything is up to you or that what you do not accomplish will result in chaos and disaster. Mercifully, the salvation of the world does not depend on you alone, even though you may sometimes feel it does.

2. You have a lot to teach others and are probably a good teacher, but do not expect others to change immediately. What is obvious to you may not be as obvious to them, especially if they are not used to being as self-disciplined and objective about themselves as you are about yourself. Many people may also want to do what is right and may agree with you in principle but for various reasons simply cannot change right away. The fact that others do not change immediately according to your prescriptions does not mean that they will not change sometime in the future. Your words and, above all, your example may do more good than you realize, although they may take longer than you expect. So have patience.

3. It is easy for you to work yourself up into a lather about the wrongdoings of others. And it may sometimes be true that they are wrong. But what is it to you? As the wise saying has it, remove the plank in your own eye before troubling yourself about the speck in your neighbor's eye. You are not without faults and shortcomings of your own, so stop watching everyone else and acknowledge your own failings.

4. It is important for you to get in touch with your feelings, particularly your unconscious impulses. You may find that you are uneasy with your emotions and your sexual and aggressive impulses—in short, with the messy hu-

man things that make us human. It might be beneficial to keep a journal or to get into some kind of group therapy or other group work both to develop your emotions and to see that others will not condemn you for having human needs and limitations.

5. Your Achilles' heel is your self-righteous anger. You get angry easily and are offended by what seems to you to be the perverse refusal of others to do the right thing — as you have defined it. Try to step back and see that you tend to play the role of "judge and jury," lecturing and moralizing to everyone else, often without much effect. Your own anger may well be giving you an ulcer or high blood pressure and is a harbinger of worse things to come.

6. One of the most difficult things for Ones is to learn to allow people to be as they are and to come to decisions on their own. It is tempting to tell people what you think they should do — and while you may well be right, the wisdom of your words will not do any good because you may not have acted wisely. Acting wisely involves knowing how much to say and when to say it; it involves knowing what your listener can accept and learn from. The wisest thoughts do no good unless others are ready to hear them. Therefore, let wisdom be your guide, not your "rightness."

7. Listen to others: they are often right, too. And even if they are not, there is almost always some kernel of truth to the point of view they are expressing. By listening to others, you not only will learn more but will become a more informed and sensitive teacher. When you speak, others will know that they are listening to a human being, not a logic machine.

8. Perfectionists drive others crazy. There is probably no single, absolutely correct way of doing everything — from washing dishes to ironing a shirt to laying out a garden

to every other activity in life. Many different things can be done differently without anything valuable suffering because of it. Moreover, perfectionism that is nothing more than a useless pickiness undermines the confidence others have in you when you advise them about something truly important. In short, it is necessary to discriminate between those times when perfection is a useful standard and when it is not.

9. Unhealthy Ones tend to be obsessive in their thoughts and compulsive in their actions, and even average Ones begin to manifest elements of these kinds of behavior. Try to resist both tendencies as soon as you become aware of them; if yielded to, they will lead you into increasingly destructive behavior. In particular, be aware of the desire for total orderliness and control of your environment since it is a harbinger of other, darker disorders. (An exaggerated orderliness is often a displacement for the fear of losing control in some other area of your life.) Try to find out what is really bothering you and tackle those problems; do not waste your energy on the thousand little annoyances you tend to spend yourself on.

10. A person does not have to be perfect to be good. Give yourself the true satisfaction of becoming human, not inhumanly perfect.

NINE

Personality, Essence, and Spirituality

SEEN FROM one viewpoint, the Enneagram describes a terrible inward spiraling into the increasingly destructive fixations of each personality type. Seen from another point of view, its movement is outward, beyond personality toward further integration once the challenge of self-transcendence has been overcome.

In my descriptions in *Personality Types*, I chronicled the first of those two movements. Like Virgil accompanying Dante through the Inferno, I led readers through each step of a journey that took us "downward" into states of ever-tighter constriction and self-destruction. As painful as these were to contemplate, seeing the negative side of each type was valuable—as the psychological equivalent of a vision of hell given to a sinner so that the sinner will be frightened into avoiding it. The emotional impact of the descriptions came, in part, because readers could see with shattering clarity what form of personal hell they would condemn themselves to if they were to continue to move down the Continuum toward neurosis—no matter how tempting and innocent that path might seem.

Even though *Personality Types* contained a great deal about the healthy Levels, much was still dark and forbidding because even the average Levels were necessarily somewhat negative—and the unhealthy Levels were a relentless playing out of neurotic entrapments. And, although *Personality Types* included accounts of the positive Directions of Integration, even these were offset by the need to include descriptions of the Directions of Disintegration. As positive as the picture was, it was always influenced by each type's potential fall into neurosis.

This was unavoidable since that book was to be not only an introduction to the psychology of the Enneagram but, on a deeper level, a work that would shock the reader into a new level of awareness. It was meant to touch the heart and in so doing help transform the person. Self-knowledge is a means toward self-transformation.

Because *Personality Types* could not contain everything, it was first necessary to give a clear and unsparing view of each type so that readers would have the self-knowledge to guide them toward that which lies beyond the ego. Those who understood the value of this knowledge also understood that it was the place to start what would ultimately become a spiritual journey.

> Naturally, it takes years of work on oneself to get to know anything real about ourselves; we may think we are finding out a great deal, through self-observation and by applying the other teachings and techniques of The Work [Gurdjieff's teaching]. . . . What we think we have discovered about ourselves is very superficial at first, so that real self-knowledge only comes after years of patient effort. But such effort is immensely worth while in every particular, because it not only transforms us, it transforms our whole life for us; because as our level of being changes, so does our life change, too. We become different people *inside*, and this is reflected by the way life treats us *outside*.
>
> This is an esoteric law . . . and explains why it is only ourselves who can make anything really worthwhile of our lives. It is no good looking to external factors or agencies to do this for us. Such things cannot change our level of being, and so

life remains just as it was before, despite whatever we may be doing or thinking. It is only when we begin to really work on ourselves, and change our habitual ways of thinking and feeling, that anything real or permanent can happen to us. For self-change is the basic pre-requisite for external change. And self-change can only come about as a result of self-knowledge and work on oneself. (Benjamin, *Basic Self-Knowledge*, 163–64).

Providing accurate knowledge of ourselves was the purpose of *Personality Types,* just as it is the purpose of the Enneagram itself. The lesson that had to be learned was the wastefulness of ego inflation. As valuable as this lesson was, there was much more to be said: the Enneagram can also guide us to spiritual dimensions by helping us move beyond personality. I have already alluded to the fact that genuine fulfillment (which is to be found primarily within a spiritual context) lies in the ability to transcend ourselves.

We must be willing and able to go beyond ego to reach out to something more, to some value outside ourselves.

Self-transcendence is difficult and fearful because it entails going into unknown territory, feeling, doing, and relating in ways foreign to our personality, contrary to our past habits, at odds with our old attitudes and identity, having begun to overcome the handicaps of our childhood. In a sense, it is a kind of rebirth, the coming into being of a new person who is learning to leave the old ways behind and strike out into a new world. . . .

In the last analysis, learning how to transcend the ego is nothing less than learning how to love. Only love has the power to save us from ourselves. Until we learn to truly love ourselves and others, there can be no hope of lasting happiness or peace or redemption. It is because we do not love ourselves properly that we lose ourselves so easily in the many illusions ego sets before us. (*PT*, 348)

Cataloguing the illusions that "ego sets before us" was the very stuff of my descriptions. It is now time to turn our attention to that other path—toward higher states that open out to us once we have transcended ourselves, to that upward spiral by which we move beyond ego into essence.

Describing "living in essence" is much more difficult than describing personality types, for one fundamental reason. Most of the ego states described in *Personality Types* are unfree; they involve degrees of compulsion, of losing ourselves in illusions and mechanical responses. Since they are relatively fixed states ("fixations"), they are also relatively easy to describe, once you know what to look for. However, self-transcendence results in states that are marked by *freedom*, and as such they are dynamic and ever-evolving—not only as an expression of life but, in a true sense, as life-giving states themselves. If we can analyze the qualities of a truly free person, of someone living in a state of liberation, we will learn more about "living in essence."

> The unfolding of essence becomes the process of living. Life is no longer a string of disconnected experiences of pleasure and pain but a flow, a stream of aliveness. One aspect manifests after another, one dimension after another, one capacity after another. There is a constant flow of understanding, insight, knowledge, and states of being. (Almaas, *Essence*, 178)

This sounds familiar; we are on solid ground, in territory we have seen before. The Enneagram has already pointed out each type's Direction of Integration. Now we understand a deeper meaning: that one's essence and the process of living in essence can be attained by moving in the Direction of Integration.

As we become more healthy by overcoming our characteristic fears and by acting on our right desires, we gradually move up the Levels of Development. To attain Level 1, the Level of Liberation, is to come into contact with our essence, our essential self, our self at its best. But it is only when we go further and transcend ourselves by moving toward the Direction of Integration that we really live within and out of our essence.

This is not done once and for all, however, as if we could be liberated from the human condition. We move to the type in our Direction of Integration and to the potentials found there—and hence into another ego state, albeit a healthy one. Thus our liberation is gradual and limited, although with the new state comes the awakening of new capacities. As Almaas says, "One aspect manifests after another, one dimension after another, one capacity after another." We do not move beyond human nature but beyond its most troublesome limitations. Living in essence becomes a matter of transcending our ego and, in so doing, of discovering and developing our truest self. The search for essence or self-transcendence is not an escape from life but the reverse: a commitment on our most profound level of consciousness to participate in our own creation.

Essence and Levels of Development

The relationship between essence and the Levels of Development can be visualized: as the person descends further "down" the Levels toward neurosis, he or she moves further away from the essential self. Conversely, as the person "ascends" the Levels, the movement is toward essence as the balance shifts from unhealthy to average to healthy states. To live in essence, we must move in the Direction of Integration, to integrate the healthy Levels found there, and then move onward yet again.

Some have mistakenly thought that to live in essence is to have left personality entirely behind. This is not the case since both personality and essence are integral parts of each other, two sides of the same coin—the whole self.

> In the best of all possible worlds the acquired habits of personality would be available to one's essential nature and would help one to function adequately in the social context in

In Direction of
ESSENCE Integration

Level 1
Level 2
Level 3

ESSENCE

Level 1
Level 2
Level 3

ESSENCE

Level 1
Level 2
Level 3

ESSENCE AND THE LEVELS OF DEVELOPMENT

which he or she lived, and for a realized being this undoubtedly is the case. The ordinary person, unfortunately, lacks the ability to make use of personality to carry out essential wishes. What is essential can manifest only in the simplest instinctive behavior and in primitive emotions. . . .

All this is not to say that essence is always noble and beautiful while personality is an alien crust of useless cultural barnacles. According to Gurdjieff, "as a rule a man's essence is either primitive, savage and childish, or else simply stupid." The essences of many are actually dead, though they continue to live seemingly normal lives. The development of essence to maturity, when it will embody everything that is true and real in a person's being, depends on work on oneself, and work on oneself depends on a balance between a relatively healthy essence and a personality that is not crushingly heavy. . . . Both are necessary for self-development, for without the acquisition of personality there will be no wish to attain higher states of consciousness, no dissatisfaction with everyday existence; and without essence there will be no basis of development." (Speeth, *The Gurdjieff Work*, 48–49)

As one becomes liberated from the negative aspects of personality, essence becomes developed. Or, more aptly, the balance between essence and personality shifts from personality to essence until more of the self is living out of its essence (that is, authentically, from the depths of its being) while the personality remains ready to be employed as a useful and necessary tool, but only as an extension and expression of the deeper, essential self—a self that, because it is "living in essence," is and always will remain unfathomable. Without personality to express the self in ordinary daily life, we could not communicate with each other and, ultimately, even our own essence would be lost or remain undeveloped.

The full development and expression of the true self is what we seek, and this cannot be done in a vacuum. Because we cannot live without form, our human essence must express itself through the forms of our personality type, just as talents must be expressed in action if talent is to be developed. A dancing master does not become so perfect a dancer that the master no longer dances. Dancing is not forsworn as evidence of having achieved perfection: on the contrary, mastery is expressed by losing the self in the dance.

Thus, personality is as necessary as essence, and it is to be used for living in the world and for contributing to it. The good aspects of personality that reveal our essence are the *healthy* personality states we find at Levels 1 to 3 for each type. Moreover, those personality states themselves develop to become finer expressions of our essential self as we continue to evolve. Once we have begun to integrate and to live in essence more habitually, we become the master of our ego and are increasingly able to express ourselves freely and appropriately. Ego no longer controls us: essence speaks through personality.

This does not mean, as some teachings have it, that the individual must experience the essential self all the time, that he must hold onto it as the most precious thing. Many systems of teaching focus on the true self, concentrate on it, identify with it, and glorify it. This will naturally bring attachment, and attachment is personality, even if it is attachment to the essential self.

What needs to happen is to free this aspect of essence for it to become a station, to become permanently available, so that it is there when its mode of operation is needed. Therefore, all of the issues around identity and selfhood must be seen and understood, including the need for or attachments to identity. The true self exposes all misunderstanding and conflicts around identity and selfhood. Resolving the issues around the essential self eliminates all identification; or rather, identification becomes a free, conscious movement. (Almaas, *Essence*, 170)

Every step in the Direction of Integration schools us for the next movement toward liberation, so that we can move yet again in self-transcendence toward more freedom and a deeper possession of our essential self. Looked at one way, this movement is from state of consciousness to state of consciousness, yet looked at another way, the movement becomes increasingly free of all attachments to those very forms.

Life continues to be a process of creative discovery. The process of learning, unfolding, and expansion never stops. Essence continues to unfold, new dimensions arise, new modes of experience and insight emerge, new capacities manifest. [see p. 9] . . .
. . . The shift of identity from personality to essence is nothing but the realization of the true self, the high self of essence. . . .
. . . Practical action becomes the action of the true being. There is efficiency, economy, simplicity, directness. One fully lives in the world but is constantly connected to the Beyond, the Supreme Reality. (Almaas, *Essence*, 179)

Still, for some, the movement in the Direction of Integration from one form of consciousness to another may seem like falling back into ego and therefore no true liberation at all. This is not so, although it is paradoxical since human beings are not (and cannot expect to be) disembodied spirits that become "liberated" into a fixed "essential" state. We do not leave behind our particular life, our past, our memories —and all that makes up the total self. The move to essence is not an escape from ourselves but the growth of freedom from those aspects of ourselves that have made us unfree and subject to suffering. The move to essence is a supremely positive thing—not a negation of our individuality, but the occasion in which we become deeply alive and in possession of ourselves. I hinted at some of this in *Personality Types*:

> Ultimately, the goal is to move completely around the Enneagram, integrating what each type symbolizes and acquiring the active use of the healthy potentials of *all the types*. The ideal is to become a balanced, fully-functioning human being, and each of the types of the Enneagram symbolizes different important aspects of what we need to achieve this end. (40)
>
> Attaining the goal of a full, happy life, ripe with experiences well used, means that each of us will become a paradox— free, yet constrained by necessity; shrewd, yet innocent; open to others, yet self-reliant; strong, yet able to yield; centered on the highest values, yet able to accept imperfection; realistic about the suffering existence imposes on us, yet full of gratitude for life as it is.
>
> The testimony of the greatest humans who have ever lived is that the way to make the most of ourselves is by transcending ourselves. We must learn to move beyond self-centeredness to make room within ourselves for others. When you transcend yourself, the fact will be confirmed by the quality of your life. You will attain—even if only momentarily—a transparency and a radiance of being which result from living both within and beyond yourself. This is the promise and the excitement of self-understanding. (45–46)

The quality of your life is confirmation that, in the moment of self-transcendence, you have attained essence—your deepest, truest self. The transparency and radiance that result from living in essence are the sign that essence is not only desirable but attainable. The state of "transparency"—of openness and unself-consciousness—makes the essential self accessible to others. And the "radiance" that results from self-transcendence—self-possession and profound happiness— emanates the many particular qualities of love.

> Enlightenment cannot be according to any system. It has to resolve and clarify your own situation. The realization must satisfy and fulfill your heart, not the standards of some system. The liberation must be of you, you personally. . . .
> The quest does not bring about improvement or perfection. It brings about a maturity, a humanity, and a wisdom. (Almaas, *Essence*, 181–82)

We have seen much the same about the limitations of any system, including the limitations of the Enneagram. While Almaas says that "the quest does not bring about improvement or perfection," surely he does not deny that "maturity . . . humanity . . . and wisdom" are improvements in our condition. But more important, Almaas seems to imply that perfection is out of the question to all but the very greatest saints—and even to them, absolute perfection belongs only to the Absolute. Perfection (even the perfection we seek in essence) must always remain an ideal. Perfection does not belong to human nature, but to God alone.

If thinking about "living in essence" sounds too esoteric, the Enneagram can help take some of the obscurity out of it. For modern sensibilities, the goal of living in essence may be strange and off-putting. But if we keep the Enneagram as our frame of reference, we will be less mystified if we think of living in essence as the same as becoming a fully functioning, integrated person. The goal is *not* to strengthen our ego but to transcend it, and in so doing not only do we become increasingly healthy but we increasingly "live in essence."

What capacities will we discover in ourselves if we move in

the Direction of Integration and begin the process of living in essence—whether we call it that or not?

The characteristics of health (and essence) are found in all the personality types, although, of course, only in the healthy Levels of Development of each.

Some of the most important healthy traits of each type are displayed on the following Enneagram. These are only some of the strengths we can learn from each other; they are particular to each type although universally accessible. Always keep in mind that many additional healthy traits exist that you will discover as you move in your own unique way beyond yourself.

Acceptance, Self-Possession,
Equanimity, Receptivity,
Patience, Unself-consciousness

Magnanimity, Self-Reliance,
Decisiveness, Mastery,
Self-Confidence, Courage

Reasonableness, Objectivity,
Tolerance, Conscientiousness,
Wisdom, Self-Discipline

Enthusiasm, Resilience,
Gratitude, Practicality,
Joyousness, Productivity

Empathy, Unselfishness,
Altruism, Kindness,
Appreciation, Generosity

Commitment, Loyalty,
Cooperation, Faithfulness,
Dedication, Reliability

Adaptability, Self-Esteem,
Admirability, Self-Assurance,
Ambition, Self-Development

Understanding, Comprehension,
Insight, Knowledge,
Involvement, Originality

Self-Awareness, Individuality,
Sensitivity, Compassion,
Creativity, Emotional Honesty

THE ENNEAGRAM OF ESSENTIAL SELF-ACTUALIZATION

Thinking about the positive image of human nature that the Enneagram holds out to us can inspire us to become more healthy. Being aware of the characteristics of health helps us recognize these traits in ourselves so that our journey toward integration will be swifter and more sure. Yet we cannot simply list the healthy traits we find in each type with the recommendation that people acquire them. The healthy potentials symbolized by the Enneagram (or by any other typology, for that matter) are not a checklist of assets that can be acquired piecemeal, like a Chinese menu of virtues from which we select one from this column and another from that. The development of the person is more complex, demanding dynamic integration and balance. As we move in the Direction of Integration, one strength balances another, new potentials come into play, and another capacity emerges to ensure the harmony of those that have already been acquired.

It is not enough to be adaptable to the environment (a trait of the healthy Three), for example, since it is possible to adapt in ways that conceal one's identity. Adaptability alone is not a sole criterion for psychological health since, under certain circumstances, the ability to adapt may well not indicate psychological growth but its reverse, a stultifying conformity. As desirable as adaptability may be, it must be *counterbalanced* by other qualities. In the case of an integrating Three, it is balanced by steadfastness to commitments, a trait of the healthy Six, the type in the Three's Direction of Integration.

The challenge is to balance all the strengths from all the types as we activate our essential self. Remarkably, the Enneagram indicates the proper progression for this balancing evolution for each type. For example, we find that the healthy Eight's self-assertion must be balanced by the healthy Two's empathy. But empathy for others alone is not enough lest it deteriorate into sentimentality. The Two's empathy must be counterbalanced by the Four's honest self-appraisal. Yet honest self-appraisal is not enough lest it deteriorate into self-absorption. The Four's self-awareness must be counterbalanced by the One's objectivity—and yet that is not enough lest objectivity deteriorate into rigid logic. We could continue this way around the Enneagram pointing out how each type's strengths are called forth to balance the strengths of the other types.

The progression of the Direction of Integration is what we need to balance our strengths and growing virtues. Thus, while acquiring the healthy traits of our type is necessary, possessing them alone is not enough for a full and balanced life. The process of living out of one's essence allows many different capacities of the psyche to emerge. There is no one state of "health" that can be prescribed for everyone, nor is there a final state of "health" common to all — but an ongoing process of growth and unfolding for each individual.

The process of growth, by whatever name it is called — living in essence, the growth of virtue, or the movement toward integration — is evolutionary, an upward spiral that has no final state of completion since to become completely possessed of all virtues would be to become God — an impossibility. (Our call, in a religious frame of reference, is to become "like God" — to attain some degree of the virtues that God alone possesses to an absolute degree.) If some see this never-ending quest for increasing virtue (or personal strengths) as a frustrating chase after an unreachable goal, it is because they have not experienced the deep fulfillment that results from self-transcendence. If integration is thought of as merely collecting a set of impractical virtues as if they were merit badges being added to a collection, then of course the enterprise will be unsatisfying.

But the true situation is far from this. Acquiring the strengths of virtue brings about the enlargement of the person. By acting virtuously and by "living in essence," the person becomes capable of living more deeply and consciously as master of the self. New depths are being opened in the integrating person. The creation of inner resources, the experience of oneself as enlarged, more potent, and creative is tremendously fulfilling. In this sense, the saying that "virtue is its own reward" has new meaning: the reward of virtue is the happiness that comes from the realization that we are living out of our essential self and that in doing so we are bringing more of ourselves into being.

Yet it will always remain true that realizing the value of self-transcendence can be found only in the individual's innermost heart. In the moment of self-transcendence, we discover that over and above liberation from the ego, self-transcendence gives us another, deeper reward by creating both the capacity and the desire for more of itself.

By integrating, we are constantly moving in the direction of increasing life. And nothing in life is more fulfilling than cooperating in the process of creation. Integrating persons become cocreators of that most vast yet intimate mystery, the human spirit.

Even from only a psychological point of view, the capacity to be a cocreator bestows on human nature enormous dignity. But from a religious point of view, this capacity has a more profound meaning because to move in the direction of increasing life is to move toward Being itself. With each step we take toward Being, we also find that Being supports our quest. In the end, the quest for the self and its deepest essence culminates in meeting the Divine.

Bibliography
Index

BIBLIOGRAPHY

Almaas, A. H. *Essence: The Diamond Approach to Inner Realization*. York Beach, Me.: Samuel Weiser, 1986.

Anthony, Dick, Bruce Ecker, and Ken Wilber, eds. *Spiritual Choices: The Problem of Recognizing Authentic Paths to Inner Transformation*. New York: Paragon House, 1987.

Bayrak al-Jerrahi al-Halveti, Skeikh Tosun. *The Most Beautiful Names*. Putney, Vt.: Threshold Books, 1985.

Benjamin, Harry. *Basic Self-Knowledge*. York Beach, Me.: Samuel Weiser, 1971.

Bennett, J. G. *Gurdjieff: Making a New World*. New York: Harper & Row, 1973.

———. *Enneagram Studies*. York Beach, Me.: Samuel Weiser, 1983.

Capps, Donald. *Deadly Sins and Saving Virtues*. Philadelphia: Fortress Press, 1987.

Danner, Victor. *The Islamic Tradition*. New York: Amity House, 1988.

Diagnostic and Statistical Manual of Mental Disorders, third edition, revised (*DSM-III[R]*). Washington, DC: American Psychiatric Association, 1987.

Faucett, Robert, and Carol Ann. *Personality and Spiritual Freedom*. New York: Doubleday, 1987.

Fine, Reuben. *A History of Psychoanalysis*. New York: Columbia University Press, 1979.

Frosch, James P., ed. *Current Perspectives on Personality Disorders*. Washington, D.C.: American Psychiatric Press, 1983.

Glasse, Cyril. *The Concise Encyclopaedia of Islam*. San Francisco: Harper & Row, 1989.

Horney, Karen. *Neurosis and Human Growth: The Struggle Toward Self-Realization*. New York: W. W. Norton, 1950.

———. *Our Inner Conflicts*. New York: W. W. Norton, 1945.

Leary, Timothy. *Interpersonal Diagnosis of Personality*. New York: Ronald Press, 1957.

Lilly, John, and Joseph Hart. "The Arica Training." In *Transpersonal Psychologies*, edited by Charles T. Tart. New York: Harper & Row, 1975.

Macquarrie, John. *In Search of Humanity*. New York: Crossroad, 1985.

Maslow, Abraham. *The Further Reaches of Human Nature*. New York: Viking Press, 1971.

Metzner, Ralph. *Know Your Type: Maps of Identity.* New York: Doubleday, 1979.

Millon, Theodore. *Disorders of Personality.* New York: John Wiley, 1981.

—— and Gerald L. Klerman, eds. *Contemporary Directions in Psychopathology: Toward the DSM-IV.* New York: Guilford Press, 1986.

Nicholi, Armand M., ed. *The Harvard Guide to Modern Psychiatry.* Cambridge: Harvard University Press, 1978.

Nicoll, Maurice. *Psychological Commentaries on the Teaching of Gurdjieff and Ouspensky.* Boulder: Shambhala, 1984.

Ouspensky, P. D. *In Search of the Miraculous.* New York: Harcourt, Brace & World, 1949.

Riordan, Kathleen. "Gurdjieff." In *Transpersonal Psychologies,* edited by Charles T. Tart. New York: Harper & Row, 1975.

Riso, Don Richard. *Personality Types: Using the Enneagram for Self-Discovery.* Boston: Houghton Mifflin, 1987.

Shapiro, David. *Neurotic Styles.* New York: Basic Books, 1965.

Shushud, Hasan. *Masters of Wisdom of Central Asia.* Moorcote, England: Coombe Springs Press, 1983.

Speeth, Kathleen Riordan. *The Gurdjieff Work.* Berkeley: And/Or Press, 1976.

—— and Ira Friedlander. *Gurdjieff: Seeker of the Truth.* New York: Harper & Row, 1980.

Tart, Charles T., ed. *Transpersonal Psychologies.* New York: Harper & Row, 1975.

——. *Waking Up: Overcoming the Obstacles to Human Potential.* Boston: Shambhala, 1986.

Waldberg, Michel. *Gurdjieff: An Approach to His Ideas.* London: Routledge & Kegan Paul, 1981.

Webb, James. *The Harmonious Circle.* New York: G. P. Putnam's Sons, 1980.

ENNEAGRAM DISSERTATIONS

Several doctoral theses have been written about the Enneagram and related matters in the last several years, and more academic work continues to be done.

Some of the following dissertations are concerned with developing and validating a questionnaire based on the Enneagram personality types, while others explore various aspects of the relation between depth psychology and the traditional Arica interpretation of the Enneagram.

This has become a fertile field in which to work at the master's and doctoral levels, and no doubt the Enneagram's correspondence with the *DSM*-III(R) personality disorders and other typologies as well as other areas of interest will continue to sustain research and scholarship.

In the following list, the author's name, title of the thesis, degree awarded, year, institution, and page length (when available) have been given; the volume and page in *Dissertation Abstracts International* and the order number have also been included with each entry. At the end of the list is information about how to order copies of these works.

Beauvais, Phyllis. "Claudio Naranjo and SAT: Modern Manifestation of Sufism." Ph.D., 1973, Hartford Seminary. 264 pages. 35/12-A, p. 8005. GAX75-13868.

Campbell, Richard. "The Relationship of Arica Training to Self-Actualization and Interpersonal Behavior." Ph.D., 1975, United States International University. 115 pages. 36/03-B, p. 1401. GAX75-20244.

Gamard, William Sumner. "Interrater Reliability and Validity of Judgments of Enneagram Personality Types." Ph.D., 1986, California Institute of Integral Studies. GAX86-25584.

Lincoln, Robert L. "The Relation Between Depth Psychology and Protoanalysis." Ph.D., 1983, California Institute of Transpersonal Psychology. 429 pages. *Research Abstracts International* LD00676.

Randall, Stephen. "Development of an Inventory to Assess Enneagram Personality Type." Ph.D., 1979, California Institute of Integral Studies. 112 pages. 40/09-B, p. 4466. GAX80-05160.

Wagner, Jerome. "A Descriptive, Reliability, and Validity Study of the Enneagram Personality Typology." Ph.D., 1981, Loyola University, Chicago. 283 pages. 41/11-A, p. 4664. GAX81-09973.

Wolf, Steven Raymond. "Effects of the Arica Training on Adult Development: A Longitudinal Study (Stage Theory)." Ph.D., 1985, Saybrook Institute. 46/11-B, p. 4040. GAX85-28854.

Zinkle, Thomas Edward. "A Pilot Study Toward the Validation of the Sufi Personality Typology." Ph.D., 1975, United States International University. 91 pages. 35/05-B, p. 2418. GAX74-24529.

For current information and to order copies, consult *Dissertation Abstracts International*, Dissertation Publishing, University Microfilm International, 300 N. Zeeb Road, P. O. Box 1764, Ann Arbor, MI 48106; or telephone: (800) 521-3042. For on-line search at libraries, use DATRIX DIRECT: (800) 233-6901, Extension 708.

Your local bookstore can provide you with copies of all of Don Richard Riso's books: *Personality Types* (1987), *Understanding the Enneagram* (1990), *Discovering Your Personality Type: The Enneagram Questionnaire* (1992), and *Enneagram Transformations* (1993). Or you can order them from the publisher by calling (800) 225-3362.

To obtain multiple copies for use in Enneagram Workshops as well as business and organizational settings, please contact Houghton Mifflin Company, Special Sales Department, 2 Park Street, Boston, Massachusetts 02108, or phone (617) 725-5969. Special discounts are available for orders of 10 copies or more.

To contact Don Richard Riso for information about his Enneagram Workshops, professional trainings, new publications, and business seminars, or to have your name added to his mailing list for workshops in your area, please call Enneagram Personality Types, Inc., at the address below.

For personal consulting or to have the *Riso Enneagram Type Indicator* interpreted by an Enneagram teacher trained and certified by Don Richard Riso, please contact Enneagram Personality Types, Inc., for a referral to a teacher in your area.

For a free brochure of Enneagram Designs products, call (800) 852-9704. Outside the United States, call (803) 548-1110.

Enneagram Personality Types, Inc.
222 Riverside Drive, Suite 10E
New York, NY 10025
(212) 932-3306